News Talk

Written by a former news reporter and editor, *News Talk* gives us an insider's view of the media, showing how journalists select and construct their news stories. Colleen Cotter goes behind the scenes, revealing how language is chosen and configured by news staff into the stories we read and hear. Tracing news stories from start to finish, she shows how the practice traditions of journalists and editors – and the constraints of news writing protocols – shape (and may distort) stories prepared with the most determined effort to be fair and accurate. Using insights from linguistics and journalism on both sides of the Atlantic, *News Talk* is a remarkable picture of a hidden world and its working practices. It will interest those involved in linguistics, journalism, language study, media and communication studies, and anyone who wants to understand how news media shape our language and our view of the world.

COLLEEN COTTER is a senior lecturer at Queen Mary University of London in the School of Languages, Linguistics and Film. She is a former daily news reporter and editor in the USA. Her previous publications include *USA Phrasebook*, *Understanding Americans and Their Culture*, 2nd edition (2001), as well as numerous articles on language and the media.

News Talk

Investigating the Language of Journalism

Colleen Cotter

CAMBRIDGE
UNIVERSITY PRESS

CAMBRIDGE UNIVERSITY PRESS
Cambridge, New York, Melbourne, Madrid, Cape Town, Singapore, São Paulo,
Delhi, Dubai, Tokyo, Mexico City

Cambridge University Press
The Edinburgh Building, Cambridge CB2 8RU, UK

Published in the United States of America by Cambridge University Press, New York

www.cambridge.org
Information on this title: www.cambridge.org/9780521525657

First published 2010
Reprinted 2011

Printed in the United Kingdom at the University Press, Cambridge

A catalogue record for this publication is available from the British Library

ISBN 978-0-521-81961-9 Hardback
ISBN 978-0-521-52565-7 Paperback

For my family…
~ Near, far
You know who you are ~

"This is the only way, we say; but there are as many ways as there can be drawn radii from one centre."   – Henry David Thoreau

Contents

Figures and tables

Acknowledgements

This book has gone through several incarnations or "editions" in its long gestation, changing to accommodate different external circumstances – journalistic, linguistic, professional, and personal. It has been an ongoing story, one that has involved rethinking and updating, assessing the latest angle, ensuring longevity-of-concept amidst an ever-changing mediascape. I could not have done this without the consistent support, insight, perspective, love, kindness, intelligence, and acts of generosity of students, colleagues, family, friends, and the news community. They have been part of a process that spans two coasts, two continents, two professions, two centuries (more or less), technological innovations, economic changes, and evolving political and cultural contexts. I am most grateful. And have a lot of people to thank. Starting with the news side.

Copy editor Bill Leach took the mentoring role seriously when I was a summer news intern, scaring me at first with grammar minutiae but later explaining the role of language in the newswriting context. Arlen Boardman was equally informative about reporting. Bill Goodyear, who gave me my first newspaper job, showed me how to cover (and photograph) a community from the news perspective, a process that Susanne Hopkins later continued in features. I learned a great deal about running a newsroom and deadline decision-making working with city editor Kip Cady, and later from editor and publisher George Thurlow, both of them keenly aware of the news media's position within the local community, whether delivering mainstream or alternative "product." Listening to and watching my colleagues at work – in print, on-air, and online – was indispensable to my understanding of day-to-day practice.

These insights, understood first as a reporter and later as a linguist, were reinforced when I left the newsroom for the classroom, particularly by my time as faculty adviser of *The Orion* at California State University, Chico, and later during my stint on the Georgetown University Media Board in Washington, DC, as well as through discussions about linguistics and journalism with scores of undergraduate and postgraduate students in classes and seminars over the years. Their questions, curiosity, counter-claims, and own research have made, and still make, teaching fun.

From the beginning, linguists have been supportive of my post-newsroom career change, starting at the University of Sussex with Ken Turner (who led me to Dwight Bolinger and radio research), Larry Trask (who helped excise newspaperese from my essays), Margaret Deuchar (who "liberated" me from the written word to which I have, via different routes, returned), and Richard Coates (who wisely had me wait to pursue "newsroom ethnography" until I knew more). The linguists at the University of California, Berkeley (especially John Gumperz, Carlos Gussenhoven, supervisor and guide Leanne Hinton, Sharon Inkelas, George Lakoff, and Robin Lakoff) also made sure I got my disciplinary bona fides, which led me to love phonology, investigate language revitalization, value the range of approaches to sociolinguistics, and learn how to keep culture and context in view.

I have been lucky to get academic jobs made felicitous by my colleagues, especially Ralph Fasold, Heidi Hamilton, Alison Mackey, Debby Schiffrin (special thanks), Ron Scollon, Natalie Schilling, J. P. Singh, Deborah Tannen, Susan Terrio, and Ande Tyler at Georgetown; and David Adger, Jenny Cheshire, Paul Elbourne, Peter Evans, Sue Harris, Erez Levon, Leigh Oakes, Michael Moriarty, and Devyani Sharma at Queen Mary, University of London. Field research was funded at different times by the graduate schools at Georgetown University and Queen Mary, University of London, and the British Academy (Award Number SG46100). I am grateful for the time that was provided for research and writing, as well as research assistance of the highest caliber (Alkisti Fleischer, Bill Jewell, Mary Madden, Dan Marschall, Aida Premilovac, Ai-Hui Tan, and Margaret Toye in the early stages; and Amy Treutel and Catherine Turner more recently).

Facilitating connections between the newsroom and the academic world were Bill Drummond at the Graduate School of Journalism at UC Berkeley and Diana Askea in the Journalism Department at CSU, Chico, who have always been there with insight, books, trenchant observations, kind consideration, and clarity. I am thankful for the support and wisdom of the late Bill Woo (then at Stanford via the *St. Louis Post-Dispatch*), who saw a great deal of potential in the intermarriage of linguistics and journalism. Equally generous have been Ben Bradlee and Barbara Feinman Todd in Washington, DC, who helped me forge a sideline identity as a "journalist's linguist." Journalists such as Bill, Barbara, and Ben, as well as Joe Cutbirth, Louis Freedberg, Declan McCullagh, and Joanna Neuman, and linguists including Allan Bell, Robin Lakoff, Otto Santa Ana, and Deborah Tannen have given freely of their time in the classroom.

Helping the academic enterprise on the fieldwork side were the editorial team at the *Oakland Tribune*, Janine Warner at *The Miami Herald/El Nuevo Herald*, Éamonn Ó Dónaill and Fionnuala MacAodha at Raidió na Life in Dublin, various editors at *USA Today*, *San Francisco Chronicle*, and washingtonpost. com, and staff at the Newseum in Arlington, VA, and Washington, DC. Ben

Bradlee at the *Washington Post*, John Diaz at the *San Francisco Chronicle*, and Bob Smith (and Alina Tyler) at the *Daily Express* in London get special thanks.

Since I have been working on this project, particularly in recent years, I have seen a rise in research on news media language, process, and practice. On this front, I have benefited tremendously from active engagement with Charles Briggs, Geert Jacobs and the Ghent group, Misty Jaffe, Sally Johnson and the Leeds group, Helen Kelly-Holmes, Lisa McEntee-Atalianis, Mark Allen Peterson, Crispin Thurlow, Will Turner, Tom Van Hout, and Wim Vandenbussche.

I am extremely grateful to those who read later-stage versions of chapters: John Damaso, John Diaz, Ann Joski, and Phil Murray. Their contributions went above-and-beyond. Sincere thanks go to the CUP team, particularly publisher Andrew Winnard and editors Helen Barton, Joanna Garbutt, and Sarah Green, as well as the anonymous readers whose insightful comments collectively enriched the whole.

And last, warm appreciation to the people who are there for me without fail: Rachel Adelson, Diana Askea, Tom and Jackie Bergman, Jennie Blomster, Julie Bridgewater, Jane Dillenberger, Joe Grady, Beverly Hill, Ann Joski, Chrissie Mullings-Lewis, Phil Murray, Kirsten Spalding, Nick Watkins, parents Mary and Jim Cotter, sister Cheri Treutel (and nieces Lauren, Amy, and Jenny), the extended Wisconsin clan, and of course Peter McGinty: partner, champion, sounding board – always ready with a quick mind, warm heart, and cups of tea.

Introduction

In this book, I consider how the process of newsgathering and daily journalistic routines work together to produce the language we see as unique to daily news and define as being journalistic. The book explores news language from the vantage point of the practitioner, focusing on the activities that journalists engage in, the knowledge they utilize, the ways they are taught to gather news and to write about or broadcast it, and the news values and other commitments that influence their decisions about the news. It gives a heretofore unexplored perspective from which to evaluate everyday news language, focusing on elements of practice and process and their relation to text, talk, and social meaning.

Linguists and journalists both have a keen interest in language, as well as descriptive protocols, audience/interlocutors, interactions, and community. Despite this shared focus, the ways each profession looks at language, audience, and community vary tremendously. The book is intended to foster a dialogue between two professions for whom language and social life are central; and for each group – the researchers and the practitioners, the academics and the journalists – to consider language in the media differently.

Goals and objectives

The main objective of the book is to develop an ethnographic view of the language of everyday journalism and an interactional sensibility in analyzing it, through which we come to understand how and what language is produced by the news community, and its relation to an intended audience.

To do this, my goals are to characterize and highlight the ***role of the practitioner in the production of news language***, an approach largely absent from existing linguistic research (see chapter 1); to more explicitly identify the ***speech events and social practice*** of the media community; and to demonstrate how ***practice and process shape*** the language of news. The larger aim is to instigate a wider application of sociolinguistics to the study of the media, to provide a fuller account of language use in a specific context, to analyze media texts and talk from the interactional perspective, to delineate the advantages of

1

an ethnographically grounded approach to media analysis, and to offer new insights for journalists and others into reading news language.

The *process* behind the production of news is worth studying because it relates to the communication of information and values throughout society. And while the news media have their own culture and their own patterns of language use, they also participate in the communicative routines of the wider society in which they are embedded. News language reflects and reinforces social norms, displays agendas, and develops identities, actions that are accomplished through language and the interaction of journalists, the public, and human and natural events. Thus, the book has the following objectives:

- to understand how news media language is produced by its practitioners;
- to consider practitioners as members of a discourse (practitioner) community within a larger speech community;
- to critically evaluate assumptions about media language by researchers;
- to consider news media data from a linguistic perspective;
- to expand the range of research possibilities in both linguistics and media-related studies.

I intend for the book to have two primary academic audiences: those with linguistic training who may be unaware of the range and potential of the news media as a site of research, and those with a media background who are unaware of the approaches and insights linguistics can offer. In general, the book is intended to appeal to anyone with an interest in the media (e.g., communications and media researchers in other social science-based disciplines such as political science and sociology). The audience for the book I hope will include not just sociolinguists, discourse analysts, and linguistic anthropologists, but also journalism educators and students, communications and media researchers, and reporters themselves.

Approach

The approach I take draws from the overlapping traditions of sociolinguistics, discourse analysis, and linguistic anthropology, building on the methods and assumptions of interactional sociolinguistics (Duranti and Goodwin 1992; Gumperz 1982a, 1992; Schiffrin 1994; Tannen 1984) and ethnography of communication (Bauman and Sherzer 1989; Duranti 1988; Gumperz and Hymes 1964, 1972; Hymes 1972b, 1974). **Ethnography of communication** utilizes anthropological field methods and linguistic analytical tools to determine the role that language plays in a community, to understand "ways of speaking" or communicating within a broad context which is itself relevant. It is a deliberately holistic approach that scrutinizes all dimensions of a communication exchange, however brief or extended, whether strictly linguistic or not.

This includes silence, signs, graphic displays, spoken and written outputs, public texts, attitudes, taboos, etc.[1]

Similarly, **interactional sociolinguistics**, which looks at naturally occurring language throughout a conversational or communicative exchange, seeks to reveal the patterns, social rules, and cultural norms that underlie communication, focusing on discourse that emerges in and is contingent on context and the identities of the participants within the interaction. (Other linguistic paradigms relating to phonological and syntactic variation, textual analysis, text-category indicators, enregisterment, metapragmatics, and multimodal dimensions will also be noted.)[2]

Viewing news practitioners from the ethnographic-linguistic framework allows us to see how the interactional and textual norms of a discourse community interrelate with the larger civic community in which they operate, as well as to understand the motivations, conventions, and rituals of a community and their output in discourse. Thus, the relation of language to social interaction and practice – and their realization on different linguistic and cultural levels – is a key premise upon which the book rests. In this way, it follows in the traditions of **linguistic anthropology** (akin to ethnolinguistics in the UK and current sociocultural paradigms more generally) for which the understanding of a community and its display of communicative competence is paramount. It is a deliberate alternative to the social science-based or social theory-based analyses customarily applied to the media, which tend to neglect or overlook the role of practice and process – and even of language – in their approaches.

The news media and its influence in society have long been scrutinized by social science scholars and political scientists, although the language dimension has been given short shrift except in the application of content analysis (a quantitative approach which codes individual words and decontextualized phrases in a restricted corpus of data). More recently, linguists and discourse analysts have begun to bring their tools to the task, on the sociolinguistic end of the spectrum examining the social message encoded in accent use, deletion of articles like "the," and the representation of social groups; and on the discourse-level end analyzing interviews, reported speech, and the framing of topics. In this book, for the purposes of disciplinary clarity, I differentiate the sociolinguistic work that involves variation and style or a similar close analysis of language from discourse research that addresses larger stretches of text and talk beyond the word or sentence level, and combine the two levels of analysis in my own approach to data.

---

[1] For example, Modan 2007; Nunberg 1990; Philips 1989; Rampton 2001; Scollon and Scollon 2003, etc.
[2] For example, Agha 2006; Bell 1991; Nunberg 1990; LeVine and Scollon 2004; Verschueren 1985, etc.

The **text** has been the primary focus of most media researchers to date, particularly as the text encodes values and ideologies that impact and reflect the larger world. (Perhaps the most robust and widely influential linguistic framework currently is that of critical discourse analysis (see chapter 1), a British-European-born approach that blends social theory with a close analysis of a selected text or set of texts to evaluate the discursive construction of power in society.) The second dimension, that of **process** – including the norms and routines of the community of news practitioners – has been on the research agenda for the past several years, but to date no significant work has been completed (but see research by Bell 1995; Cotter 1999a, 1999b, 2003; Jacobs 1999; Jacobs *et al.* 2008; Perrin 2006, Perrin and Ehrensberger-Dow 2006; Peterson 2001). With some exceptions (starting with Bell 1991 and Cotter 1996b and continuing most recently with Turner 2007 and Van Hout and Jacobs 2008) a fair amount of linguistically oriented research into media language and media discourse is compromised by a lack of knowledge about what comprises the normative routines of daily journalism. Yet it is everyday practice that shapes the language of news. It is thus a ripe area for further research, and the focus of this book.

The approach I take distinguishes itself from other work on media language in other key ways. Remarkably, there has been little comprehensive analysis of American news media by linguists, relatively few American linguists looking at the media in any other country (but see linguists and linguistic anthropologists such as Cotter 1996a, 1999c in Ireland; Jaffe 2007 in Corsica; Peterson 1996 in India; Spitulnik 1992 in Zambia; and Waugh 1995 in France, as well as a growing number of graduate students who will undoubtedly further the field), and minimal use of American news data in the existing work (since the most widely published scholars are based in Europe, the UK, and New Zealand). Nor have most researchers interested in media culture itself (sociologists and folklorists being the exception, e.g., Dégh 1994; Gans 1979) looked at much of the news "package" beyond the prestige stories that run on Page One, or at news sources beyond CNN and *The New York Times*, or at what is occurring in non-metropolitan contexts. (In the USA, the total number of daily newspapers is more than 1,400[3] – some 93 percent of these with less than 100,000 circulation[4] and 55 percent with less than 25,000 circulation[5] serving small communities. Non-daily papers number around 6,700.[6]) The book attempts to begin to address these gaps and to instigate a new focus for research on many levels

---

[3] *Editor and Publisher Yearbook* 2008 lists 1,422 in 2007; the Newspaper Association of America lists 1,408 in 2008.
[4] Friedersdorf 2006.
[5] Based on figures from Audit Bureau of Circulations, September 30, 2007.
[6] National Newspaper Association figures from 2004 and 2009. Neuharth 2008 lists 6,253 weeklies.

by theoretically and methodologically introducing ethnography of communication and the contextualization of practice, focusing on the interaction between journalists and their audiences, going into the newsroom for data, and enlarging the scope and geographical center of the inquiry. I take advantage of the fact that ethnographic observation and understanding provide evidence that is not easily available through corpora, interview, or close-text analysis.

Data

In its cross-disciplinary, holistic endeavor, the book uses a wide range of data gathered through newsroom fieldwork, interviews with practitioners, my own past experience as a daily newspaper reporter and editor, and archived news stories to look at the subject on three levels: those of language, discourse, and practice. Using examples from a variety of newsroom and field sources, primarily in the US, I touch on profession-specific speech events and processes that encompass both ideological and linguistic norms. In the interest of time and space, I rely mainly on print contexts, but also use examples from broadcast and Web news domains.

The empirical range of the book involves ethnographic interviews with practitioners, material and analysis deriving from actual newsroom observation, incorporation of various texts (trade journals, internal memos, textbooks, style guides) published specifically for and generally circulating within the community of journalists itself, and mostly print media examples – either to illustrate various linguistic and discourse-level points I am making, or to demonstrate a pattern of usage that is significant. To a limited extent, I also draw on my own insights about the profession from my experience within it.

The data and examples I use are primarily from US sources for particular reasons, including ethnographic-methodology ones:

(1) Most of the current work on media discourse is done by scholars from outside of the US and uses non-US data (with the exception of broadcast and print media like CNN, *The New York Times*, or *The Washington Post*); there is not as much linguistic research using American media examples as one would think. This means that American journalism, as journalists in the USA would see it, is not part of the broader academic discussion (although see Hill 2007, Lakoff 2000a, and Peterson 2007 for relevant discipline-situated critiques of US story coverage of interest to reporters).

(2) I discuss more than just major articles or widely familiar news stories. As I look at the relation of the news organization to the community it is covering, that means considering the local element, and "smaller" but equally recognizable stories. At the same time, I look at similarities across communities and geographical domains, and point to the differences as markers of local identities.

(3) I focus on interactional and contextual elements as much as on a body of text; I also employ the interpretive traditions of ethnography and anthropology, and orient my claims to cultural contexts and communities with which I am familiar and in which I have participated.

The ethnographic perspective has served me well. I came to England to live for a year and to study linguistics virtually the very first minute I left my news career (more on that at the end of this Introduction), and was hyper-aware – professionally at first and gradually linguistically – of what was different about the English press and the American media, as well as what was similar. After reading the Brighton *Evening Argus* for a few months, I realized that many of the issues of local coverage were identical to ones I was familiar with in the States, such as complaints about the store-owners' holiday decorations in the main shopping areas or worries about over-development, historical preservation, and area schools. In short, I saw similarities on the level of content; but variance at the level of discourse, e.g., attribution rules, and ideology. The notion of a prestige press, for instance, does not resonate in mainstream, non-journalistic USA, although the down-market association linked to "supermarket tabloids" does.

That early "making strange" ethnographic experience (cf. Agar 1980), reinforced by return visits and the past seven years living in London, means I have some intuitions about UK media in a comparative sense, and will include relevant data from the British press, the comparative element being an important analytical technique (cf. Hymes 1972a). Ultimately, though, it is well to recognize that just as there are differences between American English and British English, and the two countries' cultural norms, there are significant differences in the media paths (more about which I will explore in future research).

The newspaper data I have been collecting on a near-daily basis for a decade come from the following sources:

- *The Oakland* (Calif.) *Tribune* (Chapter 5) – editorial story meetings (field observation).
- The *San Francisco Chronicle*, *The Sacramento Bee*, *Los Angeles Times* (chapter 8) – the three main newspapers in California; to examine the depiction of a divisive state ballot initiative as it proceeded through an election cycle and beyond and to illustrate simplification rules within news discourse.
- The Redding (Calif.) *Record Searchlight* (chapters 7, 9) – a diachronic comparison of sentence-initial connectives.
- *The Washington Post* (most chapters) – to illustrate various points regarding text, relationship, and community of practice, and *The New York Times* and London metropolitan and UK national press by way of comparison.
- The *Miami Herald/El Nuevo Herald* (Spanish version) (Chapters 4, 5) – for supplementary field data.
- Wire stories transmitted by The Associated Press and Reuters.

- Metropolitan dailies in various cities, etc.
- Smaller dailies from different geographical areas, etc.
- Professional publications, newsletters, press releases.
- Relevant ephemera found in newsrooms or museums.
- Archived material from my newsroom and journalism teaching days.
- Newswriting textbooks.

Larger corpora that were used are the Lexis-Nexis Database (the General News database, which comprises major newspapers in the USA and elsewhere, e.g., London, Singapore, Bombay, Hong Kong, etc.), and a daily "news wall" at a specialist museum (formerly in Rosslyn, VA, it is now located in Washington, DC). The Newseum (an "interactive museum for news") gets electronic transmissions of the front pages of more than 500 newspapers, big and small, from around the country and the world, which are printed out in full color and at full size and displayed in a "Today's Front Pages" exhibit outside the Newseum. I use the "news wall" as a synchronic repository – to illustrate similarity and difference and their implications. (For example, in one entry in my Rosslyn-era field notes, the *Salt Lake City* (Utah) *Tribune* had two stories about the Book of Mormon and the Church of Latter-day Saints (LDS) on Page One as well as the expected stories on what was happening internationally. Any other newspaper in a state other than where the LDS headquarters are located might make brief mention of the Mormon-focus stories only in their Saturday religion page, if that.) The use of the Lexis-Nexis Database, the Newseum's "news wall," and stories selected from The Associated Press Web archives, means that I cite at least several dozen newspapers from around the US, and take care to avoid the usual fronting of more internationally known papers, or of what counts as the US's prestige media. I also attempted to choose illustrative examples that would not "date" because of topic (hence a larger number of weather stories than would be found in a typical paper).

I do not examine television in detail, except to discuss the interrelationship of the different media outlets, such as CNN or the BBC. I also talk a bit about local/ regional TV and radio and the role they play within a community inside and outside the USA, and the unique differences in news production. Broadcast "institutions" such as CNN are referred to in the same context as *USA Today* – per their historically significant role in the development of modern media, but no extensive analysis will be done. I note the evolution of the *genre* of TV news as well as how Web journalism has influenced story structure, content, and register and is causing significant discussion within the news industry – within newsrooms and within journalism schools.

Chapter organization

The book is organized according to the **phases of the newsgathering** and producing processes, from determining what counts as news, to constructing the story, to the way in which media practice influences news discourse and news language. It is divided into sections which correlate to the process: the news-community values and premises that background reporting and editing decisions and actions (Part I); conceptualizing the news (Part II); the processes of constructing the story (Part III); and dissemination of news and its impacts (Part IV). Throughout, I establish the premise that individuals who work for media organizations such as daily newspapers can be viewed as members of their own speech (or discourse or practice) community, presupposing the role of language as a primary way of marking community boundaries.

The interactional and ethnographic approach to investigating news language is set up in Chapter 1. News media discourse is best understood when the reporters, their intended audience, and the stories they write are considered as related parts contributing to a whole. Analytic approaches that allow a focus on practice, cultural and communicative competence, and an understanding of the norms and constraints of social interaction, will give a more complete view of the language that is produced by the media. Within the ethno-interactional scope, the tools of discourse analysis and sociolinguistics can be fully implemented to consider language structure, function, social organization, and worldview.

Journalists are socialized to approach their work in particular ways that both influence the shape of the text and reinforce their identities and professional roles, and this will be addressed in Chapter 2. Their work is motivated discursively in terms of craft and ideologically in terms of press freedoms and a commitment to the public. Writing and reporting well, and attending to an audience for whom the craft is intended to serve, are organizing principles that create coherence within the profession. Understanding these motivations creates alternative ways of understanding journalistic dynamics, a key step in understanding what shapes journalistic language.

Chapter 3 examines the ways reporters learn to report and editors learn to edit. The professional socialization of most journalists today begins in the classroom, where courses focus almost exclusively on learning practical skills. After that, the newsroom provides a constant reinforcement of competent practice, for both novices and veterans. Over time, the "ways of speaking" and writing in the journalistic context become internalized, functioning to formulate a professional identity as much as a news product.

The values that underlie journalistic production are the focus of Chapter 4. Newsworthiness is determined by a set of simple factors or "news values" that function as guidelines for decision-making at every step of the news process. News values are one of the most important ideological factors in understanding the shape of news stories and the decisions of journalists.

The processes of newsgathering have elements that are patterned and habitual as well as dynamic and emergent. These routinized and contingent elements are manifested in a daily, recurrent speech event specific to the news community, the "story meeting" or budget meeting, where editors talk about the stories that will appear in that day's newspaper (or broadcast). The story meeting, which I discuss in detail and illustrate with a case study in Chapter 5, is a crucial site for the emergence of values that pertain to the media context. As decisions about coverage and story play are negotiated, so are internal news values and external community values negotiated and reinforced.

Traditionally, news stories are produced with a group of listeners or readers outside the newsroom in mind (although economic factors lead to other production objectives, as Barnhurst and Nerone 2001 and Schudson 1978, for instance, have outlined over different phases of news history, and Simon 2008 has noted in the new millennium). To explore the interaction-based nature of journalism is to challenge some fundamental models of mass communication and assumptions about the way journalists relate to each other. Relying on sociolinguistic insights, in Chapter 6, I introduce the dynamic of the "pseudo-relationship" (extending Daniel Boorstin's influential 1961 notion of "pseudo-event," or a constructed, non-organic circumstance like a press conference which is reported on by the media) to characterize the relationship between the media and the public. I also demonstrate the multiple ways in which "interaction" can be identified in the journalistic context, and how the Web is making more transparent this interactive relationship (or "participant framework" as a linguist would describe it, or "interactivity" as the news community would say).

Story design and the role of the lead are described in Chapter 7. The structure of news stories follows a particular order, influenced by what reporters identify as the most important or newsworthy element. This element is emphasized in a variety of ways in the "lead," or first paragraph or beginning of a story, from the strategic use of passive voice in print to vocal emphasis in radio to the use of visuals in television. More than any other textual demand, writing a good lead is the most advanced of skills, generally acquired last by learners who have already mastered other aspects of good story design: organization, placement of attribution and quotation, and insertion of background and context.

A primary task of the reporter is to clarify and simplify the complex, a task that interacts with other discourse demands, such as maintaining neutrality, and summarizing previously reported details of a story when covering it again. "Boilerplate," the summary material that is inserted in continuing stories to remind readers of past circumstances, is one manifestation of a complex discourse demand whose implications become significant when the story is linked to more divisive issues. Using print media coverage of a contested California ballot initiative concerning the rights of illegal immigrants as an example, in Chapter 8 I characterize what was included and what was left out of boilerplate summaries of a complicated social and political issue.

Despite what outsiders might conclude, the media have a fairly conservative attitude toward language use. In Chapter 9, I orient the social and structural factors of language standardization to the practice and attitudes of the media, and examine journalism's role in relation to language style and standard language ideologies. The processes behind news reporting also create conditions in which communicative demands supersede prescriptive habits. News language both reflects what is socially acceptable usage as well as what is conventionalized and contingent within the profession.

Chapter 10 concludes with a very brief discussion of the impact of the news process on media discourse, including the **constraints of the physical world** (time and space) and ways to "read" the newspaper as a journalist does; the impacts of journalistic priorities on the representation of linguists and anthropologists in news contexts; and suggestions (and a checklist) for future research. I will reiterate my underlying motive: that journalists and linguists have a lot to talk about and learn with respect to their shared but divergent professional interests in language, and it is my wish that this book can help the discussion and collaboration along.

My background

As a former daily news reporter and assistant city editor for whom academia is a second career, one objective of my work is to do research on the media that is informed by newsroom realities. My goal is to illuminate some of the communicative conventions of the news business, for academics and journalists alike, and to show the relation of the news process to a range of outcomes and recipients.

My own interest in the language and communication routines that create and are created by the news media began when I worked for eight years as a daily newspaper reporter and editor in Northern California, and three years as a full-time journalism educator and newspaper adviser at the university level, two of them while completing my University of California-Berkeley linguistics dissertation on the use of broadcast media in endangered-language revitalization.

Not unsurprisingly, I have found myself for most of my academic career explaining linguistic concepts to journalists and journalistic concepts to linguists (and anthropologists). Meeting with the late linguist Dwight Bolinger in Palo Alto in 1989 was my inaugural attempt at this – and led to my subsequent (University of Sussex) master's thesis on broadcast prosody and an abiding regard for "the ethnographic advantage" (see Chapter 1). Numerous conversations earlier in this decade with the late editor, educator, and one-time American Society of Newspaper Editors president Bill Woo – also in Palo Alto – reinforced my sense that journalists want to know what linguists think – but in ways that illuminate the news profession's understanding of language itself (and not necessarily what contributes to the linguist's desire for elegant theory or intra-group prestige).

Both professions are interested in the work of each other, but not necessarily for reasons that either might imagine, as I will explore. This book, I hope, will provide a more powerful explanatory model of the language of the news media by synthesizing insights from both domains.

Part I

The process and practice of everyday journalism

1　An interactional and ethnographic approach to news media language

KEY POINTS

- Contradictory perceptual boundaries create the clash between the news media and the public: perceptions are developed by ongoing, shared group experiences. A reporter reads the paper differently than you do, and sees partitions in the text and presentation that you do not.
- The shape or content of media discourse is influenced by *context* (local and professional), *structure* (how news is gathered and assembled), and *interaction* (of practitioners and a community of readers or listeners).
- An interactional and ethnographic approach allows us to study the *process* of news production, the *practice* of journalists, and their relationships internally (profession or in-group) and externally (audience or out-group).
- Constraints of different orders work simultaneously to influence practice: technical, textual, relational, and sociopolitical (i.e., technology, text, audience, and ideology).

This book looks at media language through an examination of the news media as a community of practitioners, whose actions reinforce its professional identity, as well as result in the news stories we as the public read, hear, click to, digest, consume, ignore, appreciate, vilify, or rail against. The McLuhanesque meaning of the (print, broadcast, Web) "medium and the message"[1] exists because of language, as well as other cultural indexes and inferences, more about which will be said throughout the book.

The value of linguistic approaches to the analysis of news media communicative actions has the net goal of understanding news language at all levels, and

---

[1] Media theorist Marshall McLuhan's 1964 phrase, "the medium is the message," was the foundation for a significant body of communications scholarship that examined the media itself, its contribution to the formulation of content, and the meaning-bearing consequences for the recipient. See also Hall 1994 and Allan 1999.

allows for a comprehensiveness of understanding of media outputs, or news discourse. I use "language" and "discourse" somewhat interchangeably and a-theoretically in the generic sense and also to make a conscious differentiation. "Language" is used to refer to linguistic elements that are part of the structure of news language that relate to syntax (e.g., use of tense, sentence structure), phonology (e.g., intonation contour or accent), lexicon (e.g., word choice), sociolinguistics (e.g., variation, usage, language attitudes, macro-social constructs, indexicality, audience design), and pragmatics (e.g., connectives, inference, shared knowledge). And "discourse" is used to refer to longer stretches of text and talk that go beyond the segment or sentence and relate to coherence, narrative, participant structure, stance, and communicative function.

Because of the institutional power of news media, the study of media language has often been a study of bias and has predominated in the literature (see Section 1.2). It is now a good time to change focus, and to consider understanding media-language production and discursive outcomes from the perspective of journalists, from a practice or Bourdieu-derived *habitus* position[2] – in other words, from the ethnographic perspective.

The practice of journalism influences all facets of media discourse, whether it be the text (or news story) itself, the practitioner's orientation to language, the social parameters embedded within the journalistic display, and the relation of the news media, and its texts and actions, to community and society. The **orientation to media language** that I establish in this chapter, and more generally in this book, attempts to clarify and illuminate three areas:

- Scholars' or lay views vs. journalists' views of news practice and news language.
- Characteristics of news language itself and what actions and decisions are behind its construction.
- The rules of practice behind reporting and writing.

The macro question behind my undertaking here is: what affects the discourse? Thus, I examine:

- The influences on the shape and content of news *discourse*.
- The constraints that influence journalistic *practice*.
- The structure and functions of media *language*.

In other words, I examine what constitutes the dynamic behind the production of news media discourse. This means attempting to assess the patterns

---

[2] Kulick and Schieffelin 2006 define Bourdieu's notion of *habitus*, the "ways of being in the world," in relation to language socialization (Kulick and Schieffelin 2006: 349), a point relevant to the acquisition of communicative competence (cf. Gumperz 1984) and news-cultural knowledge in the journalism profession.

and interrelationships behind the newsgathering, reporting, and editing processes. The primary components underlying these dynamics are language, audience, and the practice of news professionals itself. The news media *practitioners* are primary agents, following professional roles, rules, and scripts; the *audience* are secondary agents or pseudo-interlocutors (see Chapter 6) always taken into account by the media (for whatever reason); and *language* is the instrument of delivery. Photos, graphics, visuals, actualities (radio "quotes"), and html links also play a part in the referential and symbolic presentation of news information, but will not be discussed except in passing.

In this chapter, I situate a practice-based or ethnographic approach to news media within other frameworks for news-language analysis (Section 1.2) and argue for ethnographic and interactional sociolinguistic approaches to data analysis, pointing out their advantages. I will begin to establish what constitutes journalistic process and practice, and their relation to language and salient professional relationships inside and outside the profession (Section 1.3). These dynamics will help us orient to what influences media language and discourse, and what leads to its characteristic features (Sections 1.4 and 1.5). Case examples in other chapters will further illustrate these points: e.g., attitudes toward language and language standardization (Chapter 9); the implementation of professional ideology and values in speech events such as the *story meeting* (Chapter 5); discourse outcomes such as *boilerplate* (unattributed story-internal summaries) in text and practice (Chapter 8); and impacts of the process on discourse (Chapter 10). First, however, I will make explicit the assumptions we might possess about news language and the media, and how they may function in "contradictory distribution."

1.1 Contradictory perceptions about news media behaviors

In my many years studying news discourse it has been made abundantly clear to me that there are contradictory perceptions about what the news media actually does, what it means to do, what it means, and what it achieves. My study has involved speaking with reporters, journalism educators, and colleagues from my old profession; engaging with linguists in the course of teaching and research activities within my new(er) profession; reading about the profession and its discontents, downloading news stories, taping news broadcasts, and saving reams of newsprint on behalf of research; and explaining what I do to non-linguist/journalist "others" in the talkative, data-eliciting manner of sociolinguists, e.g., while in the hairdresser's chair, on an airplane, at Thanksgiving dinner or Sunday lunch, in a taxi, donating blood, at a family reunion, etc. Each "side" – linguists, the public, journalists – have their own perspective, their own truth, as well as their own logical array of blind spots.

I see coherence in it all: the blind spots, especially, allow us to investigate the combined roles of *practice*, *text*, and *ideology*. Let me explain.

Linguists see language technically, but so far have not very thoroughly examined news media language as a reflex of a speech (or occupational or practice) community, or as discourse with structures that come from *practice* routines (but see the discussion in Section 1.2). Meanwhile, the public – the recipients, consumers, beneficiaries or victims, and critics of media outputs – has an attested "disconnect" with media (cf. ASNE 1999a), which I argue is based on the non-insider interpretation of practice/text. Finally, journalists in some sense are operating within their own world, viewing their outputs and managing the boundaries developed through practice and *ideology*, through group membership, from their own professional perspective.

Thus, relationships to *text*, or the news story, vary: the linguist looks at it as data to determine linguistic features or ideological motivations; the public sees it as information, entertainment, or evidence of power maneuvering; and journalists view it as an outcome of professional actions involving decisions and information dissemination.

The scholars' view of journalistic language is at variance with the journalists' view. Reporters see the newspaper differently than non-journalists do. It is part of their training (and socialization, see Chapter 3). They are aware of the factors that govern reporting decisions (e.g., news values, cf. Chapter 4). A news story is multi-authored; writing is differentiated from reporting; and a reporter's stance or personal position to the text is (or is supposed to be) constrained. The story itself has its own narrative structure, and its own relative value depending on the circumstances surrounding it.

As journalists look at language itself differently from linguists – they evaluate usage from the conservative-prescriptive lay perspective – so do academics look at the media from the outsider's view, similarly relying on prescriptive perspectives and stereotypes, and making assumptions about both intention and language use. For example, non-journalists have suggested that the use of passive voice in lead or opening paragraphs means the media are colluding with the powerful or trivializing victims (e.g., Lamb and Keon 1995), or that overuse of pitch contours in broadcast means playing fast and loose with given and new information structures (Bolinger 1982). Passive voice does have a role in news design (see Chapter 7), as does inference (cf. Grice 1975, Gumperz 1992), from which competing interpretations can arise. Broadcast pitch-contour configurations are different from conversational ones, but are relevant to register (cf. Cotter 1993), rather than examples of production errors (an area that Goffman 1981 also found of interest). The ethnographic perspective allows us to see the connections between media-and-language constructs and find the conceptual linguistic language to explain them.

1.2   The ethnographic advantage

A good deal of social science research devoted to the news media fails to consider how communication patterns derive from the needs or values of a particular community. But study of the community itself may reveal a better sense of what their message, behaviors, and actions mean (for influential sociological and anthropological work in this regard see Gans 1979 and Tuchman 1978). The community and how it is realized, and its interactions and communicative outputs, can be studied separately and as a synthesis of both components.

The primary orientation of an ethnographic focus is the *community*. Doing ethnography means trying to understand a community – by looking at how a community "works," by looking at norms within the community, by standing back and offering an "objective" or detached perspective, and by synthesizing what one comes to know about the community within the analytical paradigms of academia (cf. Agar 1986). The ethnographic approach used within linguistic anthropology looks at a community and what makes it cohere, what makes it unique, and the resulting structure and function of its communicative outputs and interactions. An ethnographic approach means that the situations, events, and acts that participants engage in and that comprise a community's communicative repertoire are the units of analysis.

An ethnographic and interactional approach is a holistic orientation that looks to the community and the context it inhabits: how the community itself regards its relation to language, what counts as viable text or talk, the roles and behaviors of the participants, what constitutes communicative competence, etc. It is a foundation for critical approaches. The purpose is a greater understanding of a community (speech community, micro-community, group of people, or social collective) and its particular "ways of speaking" (see Sherzer and Darnell 1972 for a brief guide to investigating ways of speaking; Hymes 1974 and 1984 for a consideration of what constitutes a community from the ethnolinguistic or linguistic anthropological perspective; Heath 1983 for a classic example of community–researcher interactions, methods, and results; and Gumperz and Hymes 1964, 1972 for foundational work in ethnography of communication). I am using the term "community" here in the sense of a micro-community, group of people, or social collective – not speech community in the strict sense (but see Morgan 2006) – as well as being aware that the news profession in different theoretical ways also constitutes a community of practice (Lave and Wenger 1991), discourse community (Swales 1990), and occupational community (Van Maanen and Barley 1984), a point discussed in greater detail in Chapter 2.

The ethnographic approach constitutes an informant-based interpretive method, reliant on participant observation, extended fieldwork, and confirmation of analytic judgments with community members themselves. What it does (and how it works) is to prioritize the community as a working, structured, rule-governed, dynamic, culturally inscribed entity. Thus, a researcher goes through a systematic process of fieldwork (and data-gathering) to understand community values, community routines, and community roles and relationships. With this understanding, the researcher can identify patterns, communicative roles, and cultural meanings.

As an analytic approach, ethnographic and interactional studies are *process-focused* and *practice-focused*, the "text" and "talk" under investigation being an output of process and practice and not examined in isolation. This context-dependent approach gives us different analytical results than non-context-based frameworks, and informs our understanding of news language, news texts, and news practice on many levels. The ethnographic approach provides an advantage in our understanding of the news media for the following reasons:

• It allows process and practice focus, on what preconditions the outputs.
• It privileges the community's understanding of its communicative ways and foci of speaking and writing.
• It allows highlighting of structural and functional features of news production.
• It identifies speech events and discourse forms characteristic of the news media.
• It reveals professional "insider ideologies" – and their constraints and impacts.

I am using, and arguing for, an ethnographic approach to the study of news language because it provides fundamental insights into journalistic ways of being, making evident the routines that underlie news practice through a focus on news process and production, the influence of news-editorial decisions on the shape of news stories, and the relation of news values to community values.

1.2.1   Past approaches to news language

The study of the media by linguists[3] is actually in a relatively early stage, compared to a longstanding body of work produced by political scientists, sociologists, and communications scholars who evaluate the media message but who seldom consider in detail what may be systematic about language itself. The earliest significant work on media language (Davis and Walton 1983; Glasgow University Media Group 1976, 1980; Kress and Hodge 1979), which has influenced the field for linguists today, tended to focus on the biased nature

---

[3] See Cotter 2001 for an extended discussion of linguistic approaches to news media discourse analysis, from which this section derives.

of the media message, and its potential for abuse, underscoring two points simultaneously: the *myth of objectivity*, a notion once held sacrosanct by reporters, and the *persuasive function* of language, a key feature of the human language system (Aitchison 1997). The critical perspective subsequently fostered within linguistics has been developed primarily by British and European linguists, notably Norman Fairclough (1995), Roger Fowler (1991), and Teun van Dijk (1985, 1988), alongside linguists at the University of Birmingham in England and the work of other media studies scholars (included in Bell and Garrett 1998). Fairclough and Fowler, especially, have made the media the cornerstone of critical linguistics, a framework informed by social theory and social justice. (More recent developments, building on the earlier work, have been initiated by Caldas-Coulthard 1997; Richardson 2007; Thurlow and Jaworski 2003; Toye 2006, etc.)

As this book attempts to demonstrate, the discourse of the news media encapsulates two key components: the news story and the process involved in producing it. The first dimension, that of the *text*, has been the primary focus of most media researchers to date, particularly as the text encodes values and ideologies that impact and reflect the larger world. The second dimension, that of *process* – including the norms and routines of the community of news practitioners – has been on the research agenda for the past several years, but only recently is significant work being done.[4]

The relative lack of attention to process, however, does not mean that the text has been examined as only a static artifact. Most linguists consider the news text from one of two vantage points: (1) that of discourse structure or linguistic function, or (2) according to its impact as ideology-bearing discourse. Either view assumes an emergent, dynamic mechanism that results in the unique display of media discourse over time, culture, and context. In the first view, Bakhtin's notions of voicing ([1953]1986), Goffman's concept of framing (1974, 1981), Bell's work on narrative structure and style (1991, 1994, 1998), and Lakoff 1990, Santa Ana 2002, and Tannen's 1998 positioning of the media as agonists and instigators of polarized public debate have led to valuable insights into discourse structure, function, and effect – and have characterized the very significant role the media play in the shaping of public, as well as media, discourse. In the latter view, the interdisciplinary framework of critical discourse analysis (CDA) – including Fairclough's deployment of social theory and intertextuality in the illumination of

---

[4] The practitioner approach underlies the innovative research projects underway at the News TextandTalk Research Centre at the University of Ghent in Belgium, and the Zurich University of Applied Sciences' Institute of Applied Media Studies in Switzerland – the site of the most significant process-oriented news-media research currently. See Jacobs *et al.* 2008; Perrin 2006; Perrin and Ehrensberger-Dow 2006, and Perrin and Ehrensberger-Dow 2008.

discourse practice (1992, 1995), Fowler's critical scan of social practice and language in the news (1991), and van Dijk's work on the relation of societal structures and discourse structures, particularly as this relation implicates racism (1991) – has been seminal, and with Bell 1991 and Bell and Garrett 1998 (see also Blommaert and Verschueren 1998) have created the foundations of the field of media discourse studies thus far.[5]

While various discourse perspectives have tended to dominate current linguistic research (see also Clayman and Heritage 2002; Greatbatch 1992), there has been a fair amount of important sociolinguistic work done on language in the news media, particularly with respect to language style and variation pioneered by Bell (1984, 2001). Given the vast repositories of media data, from databases to microfilm archives, the sociolinguistic approach allows examination of language change over time (see examples in Cotter 2003; Ungerer 2000). Equally important are cross-cultural analyses that underscore the significant sociocultural and socio-interactional dimensions of the language of the news media, particularly those that involve language policy alongside intercultural variation (see examples in Horner 2004; Jaffe 1999; Johnson and Ensslin 2007; Kelly-Holmes 2002; Knight and Nakano 1999; Naro and Scherre 1996; Pan *et al.* 2002; Satoh 2001; Scollon 1997; Vandenbussche 2008; Weizman 1984, etc.).

As the literature as a body tends to focus variously on the ideological implications of language in the media, critiques of the analyses are organized around the validity of findings of bias, whether instigated through linguistic or sociological means. (Ideology is defined and investigated differently by different researchers.) Early on, Verschueren (1985), for instance, noted that either the linguistic work was not sufficiently contextualized, ignorant of the "structural and functional properties of the news gathering and reporting process in a free press tradition" (1985: vii), or the ideology work drew obvious conclusions, "simply predictable on the basis of those structural and functional properties" (1985: vii; see also Cotter 1999b). Bell, meanwhile, has critiqued the earlier content-analytic approaches to media language analysis which in his view suffer from a "lack of sound basic linguistic analysis" (1991: 215). Approaches that are too simplistic do not advance the field, as they erroneously presume "a clearly definable relation between any given linguistic choice and a specific ideology" and assign to "newsworkers a far more deliberate ideological intervention in news than is supported by the research on news production" (Bell 1991: 214).

Which brings us back to the ethnographic approach and its process- and practice-focused ethos. Its holistic orientation allows a range of input for

---

[5] For an extended discussion of CDA, see van Dijk 2001.

analysis: it can address the "disconnect" between the public and the media, which concerns journalists, and at the same time it can address issues of ideology and power, which concern linguists. As the ethnographic (and allied interactional sociolinguistic) approach views communicative phenomena as locally realized, contingent, and complex (Duranti 1997; Schiffrin 1994), it allows multi-level and cross-disciplinary insights that can help us analytically cope with the diversity – and plethora – of media data. The aim is thus to expand our definitions of "news language" by bringing awareness of talk that occurs in the course of accomplishing communicative and discursive tasks, between and among members of a community.

1.3   Exploring news and news language from the perspective of the practitioner

The news stories we read or hear are structured in a certain way, following a set of reporting, writing, and editing rules that mainstream journalists by and large follow as a matter of course, rules of communicative practice that are taught explicitly in the classroom and the newsroom and reinforced implicitly through daily doing (Cotter 1999b, 2003; see also Bell 1991). Reporting in the print domain is generally considered to be a process of newsgathering and writing up the story; editing is a separate function, divided into "content editing" (is the story as complete as possible?) and "line editing," by which a separate team of copy editors considers and corrects elements of usage and affixes headlines.

To explore news or news language from the vantage point of the practitioner one has to be familiar with the process of news production, what is relevant to and comprises news practice, constraints influencing news practice, and the profession-instigated relationships (or participant structures) within and outside the news community. This means we can look at process and practice on the *information or propositional level*, the *text or news-story level*, and the *interactional level* – all of which I attempt to do to some degree throughout this book.

The *process* of news production involves all the steps involved in reporting, writing, editing, and disseminating a news story, and all the individuals who accomplish these steps. *Practice* is the complement of activities, actions, routines, conventions, and interactions that initiate, motivate, maintain, and orient newsroom employees to the news process. Understanding the elements of practice, which a communicatively competent practitioner does, sheds light on the way stories come into being, as well as the multiple participants they involve and roles the contributing participants occupy. Practice and its embodiments within the news culture, and their contiguities with the larger culture, are essentially what a novice reporter must learn to be a core or socialized member of the news community (see Keating and Egbert 2006;

Lave and Wenger 1991; Wortham 2005, for discussions of socialization trajectories). Practice situates communication within news culture.

Language itself, as well as visual or graphic codes, is integral to news practice in many ways beyond the obvious fact that what we read, see, or hear is comprised of words, images, and sounds that are meaningful. Language is relevant in relation to (1) the structure and semantic and social meaning of the *text*; (2) attitudes and decisions about *language use*; (3) *social reflexivity* and worldview; (4) the *community* beyond the newsroom; and (5) *display*. Display can be *deictic* (linguistically orienting our reading of a news story to place, person, time, and social context in relation to ourselves), *visual* (the form of presentation itself indexing and contributing to story meaning), and *ideological* (conveying the norms and attitudes of a ratified, vested, socialized member of the news community). Updating a story on the Web (*new information*), running a breaking-news story continuously on television (*repetition*), getting an opposing viewpoint to flesh out a story (*proposition and argument*), and asking for comments on a tragedy or loss (*phatic and personal interaction*) are all examples of ideological or socioculturally proscribed display. The text, language usage, community, display, and social reflexivity factors suggest the extended role of language in the news production process and reporting and editing activities.

As well as the "language factors," there are other constraints that operate simultaneously and influence news practice, and ultimately, the news story or news-production output. These constraints incorporate the language factors and go beyond them. These constraints include the *technical-physical*, the physical boundaries of time to deadline, space available for publication, and technology and its limitations (see chapter 10); the *text*, and the requirements necessary for well-formed news discourse (see Chapters 7 and 8); the *audience*, and the news community's relationship with it (see Chapters 5 and 6); the *ideological*, or the values that govern decisions on different levels: deciding what is news, heeding the First Amendment (in the US) or equivalent statutes elsewhere honoring "freedom of speech"; managing economics and status (see Chapters 4 and 5); and *relationships* within the profession and outside of it (see Chapters 5 and 6).

1.4   Influences on media language and discourse

A primary question underlying news practice and process is: *what affects the discourse?* Putting aside for a minute the particulars of practice and process, we can begin by looking at news discourse in relation to **context**, **structure**, and **interaction**. These elements – *contexts* of use, linguistic or discursive *structure*, and *interaction* among participants – are what one would look at in any speech situation to determine what affects the shape and content of the discourse.

The main **contexts** that are relevant to journalists, and thus the ones I look at, are *local* and *professional*. The **structure** I focus on relates to *how news is assembled* and the *narrative* forms it embodies. In terms of **interaction**, I prioritize the interaction between the *practitioner* – the community of practice (Lave and Wenger 1991) – and readers, listeners, audience, or *community of coverage* (Cotter 1999b; Chapter 3), as this interaction, which is so essential to practice elements and journalistic self-identity, is little studied or remarked upon.

Contexts, *structure*, and *interaction* are discursive operational elements in any language, and present in some form in any communicative situation, journalistic or otherwise. But there are also profession-specific factors that influence news language in particular ways. These are the ***constraints*** of the medium, journalists' consideration of ***audience***, and their ***language attitudes***. How does a reporter deal with medium constraints: the asynchrony of print, or the time-shallowness of broadcast, or the lack of visibility of radio, or the 24/7 aspect of the Web? To what extent is the audience taken into account in the everyday practice of news practitioners? How do communicative needs interact with language attitudes, and what are they? Figure 1.1 summarizes how news

---

General communicative components

Contexts →   {local
    | {professional
Structure →   {how news is assembled (reporting)
    | {narrative form (writing)
Interaction →   {news practitioner, source, community
                  {authority and friend dichotomy

Specific factors affecting news language

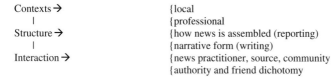

Constraints of medium on text →   {visual, oral modalities – broadcast
    | {writing and reading – print
                                    {visibility and "interactivity" – Web
Journalists' consideration of *audience* →   {writing for readers
    | {attracting attention
Language attitudes of journalists →   {prescriptive
    | {conservative and innovative
Professional *norms* (e.g., in US) →   {interlocutor-oriented/pseudo-dyad
                                               {local news privileged/attribution

Media-specific factors in relation to communicative components

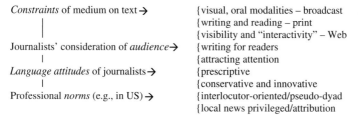

Constraints of medium   affects story **structure**
Consideration of *audience*   affects **interaction**, **contexts**, story **structure**
Language attitudes   affects writing (**structure**), influenced by **contexts**
Professional *norms*   affects **interaction**, **contexts**, **structure**

Figure 1.1 What affects news discourse?

discourse is put together and how the interrelationships of its components can be viewed.

The medium constraints affect structure: information that is most important comes first, but is also presented in ways that take advantage of or mitigate against the cognitive or apprehension constraints of reading, hearing, and seeing. Journalists' consideration of audience affects interaction (whom to talk to, what to talk and report about, what is relevant to the *community of coverage*) as well as story structure (which information elements and details to front or assign importance to) and language attitudes relating to standard-language attitudes of the larger culture (e.g., dangling participles and subject–verb agreement), local style pertinent to the community of coverage (e.g., taboo words), and language use that is pertinent to newswriting and editing.

1.5   Characteristics and tendencies of media language

Once a reporter has done her reporting, the story is composed according to a hierarchy of elements: the most important detail comes first; the others follow in descending order. This creates the "inverted pyramid" shape of the conventional story. Attribution of information is another key composition rule, as is providing sufficient context to understand why the story is important (as news) and enough background information to understand the story's position over time. The **principles of newswriting** operate on the information level, as well as applying to story structure and style (see Table 1.1). The reporter is enjoined to provide complete information accurately from an array of sources, and to construct a well-organized, well-written, and well-reported story.

Conventions of language use align with newswriting rules, the purpose being ease of comprehension for the reader, viewer, or listener and ease of time-sensitive production for the news practitioner. Attribution, for instance, is not randomly applied but follows a format (see Chapter 7 for details). The order of elements is established in a way to signify a well-formed story. Headlines are short, maximally informative, and font size or typeface a semiotic stand-in for importance. The physical rendering of the news text (in print or broadcast) has its own conventions: for instance, short paragraphs or time-brief stories, or vocal emphasis or repetition, are based on an interest in being heard, read, and understood by news consumers. The actual writing and editing rules are codified, and some version of them is found in every newswriting textbook.

Some of the writing and editing rules derive from the ideologies of the profession. For example, the widespread use of the reporting verb "said" (or "says") is part of a conscious effort by the mainstream US media to convey neutrality and balance. The language attitudes of journalists also come into play, intertwining with societal notions of good usage (see Milroy and Milroy 1999 for an account of the longstanding "complaint tradition" in public discourse).

Table 1.1 *Principles of newswriting*

Complete information (5Ws) Balance of sources Accuracy	**<On the information level**
Good lead Sentence structure Story organization (inverted pyramid) Attribution AP style	**<On the rhetorical level (structure, style)**

Table 1.2 *Characteristics of news language*

- brevity
- attribution
- quotes
- story structure
- importance of the lead
- stylistic consistency
- rhetorical accessibility
- globally accepted rules are locally interpreted

While all journalists are very conscious of language use, and of assuming a special responsibility to upholding prescriptive norms, copy editors are especially prescriptive in their approach to the language of news stories, functioning as regulators not only for the profession but to safeguard the clarity and expressive power of the standard language in general.

The result of commonly practiced, profession-specific writing rules and assumptions about usage is that news language can easily be identified as such and is visible on the style and discourse levels. Fom the news-practice perspective, **characteristics of news language** (Table 1.2) are embodied in stylistic consistency, rhetorical accessibility, and brevity as well as appropriate story structure, use of quotes and attribution, and a well-wrought lead. Indeed, the principles of newswriting themselves (Table 1.1) are relevant across the stylistic and discursive planes. A good lead, appropriate sentence structure, story organization (the inverted pyramid), and use of Associated Press style are integral to story structure and style. On the information level, complete information, a balance of sources, and accuracy are the principles that reporters' actions derive from.

It is important to see newswriting rules and parameters as a **set of "tendencies"** that inter-operate with the circumstances of reporting, deadline, access to sources, other concurrent news on that day, channel of delivery, etc. The variation we apprehend occurs as globally accepted rules are locally interpreted. Other injunctions, such as the one to convey "interest," as well as the news practitioners' orientation to audience and the variation instigated by the medium of delivery, also inter-operate with newswriting rules.

Conveying **"interest"** about news content – indicating to the reader or listener that what is newsworthy is of interest or important – has linguistic or discourse-level correlates beyond the choice of news topic. Story structure itself, the way it is patterned and organized, supports what is considered important. For example, the beginning of a news story, or lead, reinforces what is newsworthy by its position, focus, and what information elements are left out as well as included. Focus is also auditory: the "accents of interest" (cf. Bolinger 1986) or vocal emphasis in the intonation contours of radio broadcasts reinforce on the prosodic level what is of interest.

Audience orientation, as well as news-genre type, also accounts for what can be seen as patterned outcomes in media language. Early research by Bell (1991), for instance, in accounting for accent and style variation among radio broadcasters, determined that the media either respond to their audience's linguistic style or initiate a style divergent from them. Gonzalez (1991) also saw style differences as correlated to genre type in Philippine radio, variation that persisted predictably in relation to newswriting norms.

Variation also occurs across the **medium of delivery**, whether it be print, television, radio, or Web. The medium of transmission creates variation as each channel emphasizes different elements of visuality, interactivity, and comprehension. Television stories are constructed around the visual and aural; Internet journalism is guided by the potential of hypertext links, real-time interaction, and immediacy; and print stories are designed to "grab the reader" through graphic display and a (syntactically) compressed but easily understandable rendering of the information.

Some of the usage attributed only to journalistic writing is a result of the constraints of time and technology. For example, the prevailing spelling of "cigaret" and "employe" before the advent of more flexible printing technologies in the second half of the twentieth century was because each letter of each word was set in place as a physical piece of type by human hand, not by keystroke. The "inverted pyramid" style of newswriting was similarly practical: stories that were too long could be cut very quickly from the bottom up – physically on the page before it went through the press.

While variation leads us to consider the responsiveness of news practitioners to their intended audience, or the ways in which news types can be meaningfully indexed, the underlying norms of production have been *routinized and conventionalized*, accounting for a great deal of similarity across media outlets (see Chapter 3). The purpose behind these conventions is ease of comprehension for the reader or listener, and facility of production for the news practitioner.

1.6   Conclusion: process and practice – underexplored dimensions

In Chapter 1, I have presented the case for studying the dynamic, multifaceted, co-occurring aspects of news language and discourse, the elements instantiated by the process of news production and the practice of journalists that result in what is characteristic of news language, and the discursive and interactive activities surrounding news process and practice.

Contradictory perceptions about news media language can be resolved, to some degree, by utilizing ethnographic and interactional sociolinguistic approaches to the study of the news media's communicative outputs and actions. Part of the value of ethnolinguistic and sociocultural frameworks is what it yields in terms of the comprehensiveness in our understanding, of seeing journalists from within their own community, and of evaluating jointly the role of context, structure, and interaction as one element alone cannot fully account for the shape of news texts and talk. The context–structure–interaction triumvirate in the news arena means we examine – and prioritize – the interrelation of language, journalist, and audience (or text, author, and audience); hence, the utility of ethnographic/interactional tools. Exploring news and news language from the practitioner's perspective is enabled through these frameworks; it is what the ethnographic advantage affords.

The benefits of understanding what is "behind the scenes," or "the rest of the story," or why something is the way it is, are not lost on the journalist. Indeed, for the reporter it is old news. But perhaps it is not to the linguist or communications scholar. Consider this analogy: For a reporter, developing journalistic skills is similar to developing ethnographic skills. In many ways, journalists are ethnographers. They observe. They intend to make sense out of chaos. They organize a myriad of facts around the structure of stories. They seek coherence. They function as recorders and interpreters. They strive for balance. They are mindful of their subjective selves. They note hierarchical relations in their *community of coverage*. These are actions that inform their practice as they use language to create coherence on the level of text and culture.

In Chapter 2, we will come to a better understanding of journalistic practice by examining how reporters and editors view their craft and their professional role within the larger community.

2 Craft and community: Reading the ways of journalists

KEY POINTS

- Two self-referential aspects of news-practitioner habit (and *habitus*) are key to understanding journalistic discourse: their professional (internal) identity enacted through a craft ethos, and their public (external) commitments.
- Craft is important in creating a self-identity: the practice of journalism means mastering a craft and subscribing to values that the group maintains through an apprenticeship dynamic.
- Community is an important framing concept: the news media sees itself in relationship to the community they cover, as responsive and responsible, as a friend and as an authority.

Journalists are taught to approach their work in particular ways that both influence the shape of the text and reinforce their identities and professional roles. Their work is motivated discursively in terms of craft and ideologically in terms of press freedoms and a commitment to the public – in other words, in terms of responsibilities to a larger community as well as to their own. Writing and reporting well, and attending to an audience or community for whom the craft is intended to serve, are organizing principles that create coherence within the profession. Understanding this relationship creates alternative ways of understanding journalistic practitioner dynamics, a key step in understanding the shape of journalistic language.

In this chapter, I focus on the *craft ethos* that circumscribes one's identity as a reporter or editor, and on the *community factor*, which frames journalistic behaviors on many levels – discursive, ideological, and interactional. These two self-referential elements of the journalistic process are key to understanding *news texts*, the *manner of their production and outcome*, and the *journalistic behavior* behind them. Together, they work on behalf of a *socialization matrix*, which involves access to, and reinforcement of, professional norms, values, and principles. Throughout the rest of the book, I will be emphasizing the related issues of craft and practice as well as community-based and interactional elements. Thus, these are foundational concepts that bear exposition now, before closer examination of aspects of news language itself.

2.1   Articulating primary values

2.1.1   Discursive and ideological motivations

There are multiple ways to critically examine or "read" journalists as purveyors of language, as communicators. We can read journalists **linguistically** by examining their text outputs as well as how they interact. We can read journalists **professionally**, as practitioners who undergo actions and processes particular to their occupation. Along sociocultural or ethnolinguistic lines, which take into account text, interaction, and professional stance or positioning (the goal of this book), we can read journalists with respect to the **primary values** that underlie practice: the values of craft and community. Understanding the primary values attendant on craft (production) and community (recipient relationship) positions us to more accurately characterize and analyze news outputs and products – i.e., news stories – on the discourse level.

There are both discursive and ideological motivations behind news production. Discursively, practitioners follow a "craft ethos," as well as base a multitude of operational decisions on the "community factor." Together the craft ethos and community factor provide an ideological baseline. The *craft ethos* is a profession-internal value that has a direct link to the shape of news discourse: the reporting and writing of news stories is considered a craft, with identifiable, performative entailments that circumscribe a community-identified proficiency. The *community factor* is an external point of reference, one that guides decision-making in the short and long term. It is the basis of judgments about coverage and reporting competence, and helps to formulate the addressee-oriented objectives of newswriting (cf. Chapter 6). Together, the craft ethos and the community factor are foundational notions in understanding how the news media "work."

2.1.2   Privileging "craft"

Understanding the notion of "craft" in the journalism world is integral to understanding and analyzing news discourse. On the practice level, craft is privileged in the news community, and evident in the profession's metatalk (for examples, see section 2.2; see also Knudson 2000). On the analytical level, craft can be seen to be central to journalistic action (and self-identification) and that which motivates it. Craft, which can be considered a macro concept because of its scope, is relevant in the different skill areas that constitute *newswriting*: reporting and writing, entailing skills as both a journalist and a writer. *Reporting* involves gathering the facts; *writing* involves organizing and presenting the facts into a story; *writing as a journalist* means following the communicative norms and usage rules of the news community; and *writing as a writer* means utilizing language as a communicative tool following prescriptive usage rules, as well as being creative and linguistically performative within the bounds of newswriting norms.

Writing and *reporting* are referred to explicitly within the profession as relevant and related actions in the news community. *Writing as a journalist* and *writing as a writer* are not referred to in these terms, although the distinction is clearly made in the course of practice. They are designations I am putting forward from the analytical point of view to make clear that there is a professional distinction in the course of practice. This distinction has been also noted by Woo 2007, who referred to newswriting style as "institutional rules of usage and not a manner of writing that distinguishes one author from another" (Woo 2007: 103). The term *newswriting* alone generally includes the parameters of *writing as a journalist*, following "institutional rules of usage" as well as following the prescriptive writerly expectations of stylistic and grammatical "correctness" (see Chapter 9).

Reporting and *writing* work together: they are the basic "craft" actions that produce the news story. At the same time *reporting* and *writing* are viewed as separate skill sets (see Section 2.2). *Writing as a journalist* is expected, valued, and reinforced within the news community; it is the baseline from which all news discourse is evaluated within the profession. *Writing as a journalist* (or reporter) means compiling facts into a story according to news-genre norms, and following profession-lauded ideals of accuracy, balance, fairness, and truth (see Chapter 7). Any other rhetorical skill, which a journalist would call "good writing" (as opposed to "good reporting"), is appreciated and certainly valued but not necessarily essential (although journalism professors and industry language mavens make it seem so). To engage competently in *newswriting* and *reporting* is what is meant by practicing the craft. People who can both report and in addition write well are exemplars of the craft (as Examples 2.8 and 2.10 make evident).

The craft principle   In journalistic terms, *craft* can be defined in three ways: (1) craft means the standard one strives for, learns about, and achieves; craft is what one does; (2) craft is the achievement of *communicative competence* (Hymes 1972a) within the profession; (3) craft operates as a performance marker, both constrained and licensed by news-community norms. (In Bourdieu's sense, news *craft* would be a constellation of "regulated improvisations" (quoted in Duranti 2001: 29).) These three functions are the basis of understanding and analyzing news language as craft from the journalistic perspective. Knowing that a "craft principle" is at work is fundamental; it underlies a practice ethos. In terms of the academic enterprise, the *craft* concept

Table 2.1 *The craft principle*

Its critical relevance	Its journalistic relevance
• To **evaluate** journalistic/insider actions • To **explain** story design and interaction frameworks linguistically • **Self-referential** to community (ethnographic) • To **frame news outputs** linguistically and socioculturally	What one does: craft as **practice** Performance parameter: craft as **principle** Achievement of communicative competence: craft as **ethos** Standard to strive for: craft as **concept**

is useful both analytically and methodologically. *Craft* can be seen to function in four ways in this regard: (1) to *evaluate* newswriting and reporting actions and outputs as an insider might; (2) as *explanatory* of what occurs in news realms; (3) as *self-referential* to the news community; (4) as a productive way to *frame* media outputs.

To use a self-referential "insider" concept with its attendant values to evaluate, explain, and frame news outputs allows a situated understanding of the processes and ideologies behind media discourse. In other words, the craft principle can be used by academics to evaluate both practice and product as an insider might, i.e., to evaluate the journalistic *actions* (practice) that are undertaken to produce a news *story* (product). It is explanatory of what occurs (linguistically, discursively, and interactionally). It is self-referential to the news community (and thus can be ethnographically informed). It is a useful new way to frame media outputs and to consider them analytically, taking into account both language and culture (following the perspectives of social theorist Bourdieu 1977, anthropologist Geertz 1973, sociologist Goffman 1974, and philosopher and literary theorist Bakhtin 1986). Table 2.1 summarizes these points.

Irrespective of its role as a principle behind communicatively competent newswriting, craft as a theoretical notion also deserves development in the media-discourse analysis (MDA) domain. I refer in passing to the anthropological literature on craft and community (e.g., Coy 1989, Nash 1993, Terrio 2000), but orient my deployment of the notion to a greater degree to linguistic-anthropological literature on performance (cf. Bauman 1977, 1986) and socialization (Kulick and Schieffelin 2006; Ochs 2001). Already we know that different disciplines approach the analysis of news craft with different objectives. Disciplinary focal points come out of journalism and mass communication studies – which practically, descriptively, and critically evaluate journalistic *action* – as well as linguistics, ethnography of communication, linguistic anthropology (all noted in Chapter 1), and sociology and anthropology (e.g., Bird 1992, 1999; Gans 1979; Peterson 2003; Tuchman 1978).

Expanding the craft concept theoretically would be a productive course of action in future scholarly work on the news media but it is beyond the remit of this book to give the theory of craft more than a passing mention. One theoretical point, however, is relevant: Craft can also be viewed as a tension between cultural knowledge and symbolic competence and those who manage this tension viewed as "symbolic specialists" (Mark Peterson, citing William Beeman, personal communication). I am not characterizing *news craft* in terms of this tension but instead as a constrained performance, a "regulated improvisation" within a macro-cultural context for which a set of skills is requisite (as Bourdieu, cited in Duranti 2001: 29, or indeed Beeman 2007 might). Where "symbolic specialist" insights *would* prove advantageous critically is outside of actual daily news reporting, in the realms of news practitioners who are licensed to operate to some degree outside reporting norms: the columnists and editorial-writers (and bloggers who appear on news-outlet websites). Granted a greater freedom to display personal opinion and "slant," columnists and editorial-writers more actively milk this tension to present supported positions; they are *active* symbolic specialists. (To a lesser degree, mainstream news reporters could possibly be seen as "symbolic specialists" in their own right in the sense that they understand and operate between the symbols of their own internal news-community culture and the larger culture.)

In the meantime, linguistic and anthropological approaches can get further in their critical and analytical research goals with the **craft concept** to hand. It is an additional, attested, contestable, and viable parameter – like the notions of *speech community*, *turn-taking*, and *indexicality*, to name three – that can be used to increase our understanding of social phenomena and to help linguists understand the patterns and motivations behind language in use in the news realm. As Coy notes: "Craftsmanship involves more than the performance of specialized tasks. Craftsmanship also refers to the code of normative behavior, often unwritten, that is expected of craftsmen" (Coy 1989: 2).

2.1.3   Intersecting communities

As with craft and its relevance to practice on multiple levels, the *community* concept is equally encompassing. The notion of "community" that I refer to and develop is multi-tiered, and the various subcomponents intersect. At its simplest it is binary: there is the **community of journalists**, the practitioners; and separate from them is the **community of readers or listeners** that comprise the audience (more about which will be said in Section 2.3).

From the news media's perspective, the latter community also includes the people who are not necessarily readers but who live in the news media outlet's geographical region or would have exposure to it. These communities overlap in the day-to-day, especially if one considers that the reporters themselves come

Table 2.2 *News practice-relevant communities*

Community sphere	Comprised of	Designation
Professional	Journalists/practitioners	Community of practice
Audience	Readers/listeners	Community of coverage
Residents	Inhabitants of geographical area	Local community
"Society"	The larger social world	Society/culture

from or reside in the inhabitant/geographical community. Ties within the community network can be both *dense*, or related, and *multiplex*, or interlinked (cf. Milroy 1987). (Evaluating news practice according to network theory would be another informative line of inquiry in future work.) Both journalists and news recipients coexist in the larger social world, operating within the larger context of "society" with its temporal and cultural contiguities and dislocations, experiencing a shared social history. Table 2.2 summarizes the community typologies that are relevant to us in terms of journalists' community spheres, who comprises it, and how it can be referred to.

Theoretically, methodologically, functionally, and pragmatically, the notion of "community" is best seen in its variation and subdivision, through its capacities to intersect and overlap; it is not restricted to one amorphous entity, to a single "tribe" or constituent (Hymes 1984), nor defined according to any one parameter. The best way to view community for our purposes here is to use a complement of theoretical tools, as each framework accomplishes just part of the analytical work. Individuals who work for media organizations such as daily newspapers or broadcast outlets can be viewed as members of their own *speech (or discourse) community*. "Speech community" is a term that presupposes the role of language and linguistic competence as a primary way of marking community boundaries (cf. Gumperz 1968; Morgan 2006); a "discourse community" is a subcategory in which the shared purpose for engagement predominates over other interactional factors. Given that the workplace in general is a localized network of attitude, practice, talk, text, and social relations that inscribes both individual and group identities, other designations that encompass these sociocultural sets of characteristics such as *occupational community* (cf. Van Maanen and Barley 1984) and *community of practice* (cf. Lave and Wenger 1991; Wenger 1998) can also be applied to the news media community aggregate. They are compatible theoretical constructs that allow an examination of language use and its social and ideological entailments within institutional contexts (cf. Cotter and Marschall 2006).

For simplicity, and as a type of disciplinary shorthand, throughout the book I refer somewhat a-theoretically to journalists as being members of a speech community or discourse community, or, at its most a-theoretical and descriptive, *news community.* That said, in upcoming chapters I will also refer to *speech community* when looking at news style or sociolinguistic variables; *discourse community* when I examine discourse correlates such as the news community–audience participant relationship and communicative goals; *occupational community* when the workplace elements and professional identities are in focus; and *community of practice* when I detail the mechanisms behind the production of news outputs and the actions of the news practitioner. (See Chapter 1 for additional discussion of these theoretical community designations.)

2.2   The craft ethos

The craft dimension has long been embedded in US news-practitioner identity. Indeed, the journalists' labor union, founded in 1933, is called the Newspaper Guild, evoking the master–apprentice relationship of the Middle Ages. Similar to the medieval craft setup, there is a seven-year period of de facto apprenticeship before one can be referred to as a "journeyman," a term that is still in use in some US newsrooms. In that sense, reporters to some degree can be viewed as contemporary artisans (a point that Aitchison 2007 makes in historical terms). As noted earlier, journalistic craft is a combination of *reporting* (gather the facts and talk to people, and report what is said) and *writing* (telling the story according to news style). It is also achieving and maintaining larger news-community goals such as *accuracy* (including the micro goals of factual and grammatical precision) and its more abstract consequence, *credibility*, a macro goal that exists alongside and is supported by explicit news-community values of fairness and balance.

Behind news reporting and writing is the **craft ethos**, signaled and measured in large part by the **communicative competence** of the news practitioner. Within the journalist/news community, "craft" works in many ways: it is a *term* of reference, a *concept* of practice, a *principle* that underscores practitioner identity, and an *ethos* of communicative competence – an operating standard – which conveys in the abstract sense a target ideal to meet. In this way, "craft" can be seen to operate as micro- and macro-level motivations similar to what occurs with a standard language ideology, cf. Cameron 1995; Lippi-Green 1997; Milroy and Milroy 1999.

Craft means both the nitty-gritty of writing well, as well as conveying a *journalistic stance* that involves macro ideals of objectivity and ethics. Craft means both the discursive and the ideological. Within the news profession, craft is a word that indexes these micro and macro objectives and ideals, as in the profession-common phrase, "the demands of the craft," as in Example 2.1:

Example 2.1
The demands of the craft, the attention span of our readers, and the limits of available space can conspire against us.

(Declan McCullagh, March 7, 2002, emphasis added)

In Example 2.1, McCullagh lists what elements influence reporting outcomes: physical limitations ("space"), claims on readers' time and attention ("attention span"), and the multiple obligations of practice ("craft"). He refers to the process not as the "demands of newswriting and reporting," but as the demands of the "craft."

Similarly, the journalist Marvin Kalb, quoted in Example 2.2, also refers to the "challenges of the craft" – situating these challenges in terms of larger-society changes that inevitably occur and impact the news community.

Example 2.2
"Once a journalist, always a journalist? Sort of," said Kalb. "But one would hope a better journalist, with better training to meet the new challenges of the craft and the age. [...] Shouldn't news organizations and foundations be doing more?"
(Press release, George Washington University, December 2002, emphasis added)

Kalb poses questions to the profession in an effort to particularize the challenge, to become a "better journalist." In so doing, he makes evident the notion of a standard to maintain that is embedded in the craft ethos, as in Example 2.3:

Example 2.3
When it works like it should, the American news machine is the most informative, insightful, and useful operation in the world [...] if the media are capable of such high standards, why does so much of what we typically see, read, and hear fall so far below the bar?
(Press release, American News Women's Club and World Affairs Council of Washington, DC, March 6, 2002, emphasis added)

In Example 2.3, from a press release announcing a panel hosted by the American News Women's Club and World Affairs Council of Washington, DC, the author establishes a position that there is a standard ("when it works like it should") and the very real chance that news media achievement of that standard can "fall so far below the bar," the "bar" being an ideal against which to measure perform-ance. When the "American news machine" operates appropriately it informs and illuminates. It is this standard that requires active intra-professional work to question, troubleshoot, and ultimately maintain, particularly "if the media are capable of such high standards."

As an aside, the metaphor of the "news machine" suggests an evolution of the craft ethos to one of industrial production, but it is still a model in which "high standards" wrought by journalists with the capacity to maintain them are meant to prevail. The example also is US-centric in its consideration of the impact of news craft, which is interesting to me not only because it indexes US-centrism but because it reflects a professional participatory pride, an attitude of excellence worth striving for that is commonly expostulated in media self-critiques in the US.

Both Examples 2.2 and 2.3 pose questions to their news-community audi-ence: "Shouldn't news organizations and foundations be doing more [regarding training]?" "[W]hy does so much of what we typically [produce] fall so far below the bar?" The act of questioning the elements of craft, of what "works," on behalf of a successful integration of all that comprises the complexity of the craft, is one community-internal device employed to both *maintain* the standard of the news community, as well as to *challenge* community-internal assumptions of practice. Kalb's "sort of" answer makes this community-internal tension clear: "Once a journalist, always a journalist? Sort of."

2.2.1   Reporting – with respect to craft

Reporting is on the face of it a simple set of actions and skills: finding information, asking questions, "getting the story." There is also the expectation that a reporter will go beyond the superficial, "dig" for the "real story," go "the extra mile." These expectations hold whether the story is slight and has minimal impact, or is an investigative enterprise geared toward "uncovering truth." These expectations are behind the application of "the old-fashioned virtues of good journalism," quoted in Example 2.4 below. This is because beyond reporting actions is a practice-oriented or instrumental ideology (one with entailments we will not consider at the moment) that is inherently associated with "virtue" and "good journalism." That these virtues are "old-fashioned" hearkens to a prototype forged in the idealized past that has, according to the utopian journalistic worldview, stood the test of time (although see Schudson 1978 and 1987 for a more realistic historical perspective).

Examples 2.4, 2.5, and 2.6 are drawn from different industry-relevant sources – a specialist journal in Example 2.4, a professional journal in Example 2.5, and a newspaper obituary in Example 2.6. They are similar in the ways they present the features that are relevant to "good" reporting, features that variously encompass craft elements and actions, ideology, and practice competence.

Example 2.4 [craft and ideology]
"Reporting isn't just finding [Web] links!" they cry. "It's interviewing people. Checking sources. Digging for the truth." To which the only sane answer is: of course. No one's suggesting that weblogs are any sort of replacement for the old-fashioned virtues of good journalism.   (Scott Rosenberg, Salon.com, May 28, 1999, emphasis added)

Example 2.5 [ideology and practice]
We [newspapers] collect and present information that people want or need, and we deliver it in a way they find both useful and believable. We offer up more of this wanted, needed, useful, believable information than any other medium, by far.
                                        (Eugene Robinson 2007: 17, emphasis added)

Example 2.6 [practice competence]
"Danny was a reporter's reporter," said Lewis Cuyler, Mr. Pearl's editor at The Berkshire Eagle, where he worked in the late 1980s. "He really got wrapped up in it and it drove the managing editor nuts because Danny was reporting it right until deadline. He added that Mr. Pearl "always had another call to make. I had to tell him, 'Dammit, Danny, write! No

more calls.' He always wanted to make more calls because there were so many dimensions of the story he was curious about."

         (Susan Saulny, NYTimes.com, February 22, 2002, emphasis added)

Example 2.4 is an insider's response to an insider's complaint about the Web, and the potential damage Internet technologies may be doing to the reporting craft. (The other view is that the Web increases the expectation of good writing and reporting.) This example lists what reporting entails: "interviewing," "checking sources" (ensuring that they are sound and appropriate), "digging for the truth." That these reporting basics are explicitly mentioned in this insider context reminds the complainants that the "old-fashioned virtues" of reporting are still part of the ethos, despite the options and incursions of the Internet, and in the process tells the outsider what counts as "old-fashioned virtues."

Example 2.5 specifies very clearly that **reporter actions** – insider units of analysis – involve *collecting*, *presenting*, and *delivering* information; that the **participants** in the exchange are the news media, particularly editors ("we"), and the "people" who receive the news; that the **interactional goals** are presenting and collecting information that recipients *want* or *need* (what can be inferred is the fact that this is an assumption the news community makes and an agenda it sets); that the **manner** of delivery is constructed in a way that the recipient finds "useful" and "believable"; and that the **element of exchange** is *information*. (Note that "collect," "present," and "deliver" correlate to the "facts–story–page" triumvirate of the news process described in chapter 3; see Figure 3.1.)

Example 2.6, an account of the late *Wall Street Journal* reporter Daniel Pearl's newsroom persona, also lists, and thus exemplifies, what it takes to be a "reporter's reporter." A "reporter's reporter" is one who operates in the top tier of practice, who "always [has] another call to make," who will not be deterred from "reporting [a story] right until deadline." It reinforces for the fellow news colleagues who are reading the obituary what reporters do. It reminds them of the familiar, and makes Pearl familiar to them: no self-respecting, competent reporter is *not* going to report until deadline, not make as many calls as possible, or not negotiate with the editor about deadline. In the process, the obituary account (within the narrative routines of the obituary) tells "outsiders" what goes on in the newsroom, depicting Pearl as he projected himself as a newsman. In effect, it tells us that he did not just report, but *went the extra mile* (another value, and phrase, that is used to compliment good reporters) by saying that he "really got wrapped up in it," and that he saw stories as multi-dimensional: "He always wanted to make more calls because there were so many dimensions of the story he was curious about." *Curiosity* is another defining trait of a good reporter: someone who is curious will not take information given to them at face value. They will try to understand a story not just from two sides, but from as many as possible.

Example 2.7, extracted from a "farewell column" written when reporter McCullagh left Wired News, outlines the **multiple touchpoints** that reporters rely on in going about the daily business underpinning the practice of craft and "solid journalism":

Example 2.7
I owe my **editors** a considerable debt for their good humor and commitment to solid journalism. I owe my **readers** an equal debt for their commitment to keeping journalists in line: It's humbling to know that readers often know far more about a subject than the writer. I'm grateful to my **fellow reporters** at Wired News for the chance to work with them in chronicling the evolution of technology, society and politics. Keep up the fierce, intrepid reporting!   (Declan McCullagh, June 14, 2002, emphasis added)

Editors, readers, and reporters are all acknowledged: editors for commitment to "solid journalism," readers for their supplemental but integral knowledge, and reporters for collegial fellowship in a shared enterprise, in McCullagh's particular case, "chronicling the evolution of technology, society and politics." It is relevant (as we will see in subsequent chapters, especially Chapters 3, 5, and 6) that McCullagh acknowledges a "considerable debt" to his editors, who have an attested hands-on role in the production of news, and an "equal debt" to readers. He puts the contributions from readers on par with the input from editors. The readers are equally integral to the process. In McCullagh's view, they are necessary for "keeping journalists in line," for ensuring that journalists maintain factual integrity, by providing additional knowledge. (That readers are not just passive recipients, but actively engaged in the news-construction process and its outputs, is discussed in Chapters 5 and 6.)

Within McCullagh's acknowledgement of the multiple contributors to his journalistic development and practice outcomes, he situates his actions within the domain of reporting, indicating the expectations on reporters to be "fierce" and "intrepid," uncowed by the machinations of the powerful – personal values and approaches that are essential to being a good reporter, and necessary for acting according to the responsibilities of the profession.

2.2.2   Writing – with respect to craft

Writing is the second primary skill arena that marks journalistic competence. Good newswriting, however, follows combined standards that draw from larger society and from within the news community of practice. As I discuss in detail in chapter 9, news practitioners heed what I call the "prescriptive imperative," the requirement to follow the norms of standard usage within mainstream society, from grammar, word choice, and pronunciation, to more complex discourse-based elements of register and style. Following the *prescriptive imperative* means that one's writing is "correct." When one editor with whom I conducted ethnographic interviews heard I was a linguist she told me: "You can teach us to write." She meant clarity of style, accuracy of expression, and "correctness" of grammar and lexical choice (more on this in Chapter 9). She was referring to the basic writing skills that make a good reporter. Her comment is an indication of the expectation that writing is a skill that is valued, needs work, and needs mentoring. Equally importantly, on the journalistic as well as stylistic level, writing must be "accurate" – factually as well as grammatically and semantically. Reporters are taught to heed nineteenth-/early-twentieth-century newspaper publisher Joseph Pulitzer's three-word objective: "Accuracy! Accuracy! Accuracy!"

Writing thus comprises a somewhat different skill set than reporting (which as noted above includes interviewing, checking sources, locating information), and news practitioners tend to keep these skill sets separate at various points. One can be a "good reporter" (which implies but backgrounds that one follows usage norms appropriately) or a "good reporter and writer," which means one also possesses the rhetorical finesse noted earlier when one *writes as a writer*. Example 2.8 demonstrates the validity of this distinction explicitly, and Example 2.9 implicitly.

Example 2.8
Pearl started in the Journal's Atlanta bureau [...] he quickly established himself as a <u>good reporter and writer</u> and was initially known for producing what the Journal calls "A-heads" – offbeat, often quirky feature stories that run in the middle of the front page.
(David Shaw, *Los Angeles Times*, February 22, 2002, emphasis added)

Example 2.9
[... Pearl] built a reputation on the witty strength of his feature stories.
(Susan Saulny, NYTimes.com, February 22, 2002)

In Example 2.8, the obituary writer describes Pearl as "a good reporter and writer," keeping the two skill-sets separate. He also gives evidence of what made Pearl a good writer in the elaborated sense, citing his beginnings in the *Wall Street Journal* Atlanta bureau. There, Pearl came up with "offbeat, often quirky feature stories" that have a particular position on the front page of the *Wall Street Journal*. (The *Journal* calls these offbeat stories "A-heads"; other news organizations refer to them as "brites" or "readers.") Example 2.9 implicitly underscores the point that peers are making about Pearl's ability and discursive strengths.

Feature stories, because the news peg or time-relevance may be more tenuous than a hard news or breaking-news story (see Chapter 7 for differentiations between news and features), tend to lean more heavily on how a story is composed and on the stylistic use of language to enhance its journalistic value and reader interest. As stories on Page One are particularly valued in the news hierarchy, when features stories make Page One it is through some reportorial or writerly inventiveness on the part of the author, or a curiosity factor that is inherent in the news itself (see Chapters 5 and 7).

2.2.3   The "credibility" dimension

As one goes about reporting and writing news, there are other values and key elements that a communicatively competent news practitioner must keep in mind, chief among them is maintaining *credibility*. Errors in both reporting (the wrong facts) and writing (the misuse of language) work against the maintenance of credibility in reporters' eyes. *Accuracy* in both reporting and writing domains is of the essence, and is a basis of maintaining credibility. *Credibility* is thus an identity factor in the news community, and language plays a role, as Example 2.10 illustrates (see also Woo 1999):

Example 2.10
We hear less about another offense to credibility that immediately impairs the journalist's authority and the reader's trust. That offense is second-rate language skill.
(Paula LaRocque 1999: 38, emphasis added)

Paula LaRocque is a well-known news-industry writing coach in the US, with regular columns in industry magazines, who is called on frequently to give seminars at conferences and professional meetings. She and other prominent writing coaches like Roy Harris Clark call professionals to task for their language lapses (see her reference to the "giddy disregard" of proper use of language in Example 2.11). In Example 2.10, LaRocque makes clear the reporter's responsibility to use language skillfully, the connection between language and credibility ("second-rate skill" is "an offense to credibility"), and the connection between "language skill" and "reader's trust." An absence of language skill erodes journalistic "authority," minimizing the potential impact of reporters' words, as she elaborates on in Example 2.11:

Example 2.11
I know of no other profession that has at its command only one tool and yet has such giddy disregard of that tool's proper use. Wordsmiths should know words, surely: Between writer and reader stands only the language, and its skillful use should be a given.
(Paula LaRocque 1999: 38, emphasis added)

Example 2.11 captures the attitudes that most news practitioners and particularly journalism educators maintain about language. She refers to language as a tool. She refers to members of the news community, who use words as their "tool," as "wordsmiths" – craft-oriented artisans. As so-called wordsmiths, it goes without saying that they "should know words" and how they work, how to use their "one tool." She refers to the relationship between the writer and reader by observing that "only the language" stands in between them (evoking the "conduit" metaphor that is standard in mass communication/journalism conceptions of the news-community relationship; but see chapter 6 for a counterexample). Her argument is: because language is all that stands between the writer and reader (note that she doesn't use "reporter," to further constrain the interpretation of her edict to the writing skill set), "its skillful use should be a given," it should be an act unmarked in the praxis context.

The title of the article from which Example 2.11 is extracted, "Language and lost credibility: Poor writing skills can jeopardize reader trust," makes clear the interconnections of the role of language and credibility, reporter responsibility, and audience. A reporter with "poor writing skills" not only has problems utilizing his or her primary tool, but the poor writing skills carry the additional consequence of "jeopardiz[ing] reader trust." Thus, "lost credibility" – a consequence no self-respecting practitioner wants to occur – is related consciously and directly to "language." LaRocque refines her point further in Example 2.12, correlating "mistakes" by reporters with loss of "credibility" with readers, indicating that *actions* by reporters have *consequences* as determined by readers.

Example 2.12
The mistakes the readers find hard to forgive and that ultimately destroy our credibility are those that seem to occur either because we don't know or because we don't care.
(Paula LaRocque 1999: 38, emphasis added)

In Example 2.12, she characterizes the worst mistakes as the consequence of ignorance ("we don't know") and inertia ("we don't care") – positions that can be rectified with appropriate communicative action. Her argument is that ignorance/inertia mistakes have negative impacts on the reporter–reader relationship (they find these kinds "hard to forgive," as opposed to, one might guess, normal human error), as well as negative results through "ultimately destroy[ing]" the profession's primary value of credibility.

2.3   The community factor

2.3.1   Professional responsibilities

LaRocque's points are small examples of how the news community explicitly lays out its professional responsibilities to the community on which it reports. Professional responsibilities, and with them modes of practice and interpretation, are expected to be met in two domains: on behalf of source and community, that is, source of information and *community of coverage*. At the same time, the news media are concerned about their role within the local or geographical community, as well as their position of authority and attendant responsibility (as

Examples 2.10–2.12 illustrate). Intended to guide these responsibilities alongside the community-internal practices that are part of everyday discourse and relationship management are the more backgrounded but familiar commitments to press freedoms and ethics. In the US, the Society of Professional Journalists' Code of Ethics (see Appendix 3) and the First Amendment to the Constitution (which includes Freedom of the Press) are often referred to in industry discussions.

Beyond the professional responsibilities that address the ethics of practice and support journalistic ideologies are the issues that individual reporters face in the course of their daily reporting, and the responsibilities they assume as they manage the addressee-oriented goals of newswriting and the situations in which interactions with the community outside the newsroom occur (cf. Chapter 6). Example 2.13 provides a comprehensive rundown of the prototypical reporter's multiple objectives:

Example 2.13
As a print reporter, I felt a responsibility to the people I was quoting, to those involved in the subject I was covering, and to the ideals of my profession – mainly, objectivity and fairness. I also felt a responsibility to the readers, but that responsibility basically revolved around the same ideals. It was my job to bring them both sides of the issue, and they would make up their own minds from there.   (Cupaiuolo 2000)

In this comment, the reporter makes fine-grained distinctions as she recalls her sense of responsibility to her sources as well as to the people involved in the subject – not just the people who had a quotable comment on a topic but the people whom the story was about. She also talks of a responsibility to the "ideals" of the profession, citing "objectivity" and "fairness" in the context of reporting, connecting a responsibility "to the readers" to the same set of ideals – to be objective and fair.

Cupaiuolo also articulates a sensibility that is familiar to me as a former reporter but is not part of the discussion of journalistic practice *outside* of the news community (e.g., the academic community): that she considered it her "job" to provide "both sides of the issue" to the reader, allowing the readers to then make their own judgments, to "make up their own minds from there." Implicit in this objective is that the information provided is done so responsibly, with as much "objectivity and fairness" as humanly possible. She echoes McCullagh's points about the process (in Example 2.7 above), the manner in which Pearl met his responsibilities to the reader, the subject, and the profession (in Example 2.14 below), and the standards with respect to the *community of coverage* that industry gate-keepers like LaRocque remind practitioners to achieve (in Example 2.15).

Example 2.14
Colleagues and friends said that the work the 38-year-old Mr. Pearl left behind shows where his talents lay: in doggedly pursuing and explaining obscure topics, or

superficially simple ones, with <u>sensitivity</u> and <u>nuance</u>. He saw that as his <u>mission</u>, friends said, and he died pursuing it.
(Susan Saulny, NYTimes.com, February 22, 2002, emphasis added)

Example 2.15
Must we be perfect? We must try [...] Perfection is unreachable, but that goal is the only way to <u>keep our standards as high</u> as they must be to <u>serve our audience</u>.
Although the reader's intelligence is often maligned in newsrooms, that's an attitude as misinformed as it is arrogant.   (Paula LaRocque 1999: 38, emphasis added)

These examples capture several facets relevant to the reporter's sense of responsibility to the community: Cupaiuolo (in Example 2.13) captures and summarizes the multiple elements comprising the *reporter ideology* that is a basis for reporting actions, while McCullagh acknowledges his debt to readers "for keeping [him] in line" and on the journalistic straight-and-narrow (in Example 2.7). Pearl's colleagues (in Example 2.14) attributed his actions to his indefatigable attempts to illuminate the "obscure" or "superficially simple," and to maintain "sensitivity and nuance" in his reporting, highlighting an external and socially aware "mission" rather than personal ego gratification as motive. And LaRocque reminds the news community that journalistic "standards" are there to "serve our audience," chastising them for arrogance if they think or do otherwise (in Example 2.15). Her point about the intelligence of readers being "maligned in newsrooms" does not contraindicate my contention that reporters feel responsible to the readers, but is additional evidence that the news community can be viewed as a community in its own right, that as a community its members utilize non-profession-specific ways of marking community boundaries. Judging "others" in less than positive ways, as well as telling jokes about them – discursive maneuvers that I have witnessed in numerous field situations outside of my news research (cf. Cotter 1996a) – particularly when these comments are meant to circulate only within the community – is a way of managing and maintaining community boundaries and identity (see also Tyler 2006 on the role of newsroom humor in this regard).

2.3.2   Local values

The news industry has developed several ways to incorporate the local, or the immediate vicinity, into their reporting ethos. For nearly fifty years, "civic journalism," in which the local-community infrastructures and institutions are reported on, has been one way of reminding practitioners of what can count as responsible journalism. Reaching readers by reporting "news you can use" is another decades-old approach that has led to, for instance, numerous consumer- or health-related stories in print and broadcast (and in the process expanding the genre typology of news stories). With the advent of the Internet has come "citizen journalism," which ostensibly allows a greater role for news consumers, particularly those within the local community. These are domains that have been and are continuing to be discussed in detail within the profession (but which I will only mention in passing).

Instead I want to highlight "local values," which are more intrinsically fixed within the news community, and are somewhat more interesting analytically (for the linguistic community) as the notion of the "local" contains with it locations for interaction as well as the many reporting rules, coverage attitudes, professional assumptions, and craft elements behind it. The primary motivation within the news community is that its work must be relevant to the *community of coverage*, to the people who live where they are reporting (but not necessarily to all readers). "Local values" help focus this work across multiple communicative domains, as well as within the news community (see ASNE 1999a, 1999b; Conboy 2006, Howley 2005, and Kaniss 1991 for industry and academic discussion of local coverage; Cotter 1996a, Dorgan 1993, and Husband and Chouhan 1985 for discussions of local radio and the community; as well as chapters 5, 6, and 7 for examples that illustrate community of coverage reporting motivations).

Indeed, "local values" as they are embodied in local news outlets influence the shape of the news product on the discourse level, especially in terms of topic and context, a point that is particularly relevant in American journalism. As *Washington Post* editors Downie and Kaiser 2002 observe:

> The local newspaper will provide more – a lot more local news, plus lifestyle, sports and financial news. In a relatively few cities the paper also contains significant national and foreign news. Most of the stories are about events – speeches, news conferences, court decisions, athletic contests. A good paper will also publish revelations, information discovered by good journalists that wasn't handed out in a press release or at a news conference. Some mornings good newspapers will surprise their readers with unexpected reports that are deep, thorough and engaging. [...] In the evening the local television news reports a few stories of local events of the day, primarily those that are photogenic. [...] Then just before bedtime the local stations return with the day's last news: usually a crime story to begin, then a recap of some of the day's news events, the ball scores, the next day's weather.   (Downie and Kaiser 2002: 220–221)

This topic rundown holds even in the Internet age: "It's the same formula that's kept newspapers alive in this country [the US] since the horse-and-buggy days. Local news" (Mahoney 2007: 5). "Local news," as I outline in chapters 5 and 6, is what is considered relevant to the community, and thus relevant to journalists. (Its relevance is manifested in regular articles in trade publications about its interpretation, what constitutes its practice, who successfully exemplifies it, and reminders about its importance in sustaining professional identity.) By extension, "local media" is also relevant within its community. (A significant majority of Americans "(80 percent or more) feel positively about local TV news, local newspapers, and network TV news" (Schudson and Haas 2007: 70), which has a local subjectivity.)

2.3.3   The audience as co-participant: community of coverage

The extent to which the "audience" is a relevant component in the practice of newswriting and reporting will be discussed at length in chapter 6. At this point, I merely want to position the "community factor" as relevant to our understanding of news discourse. The examples above to varying degrees make the journalistic awareness of "community," "local," "readers," and "audience" evident.

One of my objectives, as Chapter 6 will detail, is to indicate new ways in which the role of the audience can be characterized, and to more fully understand its role in our discussions of news discourse and news practice. My approach (informed by context-based discourse analysis, linguistic anthropology, and ethnography of communication) is to view the audience as a co-participant in the construction of news discourse. I have in earlier research referred to the participant structure between the news media and the coverage community as a "pseudo-dyad," a point I will elaborate on in Chapter 6. (This runs counter to traditional mass communication approaches that involve the one-to-many model, in which the audience is the recipient – most often the passive recipient.) Utilizing the concepts of *occupational community* and *community of practice*, as I mentioned earlier, allows us to set up a new designation for the audience: the *community of coverage*.

Other linguists such as Allan Bell (1984) have captured insights into the relationship of the audience on news language (his audience design framework has been influential in demonstrating the role that the audience context plays in style changes and language variation on the radio). With an equal degree of success, concepts of framing (Goffman 1974) and positioning (Davies and Harré 1990) have been usefully deployed by researchers aiming to evaluate the interactions among various media participants and their alignments to the message in a range of news media contexts within and beyond news production (e.g., Cappella and Jamieson 1997; Clayman 1992; G. Lakoff 2006; R. Lakoff 2000a; Suleiman 1999, 2000, etc.).

2.4   Conclusion: locating and understanding news priorities

In this chapter, I looked at the elements behind the *craft ethos*, its role in maintaining credibility (an essential professional commodity in American journalism), distinctions between writing and reporting, the role of the *community of coverage* or news consumer-recipients in guiding decisions, and discourse correlates such as the participant relationship and addressee-oriented goals that can be examined in relation to the *community factor*. I also mentioned, briefly, theories of craft and performance and propose that linguists (from any subdiscipline) develop the craft angle as a way to "read" journalists and their language.

Craft and *community* are fundamental to understanding news priorities; to some degree, the craft ethos and the community factor are embedded in every decision, and members of the news community are expected to consider them in terms of their own communicative outputs and motivations. The privileging of craft is of relevance to journalistic identity, encompassing how things are done and said, and it is the perspective from which the news community monitors its potential effect on the recipient community, framing both discursive and interactional processes. Craft and community are two profession-referential elements that are key to "reading" news practitioners, relating as they do to insider performance expectations and operating in multiple domains. Reporters and editors learn how to ply their craft, how to respond to their local or coverage community over time, and through education and experience. Their learning process and socialization in the news community is the subject of Chapter 3.

3 The ways reporters learn to report and editors learn to edit

KEY POINTS

● Nowadays, reporters learn their craft in college or university in undergraduate or master's-level journalism programs, from textbooks, through newsroom internships, and on-the-job, the last functioning as a daily renewal of skills, values, and priorities throughout the duration of a career.
● Socialization into the profession is a complex process, involving internalizing a set of assumptions of practice and professional identity.
● The journalistic community makes distinctions between "reporting" and "writing," emphasizing process-oriented "reporting" as a value; and between different types of editing (either for content and story organization or for usage and style). It prioritizes "local" news over international or other types of *cognitively distant* news.

Old reporters never retire: they live on in emails that contain spellings like "adviser," series with the last comma deleted[,] and a sensitivity to relative pronouns; or they retain their radio-trained mode of listening in conversation without making response noise. People in the news business learn to report, edit, produce, and think about the news in ways that become habitual and a reflexive part of their everyday actions. While there is ample variation among news outlets, there is enough unanimity such that journalists in Florida could easily practice their craft in Alaska or the UK. The professional socialization of most journalists today begins in the classroom, where courses focus almost exclusively on learning practical skills. After that, the newsroom provides a constant reinforcement of competent practice, for both novices and veterans. Over time, the "ways of speaking" and writing in the journalistic context become internalized, functioning to formulate a professional identity as much as a news product.

How does this happen? In this chapter, I will look at what, how, and where reporters and editors learn. *What* they learn are the primary skills of reporting and editing and other competencies such as maintaining credibility (as noted in Chapter 2); *how* they learn is through socialization into a news culture that effects its own particular discriminations (in text, practice, and relationship) that are purely journalistic, and in the situations *where* this knowledge is imparted. Finally, values of craft (as was noted in Chapter 2), use of language (as will be addressed at length in Chapter 8), and the mechanisms that lead to a well-formed story (as described in Chapter 7) will be discussed in relation to the "apprentice model" that is behind journalistic practice.

3.1   "Ways of speaking"

Reporters learn how to be reporters and are socialized into the profession in three primary realms: first, through **practice** – in other words, through *doing* journalism (i.e., the actual acts of reporting and editing); second, through a reinforcement of a professional **identity** – by *being* a reporter, by incorporating a professional stance, role, position, and worldview as one engages in news practice; and third, through institutional and professionally constituted **loci of learning** – through education and performance within and outside the newsroom.

3.1.1   Primary skills

The primary skills reporters must learn include reporting, writing, editing, and interviewing; all else falls out from these skill sets. These skills are recognized in and of themselves, as well as in relation to the news story objectives and outcomes (cf. Chapter 7). **Reporting** involves newsgathering: asking questions and interviewing sources being primary ways to gather information. Behind reporting are multiple tasks, more or less obvious, such as finding sources to be interviewed, the actual writing of the story, and the editing and rewriting stage. Judgments about balance and objectivity motivate or are expected to motivate reporting, writing, editing, and interviewing actions. **Newswriting** has its specific rhetorical demands (as noted in Chapters 2 and 7), key among them *attribution of information* and appropriate *order of information* (the news hierarchy). **Editing** rules range from technical requirements (maintaining headline enjambment or local style) to the content itself (keeping track of story structure and news values, cf. Chapters 4 and 7). **Interviewing** techniques embody the ultimate goal of getting the story as well as maintaining a journalistic focus. Reporters and editors also learn to use reporting aids and other resources such as phonebooks, trademark guides, the penal code, the Internet, and relevant style guides.

3.1.2   Other journalistic competencies

Maintaining **credibility** is a larger journalistic goal that is always referred to in relation to appropriate practice. Maintaining credibility occurs, in the journalistic view, through practice-based actions involving *accuracy, balance,* and *getting the other side. Accuracy* – of information and language use – is a goal behind the text/news story (cf. Chapter 2); *balance* of positions is both a reporting and text goal; and *getting the other side,* getting sufficient points of view for a story, is a reporting goal. Maintaining credibility with one's sources – *not burning a source* – is another reporting competency. Beyond these specifics, maintaining credibility relates to journalistic identity, to being a good reporter or news professional.

Learning about roles, relationships, and hierarchies within the news community, as well as one's **professional role** with respect to the community of coverage, are other areas of education and socialization. Equally important are learning the **"issues" of news text production** that range from dealing with limited time and space to "writing around" a gap in a news story when information is not forthcoming. **Ethics** are emphasized from the beginning in the classroom and subsequently in the newsroom and involve learning to follow professional guidelines about making ethical decisions (see Appendix 3 for the Society of Professional Journalists ethics code). Ethical decisions vary from the naming of victims of crimes and quoting children and vulnerable adults, to whether to accept "freebies" or not, from prohibitions on paying for information, to libel issues and managing Freedom of Information and First Amendment objectives.

3.1.3   Interactional skills

A novice reporter also learns a range of interactional skills that are necessary for engaging in the reporting and editing tasks requisite for producing a well-formed news story. In turn, the interactional skills and the way in which one engages with them become part of the round of routines that signify membership in the news community. In interview situations a reporter learns to talk like a journalist and respond like a journalist (as opposed to, for instance, a student or an academic). Keeping opinions to oneself (and learning to use neutral response cues) is one requirement, as is asking the type of questions, "hard questions" which are essentially face-threatening for both interlocutors, not necessarily posed in a social setting. Reporters also learn the appropriate set of questions for the different news reporting genres (e.g., cops or courts or education or sports or business) and the insider language necessary to be taken seriously in those domains. To manage interactions with these "outside" interlocutors, reporters learn the beats they cover to understand the communicative norms, interactional styles, and roles, values, and actors – as well as the jargon – that go along with the community or beat they are covering. It is a familiarization process similar to that undertaken by ethnographers spending time in the field, or by socioculturally minded linguists coming to understand and more accurately analyze the empirical data they have elicited within social contexts of use.

Across numerous situations, a reporter learns how to make it past the "secretary barrier" to achieve actual telephone or in-person time (and valuable quotes) with a primary news source. Most reporters will say that this means respecting the competence and knowledge that these "gate-keepers" have in organizations. It is the result of developing a relationship over time, the basis of which is built on repeated interactions and trust – similar to any extended professional encounter such as linguists and anthropologists, for instance, experience with informants and consultants in the field.

3.2   Socialization into news culture

Socialization into the news culture means understanding how to place the skills one has learned within a context, and to employ them alongside the daily exigencies of practice. (For this reason, newsroom internships are de rigueur for journalism students who want to continue in the profession.) Referring to other situations of apprenticeship, Coy's description is apt for the journalistic context: "What this privileged knowledge provides for practitioners goes beyond practical aspects of production and creates a sense of identity, a notion of distinctiveness" (Coy 1989: 3). The socialization process involves the "interactions that conjoin less and more experienced persons in the structuring of knowledge, emotion, and social action" (Ochs 2001: 227). It also invokes learning what comprises the ideology behind the practice; the conceptual boundaries of interpretation of group and individual beliefs, values, and intentions, and how they are marked discursively.[1]

From an ethnographic and interactional analytic perspective,[2] a prospective member of the news profession learns about the news process by learning the *act sequences* that are relevant to practitioner communicative objectives and position within the news community; the *participant roles* that exist within the news community and what communicative constraints and expectations come with the roles; and a broad range of both practical and ideological values or *norms* that become integral to participation in the news community and are thus

[1]   See discussion of these points in Bucholtz and Hall 2006; Milroy and Milroy 1999; Philips 1998; Schieffelin *et al.* 1998, etc.
[2]   See Duranti 1997; Hymes 1972b; Kulick and Schieffelin 2006; Saville-Troike 2002 [1989]; Schieffelin and Ochs 1986, 1996.

reflected in "insider" communicative behaviors, language use, and genre forms. A variety of discursive skills – interactional, monologic, evidential, multi-authorial, rhetorical, performative, linguistically prescriptive – are required to become a communicatively competent journalist, as the chapters throughout this book make evident.

The socialization process involves learning about **boundaries** and **distinctions** in terms of both personal behavior and what is appropriate ethically, interactionally, and professionally, and the rationales behind textual norms (most non-journalists are unaware of the emphasis on these points). There is a profession-maintained *position with respect to the public charge*. This is a position that changes cross-culturally as well as across different media modalities (cf. Jaffe 2007; Knight and Nakano 1999; Leitner 1980, 1984; Meinhof 1994; Satoh 2001; Scollon 1997; Spitulnik 2001), which leads to different subsets of practice, actions, and outcomes. There is also the inculcation of *news values*, which help to focus reporting and coverage decisions (see Chapter 4) and ideological values in general.

Language socialization is also integral to journalistic identity, to "becoming an active, competent participant" (Ochs 2001: 227) in the news community. The journalist's particular *role with respect to language* is reinforced (see Chapter 9) in ways that are particular to journalism. At a fundamental level, reporting skills trump writing, but language use in the *prescriptive* (linguistic), *functional* (discursive, multimodal), or *accuracy* (journalistic) sense is important. *Prescriptive* norms are especially valued in print contexts; *functional* motivations relate to the spoken, written, visual, aural, and interactional dimensions of different media modes and how these dimensions guide narrative organization and presentation; and *accuracy* objectives in view of facts and usage are relevant in all news media domains, whether the actual outcomes support or belie this or not.

3.2.1   News process

The news process involves newsgathering, reporting, writing, editing, and publication. At its most basic, it starts with the story tip and ends with the story in print or on the air or Internet. The news process can be broken down in two related ways: in terms of the *story components* and its *discourse-level features*. How the component elements fit together varies according to the medium, with radio, television, Web, and print media relying differently on aural, visual, spoken, written, graphic, and real-time modes and mechanisms of delivery.

The **story components** include what is involved, journalistically, in writing the story. In brief, this involves: *news tip, sources, news values, writing, editing, headline*, and story *placement*. The news process schema (see Figure 3.1)

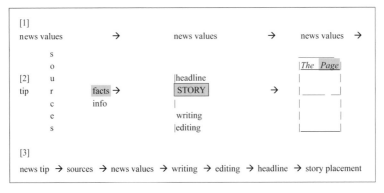

Figure 3.1 The news process schema

shows more graphically how the story components are related (Sequence [3]) and how once a news tip is established, *facts* comprise the *story* on the *page* (Sequence [2]).

The news *tip* a reporter receives or uncovers generates follow-up: interviewing sources to gather *facts* or *information* sufficient to write the *story*. After the reporter has written the story, and it has been edited (by a section editor) for content, it goes to the copy (or sub-) editor for *editing* for style and usage. The copy editor generally puts the *headline* on the story. The story's importance determines where on the page the story is *placed*, or at what point in the broadcast the story is heard. *News values* are relevant and guide decisions throughout (Sequence [1] in Figure 3.1); they are utilized to determine the news *tip*'s relevance, the *facts* to include, organization of the *story*, and its *placement* on the page.

At its simplest, the news process can be summarized as the triumvirate of facts–story–page: of *facts* (comprising the) *story* (on the) *page*. Facts–story–page correlate to the acts of reporting, writing, and transmission, and to the parallel discourse typology of information, narrative, and presentation or display.

The news process and its components can also be characterized more directly according to its **discourse-level features**. The discourse-level features behind these story components include but are not limited to the list in Figure 3.2. In newswriting, a *reporter tells a story*, on the surface level following a particular *narrative structure* indigenous to the news community, and integrating *cultural attitudes or schemas* within the story. (In other media contexts, see Kelly-Holmes and Atkinson 2007 for examples of cultural attitudes in radio satire, and Dégh 1994 for examples of folk schemas embedded in newspaper death-notice narratives.) News tip in hand, a reporter relies on sources to confirm information and provide facts, a preliminary filter in the *topic selection*

Discourse-level features	Story components
General	
• Telling a story	Newswriting
• Narrative structure	
• Integration of cultural schemas	
Specific	
• Topic selection	News tip
• Multiple authors	Sources
• Authorial roles	
• Internalized assumptions	News values
• Coherence	Editing
• Local norms	
• Information hierarchy	The headline
• Conventionalization, routine	
• Salience in physical domain	Story placement

Figure 3.2 The news process: discourse-level features and the story

process. The reporter also relies on the shared knowledge of the news community, talking about the story with editors and peers, which influences the discursive outcome.

Between sources, editors, fellow reporters, and prior discourse between and among them (formal and informal, spoken or written), the story is in effect constructed by *multiple authors*, each of whom has a different *authorial role* in the Goffmanian sense. Goffman 1981 distinguished speaker roles such as *principal* (the person who stands behind the words and their meaning), *author* (the person who chooses the means of expressing them), and *animator* (the conveyor, "an individual active in … utterance production," p. 144).[3] In the news production process, the authorial roles are similarly multifaceted. On the simplest level, "principals" are the people quoted and reported on, reporters

---

[3] As a case in point, an official's speechwriter is the text's *author* (choosing and devising the means of expression); the official is the *principal* (committed to the words that are attributed to him or her); the news outlet which transmits the speech is the *animator* (the conveyor or, in Goffman's words, the "sounding box" (Goffman 1981: 144)). In my own citation and quotation of Goffman here, he is the principal – they are his words and meanings; I am the author – I am expressing them; and the publisher of this book is the animator, responsible for conveying them to the recipient reader.

function as "authors" of the principals' words as well as "animators" who get the words or message to the recipient.

Supporting the news community's decisions about the newsworthiness of the story, at each stage, are news values, *internalized assumptions* about what is important to transmit (see Chapter 4 for an extended discussion). These profession-embedded assumptions influence story length and placement and the time taken in reporting.

Both section editors and copy editors edit the story – they are part of the story's multiple-author "biography." Section editors scrutinize the story on the propositional level, looking at content for the story's relative newsworthiness, ensuring that the narrative structure is in place or that the story elements "flow," and ensuring that the most important news element is fronted. Copy editors edit for style, usage, propositional and narrative coherence overall, and to ensure that *local style norms* are followed (e.g., how place names are referred to, whether courtesy titles are used, etc.). They are generally the ones who add the headline, which must distill what is newsworthy about the story or why it would want to be read or listened to. Given limited space and time, there is a great deal of *conventionalization* and *routine* behind headline writing, as there is within the news narrative itself. For example, on the lexical level, copy editors have a stable of short words standing in for physically longer synonyms (words like "tot" for child or "solon" for legislator or, less auspiciously, "Gitmo" for Guantánamo).

On the page itself, the headline, like the story, reflects a contingent *information hierarchy* – the hierarchy of information in place. The size of the headline and number of lines (or decks) are a preliminary indicator of the importance of the story. Depending on what else is happening that day, the story is placed on the page, its placement reflecting news *salience in the physical domain*. A story above the fold on Page One is more important than one buried in the back pages. This salience is aurally relevant as well as visually, extending to broadcast, as well: "Top of the news" (following the conceptual metaphor of "top" entailing "first" or "best") is a common phrase used in broadcasts, orienting to the listener in the same way a reader is oriented to the top of a newspaper page. (For more on Page One considerations and the information hierarchy, see Chapter 5.)

To illustrate the news process to both novice reporters and linguists, I have used the Jack and Jill nursery rhyme over the years as a case-in-point (Figure 3.3), its familiarity masking its propositional drama.[4]

---

[4] Student reporters, as well as novice fieldworkers, systematically learn to "problematize the everyday," to find stories and explanations behind the obvious and the culturally unmarked, as discussed in chapter 4.

NEWS PROCESS... ...involving the story:	DISCOURSE-LEVEL POINTS... ...manifested by the reporter:

The tip:
    Jack and Jill went up the hill
    to fetch a pail of water.
    Jack fell down and broke his crown
    and Jill came tumbling after.
	• telling a story
	• narrative structure
	• cultural schemas
	• folklore relationships

List of sources [suggested]:
    police dispatcher
    Jill
    sergeant at scene
    onlooker
    hospital spokesperson
    nursery-rhyme expert
	• multiple authors
	• authorial roles

News values:
    proximity
    importance
    currency
    prominence
    (conflict)
    (information)
	• embedded assumptions

Editing:
    content (city desk)
    style (news desk)
	• coherence
	• local norms

The headline [suggested]: *Character in coma following tumble at Hill/* *Water in bucket shifts, throws boy off balance*	• information hierarchy • conventionalization, routine
Story placement	• salience in physical domain

Figure 3.3 Jack and Jill: illustrating the news process

As the Jack and Jill schema shows, the elements of the news process involving the story have related discourse-level points initiated and manifested by the news practitioners that are also part of the reporting process. I have associated the discourse-level features and story components noted earlier in Figure 3.2 (tip, sources, news values, editing, placement) with the "news elements" in the Jack and Jill illustration, elaborating a bit on the sources a responsible reporter would have to contact and the headline a copy editor might write.

3.2.2 Roles and participant relationships

The primary roles in the newsroom are reporters and editors. Reporters go out in the world and gather the news, report, and write. Editors monitor reporter production, comment, mentor, and edit. (By and large, copy editors or sub-editors look to language; section editors look to content.) Reporters have beats or jurisdictions they cover (news, sports, features, crime, courts, regional, business, etc.). Editors manage their respective sections (news, sports, features, photo, graphic, etc.). The News Editor manages the copy editors. The City Editor oversees the news reporters. The Managing Editor oversees the section editors. The Editor-in-Chief or Opinion-Page Editor oversees the columnists, editorial writers, and content on the opinion pages. Photographers and graphic designers work with reporters and editors; their outputs enhance, clarify, and add the visual "thousand words" to the reporter's story, or function alone as a visual narrative.

News practitioners who self-identify as "reporters" see themselves as more workaday, news-oriented, and behind-the-scenes in the public sense than people who self-identify as "journalists." That said, "journalist" is a useful generic term that captures a role or occupational designation outside the news community as well as within it. It is used (as I do here) when one does not need to or want to make a distinction between "reporter" and "editor."

Participant roles set up relationships in the news community and outside of it. The primary participant relationships in the newsroom are reporter–editor and reporter–reporter. Outside of the newsroom, it is reporter–source (or reporter–coverage community and editor–coverage community). Journalism as a profession occupies a role and relationship with respect to the public (see Chapter 2 for initial discussion about this "community factor").

Complexities   In the newsroom, a conscious division between news-community and outside-community membership and alliance comes about when issues of "conflict of interest" arise. A reporter who has some personal engagement with the news story, or with someone interviewed for it, is expected to declare that "conflict of interest" either through a statement within the story, or to absent himself or herself from covering it.

As in any relationship, there are tensions between managing a balance between autonomy or authority and connection or accessibility. News organizations try to maintain a voice of authority in terms of story coverage, position within the larger community, and stance in relation to news delivery – which is where maintaining credibility comes in. At the same time they actively try to function as the "voice of community," developing a one-to-one, de-hierarchized, approachable, more symmetrical relationship. Phrases that suggest this purpose are often found on the front-page nameplate or flag (not "masthead," which is the box inside that lists the staff and contact information). For example: *The Oakland Tribune* (Oakland and the East Bay, California): "Serving Oakland for 136 years" (2010); *Chesterton Tribune* (Chesterton and Porter County, Indiana): "Duneland Community Newspaper Since 1884";

News-Leader (Fernandina Beach and Amelia Island, Florida): "Proudly serving the community for over 150 years"; *The Daily Star* (Oneonta, New York, and surrounding counties): "The Newspaper for the Heartland of New York"; The Kiowa News (Kiowa, Kansas): "Serving the Stateline Area for 117 Years" (2010); the former *Cleveland* (Ohio) *Press*: "The Newspaper that Serves Its Readers"; the former *Atlanta* (Georgia) *Journal*: "Covers Dixie like the Dew"; and perhaps most notoriously in recent years (quoted in AJR 2000 and Lauterer 2006), the *Mason Valley News* (Yerington, Nevada): "The only newspaper in the world that gives a damn about Yerington."[5]

3.2.3   Values: journalistic distinctions

Motivating journalistic practice are profession-specific values that translate into profession-specific distinctions governing practice. For example, the inculcation of *news values* allows distinctions between what counts as relevant to report on (as will be addressed in Chapter 4). More ideologically, the news community's self-policed *position with respect to the public charge* is intended to constrain behaviors that might contravene public benefit. Boundaries and *firewalls* are in place to keep the commercial and journalistic strands of the news media separate, in an effort to maintain editorial objectivity and avoid conflict of interest.

    Reporting priorities   As noted in Chapter 2, the news community also makes distinctions between "reporting" and "writing" (emphasizing process-oriented "reporting" as a value, although appropriate language use is valued); between content and style editing, both of which are prized, but for different reasons. "Local" news, because of its relevance to the *community of coverage*, is prioritized over other types of news (cf. Chapters 2 and 5).

    A "scoop" – getting the story first – is another value, as to a lesser extent is the "exclusive." It is not just the obvious big-ticket story (uncovering malfeasance, an interview with a reticent newsmaker, an eye-witness experience like watching the Hindenburg explode, etc.). As most newsrooms deal with the day-to-day of their respective communities, no matter how small they are, scooping the other media in the area or being first with an important, more complicated story may also be realized in being first with something as small as a police blotter item or as localized as a planning department decision. In my own experience, being first with the news – by having the necessary facts with which to run a

---

[5] The *Mason Valley News* can be found online at https://secure.rgj.com/yerington/, which once was billed as "The Only Website in the World that gives a Damn about Lyon County" (accessed October 22, 2009); Yerington is in Lyon County. (The paper was purchased in 2000 by the *Reno Gazette-Journal.*)

story – became part of the daily motivation to do "good journalism." This value was reinforced by editors quizzing me when the local radio had a news item I did not get, e.g., a burglary at a major store, or praising me when I got an important complex story, like a pyramid scheme involving hundreds of "victims," before the larger regional paper did.

As the Internet is changing some of the time factors that daily papers traditionally labored under, some editors have observed that the scoop priority is being supplanted to some degree by other requirements, such as quality of writing, depth of coverage, and presentation of contextual knowledge that experience and practice can provide (John Diaz, personal communication).

Firewalls   "Firewalls" are the boundaries that exist within the news profession that a reliable news reporter or editor is not supposed to transgress. Key among them is not blurring the boundary between the enterprise of reporting and the business of selling newspapers, between advertising and "editorial." (Confusingly "editorial" is the term for everything that comprises the "news side" that involves editors, reporters, and photographers, including the op-ed ("opinion-editorial") pages and the actual editorials and opinion columns. More confusingly, "news-ed," a short form of "news-editorial," is the term used to keep the "news" and "opinion" distinctions clear.) The "firewall" is also the psychological boundary that exists, often within the actual physical setting where newsrooms and ad departments coexist in open-plan fashion, to help to maintain reportorial objectivity, to retain one's ethical grounding. The production staff, the design and pressroom people responsible for the physical outcome, are also aware of the firewall. As newspaper veteran Judith Martin, who writes the syndicated "Miss Manners" column and reminds readers of the standards behind one's social obligation and ethical duty, recollects:

When Miss Manners was a budding young journalist, a fiercely strict distinction was made between news and advertising. They shared pages, and cynical readers assumed that advertising dollars influenced the news, but honest journalists did not permit this.
(Judith Martin, *Washington Post*, December 26, 2007: C10)

To maintain the firewall, there are general rules, such as no "editorializing" (meaning no insertion of personal opinion in a news story by the reporter) and no ads on Page One, although this does happen, but usually either because it has been done historically, or only after a great deal of editorial discussion, economic justification, and restriction. Ads are kept separate from "editorial" content, and clearly marked, e.g., "advertisement," "advertising supplement," "this notice paid by [X]," etc. News stories that may contain an element of legitimate "editorializing" are supposed to be marked as "news analysis." The firewall is cited within the newsroom when coverage decisions come too close to favoring an advertiser, e.g., when a major advertiser wants his drunken-driving arrest quashed. One's news-professional identity is supposed to be distinct and separate from the newspaper's bottom line; one's news decisions are not supposed to be economically motivated. In my experience (corroborated by others), it is a distinction that is more black-and-white at the reporter level, amongst the journalistic "foot soldiers" whose ideals may not have not been challenged, than further up the management chain.

The boundaries obviously are negotiable, and the outcomes reflective of the particular news organization's ethos (most major newspapers do not, for instance, accept "freebies" of any sort or free tickets to events they cover, although some do), and of the individuals at the helm. In that sense, the interpretations and realizations behind firewall maintenance are ongoing and emergent – to the extent that their violation is of active concern to the larger journalism community, and frequently addressed in trade publications. A prime example of this policing is the regular "Darts and Laurels" column in the bimonthly *Columbia Journalism Review*, which either praises news practice that enlightens, or chastises acts that run counter to the profession's ideals (specific incidences of, for example, not holding a politician accountable, or catering to an advertiser).

Boundary blurring   Other boundaries are also "blur-able." Critics from both within and outside the news community cite with chagrin the rise of an entertainment focus over the past several decades and the subsequent blurring of the news–entertainment boundaries. (It is a newsroom cliché that print journalists attribute the rise of this dynamic to television; and television journalists attribute the blurring to the lowered expectations of society as a whole.) More thoughtful analyses look at the role of the economy and the changing structure of the news business – the closures of independently owned media outlets, for instance – as influences. In possibly more interesting ways, from the discourse analytic perspective, there are seepages of one media form to another, "modality bleeds" that come about through changes in media technology. This is most evident in daily newspapers' inclusion of video on their websites; radio stations' inclusion of pictures and visual elements on their websites; and television stations including the written word on the screen, as well as the development of multimedia platforms on the Web.

3.3   Loci of learning

News professionals learn their journalistic ways of being and responding in two primary institutional "sites": journalism school, where they are taught by journalism professors who have practical experience in the profession, and the newsroom, where their instruction, socialization, and shared knowledge base develops through contact with peers and editors. Other sites of institutional learning are publications (e.g., *Columbia Journalism Review, American Journalism Review, Quill*, or *Editor & Publisher*), organizations (e.g., the Society of Professional Journalists and minority journalism organizations), and conferences (e.g., the annual Public Radio Conference and Unity Convention, and regional Associated Collegiate Press and Radio-Television News Directors Association meetings). Journalism educators have their own sub-community, publications, and organizations (the Association for Education in Journalism and Mass Communications, and College Media Advisers prime among them) related to education as well as journalism.

In practical classes in university journalism programs in the US, student reporters acquire basic skill sets involving reporting, writing, editing, interviewing, design and layout. They learn these skills by doing them, often in tandem with participation on laboratory newspapers and news websites or radio or television projects and programs. News media ethics, access and open government (Freedom of Information Act and the "Sunshine Act"), libel law, and using the Internet and public records for reporting are also components in beginning newswriting classes as well as advanced subjects on their own. Newsroom internships are essential steps to put into practice what has been learned, and to start the newsroom socialization process.

Newswriting parameters and rules for producing well-formed stories are set out in textbooks and workbooks. Most teachers, lecturers, and professors have been or still are practicing journalists. Alongside learning about and acquiring the requisite skills involving language (standard usage and news style), discourse (story structure), and interaction (whom to interview, what to ask about, and how to conduct interviews), there is the overarching pedagogical aim – which relates directly to developing a professional identity and internalizing the news community's practice-oriented values – to have students hone their "nose for news," their ability to register what is considered important to report on, to observe, and interpret.

Beyond the formal education process, there is also knowledge that is informally conveyed through comments from teachers and later on from colleagues in the newsroom. Esoteric skills such as learning how to read upside down (an "advanced" observation skill) and more fundamental nuances like appropriate telephone voice come through informal socialization and imitation of newsroom peers and editors (for discussion of workplace practice beyond the socialization process, as well as examples of interaction across multiple workplace contexts and cultures, see Cotter and Marschall 2006; Drew and Heritage 1992; Holmes and Marra 2005; McElhinny 1998; Schnurr *et al.* 2007; and Tannen 1994).

Socialization in news culture and learning how to be a communicatively competent member of the news community come through acquisition of the range of practice-related skills (learning how to determine what makes something news and how to report on it) as well as acquiring the values under-lying them (assimilating a professional identity of reporter). Roles and relation-ships within and outside of the newsroom, hierarchies within the profession, issues that influence the production of news stories, story construction, relations with the *community of coverage*, and all the constituent parts of the news process itself comprise the learning curve.

The "apprentice model" is the operative learning format in the journalist's world. It involves steps and stages of proficiency acquisition which are marked by guideposts within the profession. It orients to a consideration of practice and performance of news craft. It relies on peers, teachers, mentors, and individuals with experience to develop and maintain the communicative competence of the newsroom novice. The apprentice model is familiar in the Western world; for instance, medicine, business, and academia all have their apprentice routines. The apprentice model has historical evocations of the medieval guild culture of craftsmen (and women) which exists in the modern day (see Lakoff 1990 for points about academia in the US and Terrio 2000 for a discussion of craft and commerce in modern-day France), as well as pop-culture incarnations on tele-vision currently (episodes of *The Apprentice* illustrate in edited and entertain-ment form some of the factors that are relevant).

In the newsroom, the apprentice model situates learning with practice, and associates the outcomes of performance with communicative competence as a journalist. It also accounts for individual development within the news-profession culture and acquisition of the "mature subjectivity" required of good decision-making, a subjectivity "tempered by encounters with, and regard for, the views of significant others in the profession; and subjectivity aged by encounters with, and regard for, the facts of the world. There is no text for this" (Schudson 1978: 192).

3.4   Conclusion: the apprentice model and journalistic practice

In this chapter, I looked at aspects of socialization and learning within the news profession, citing the focus on practice and craft, and proposing that an "apprentice model" best characterizes the process by which news practitioners come to learn their craft and perform according to intra-community standards. It is another dimension and way to consider the notion of craft discussed in Chapter 2.

The elements that a novice must learn involve more than the ostensibly simple construction of a news story, or even the more complex understanding of the news process, and they ultimately allow the development and presenta-tion of a news practitioner *identity* that obtains alongside practitioner *actions*. Distinctions and "firewalls" on the discourse and ideological levels, priorities within the text and its outcomes, understanding the roles and relationships within the newsroom, as well as the need for a cognitive distance in relationships with sources and in the local community are part of the learning package that one acquires through practice.

Behind the news story, the most important concept a novice reporter must learn is the role of news values and their use in deciding what to write about, who to talk to, what to prioritize, and how to present and edit it. Chapter 4 focuses on the all-important concept of news values.

Part II

Conceptualizing the news

4   News values and their significance in text and practice

KEY POINTS

- News values – the qualities that make a news item "newsworthy" – become embedded in text and govern practice.
- News values "shape texts" by providing decision-making parameters, limiting the scope of possibility.
- News values are agreed to in the abstract, as a list of motivations for coverage decisions, but are interpreted differently across publications and editors and through time.
- News values look different from the inside vs. the outside: a reporter's list varies from an outsider's.

Why does a monsoon in India that kills thousands of people get buried on Page Z99 when a meteorological threat of a lesser degree in the next county gets A1 play and plenty of television broadcast time? Why in US papers do the politics of Eastern Europe get less attention than the decision of the local zoning committee? What counts as news? What makes a story newsworthy? Newsworthiness is determined by a set of simple factors or "news values" that include proximity, impact, change, prominence, conflict, timeliness, usefulness, and the unusual. News values function as *guidelines for decision-making* and are invoked, unconsciously or explicitly, at every step of the news process. News values are one of the most important *practice-based and ideological* factors in understanding the focus and shape of news stories and the decisions of journalists.

News values are more than a list of qualities that explain what counts as news. Knowing about news values means one can look at how a story is interpreted from the journalist's perspective. News values govern **practice** by affording decision-making parameters, and are thus embedded in **text**. As such, they shape text by reinforcing an "ideology" about what counts as news and, consequently, by organizing story design: story form and news values go hand-in-hand.

In this chapter, I specify the significance of news values within both text (editorial outcomes) and practice (routines and decisions by editors and reporters) by describing how they are operationalized, how they are more than an inert or idealized list found in journalism textbooks. I note how they function as a heuristic to determine what counts as news; where they play a role in governing practice as well as promoting journalistic identity; and, as with other more general speech community values like prescriptive usage, the extent to which they function as norms in the abstract, allowing for interpretation and variation in the outcomes we see as news stories.

4.1   Determining "newsworthiness"

4.1.1   What are news values?

Ask reporters or editors to define "news values" and they will immediately come up with a list of qualities or elements that a news story must possess to be viable for publication: the story must be timely, important, relevant, about change or conflict, etc. The question that is really being asked is, "What is news?," the objective of which is to determine when something (an event, change, occasion, act) is "newsworthy." It is at the heart of news practice and process, and is central to reporter and editor actions. British news veteran David Randall put it succinctly: "A newspaper's role is to find fresh information on matters of public interest and to relay it as quickly and accurately as possible to readers in an honest and balanced way. That's it" (Randall 2000: 22). "Fresh information" contributes to the newsworthiness dynamic.

Although "there is no easy formula that can determine whether something is newsworthy" (Lorenz and Vivian 1996: 22), textbook authors give nearly identical lists of characteristics when defining what news is: it is unusual, timely, local or nearby, surprising, about change, conflict and people, has impact, evokes human interest, and conveys information. In short, would a reader care to hear about it? (cf. Cotter 1999b). As one author summarizes: "News is often defined by its qualities, and the qualities often mentioned are timeliness, proximity, prominence, rarity and human interest" (Hough 1988: 3).

As news values are so fundamental to determining what counts as relevant in the news context, they are one of the first topics that is addressed – in list form accompanied by explanation – in journalism textbooks. These lists of news values, which are established, operationalized, interpreted, and reinforced by the community itself, can be viewed as "in-group taxonomies." I am taking care to differentiate in-group lists from outsider lists (such as those compiled by researchers such as van Dijk 1988). To start with textbook definitions is to start with what practitioners and experts in the field have distilled, as well as to understand student reporters' first exposure to the foundational, practice-specific values of the journalist in-group to which they are seeking membership. Table 4.1 summarizes lists of news values from five randomly selected newswriting text-books sent as examination copies by publishers to university journalism depart-ments (two of which are used as primary textbooks in undergraduate newswriting

Table 4.1 *News values: textbook lists (in-group taxonomy)*

Textbook 1	Textbook 2	Textbook 3	Textbook 4	Textbook 5
Impact	Timeliness	Timeliness	Timeliness	Timeliness
Proximity	Impact	Proximity	Proximity	Proximity
Timeliness	Prominence	Conflict	Prominence	Prominence
Prominence	Proximity	Eminence & prominence	Currency	Rarity
Novelty or deviance	Conflict	Consequence & impact	Drama	Human interest
Conflict	The unusual Currency ("Conscience")	Human interest	Consequence Novelty	
Bunton et al. 1999	**Mencher 1997, 2006**	**Itule & Anderson 1991**	**Lorenz & Vivian 1996**	**Hough 1988**

classes at California universities). The news values in the table are listed in the order in which the authors present them in their textbooks.

Timeliness, proximity, and *prominence* are key news values, in the "top four" of each textbook listing in Table 4.1, as well as in the "top three" in Textbooks 4 and 5. *Timeliness*, simply, is whether the story is new or old, or relevant in some way to the calendar (holiday or anniversary stories, for instance). *Proximity* is the extent to which the story has occurred locally or, if it occurred elsewhere, is relevant to readers locally (federal government edicts with local impacts, for instance). *Prominence* gauges the standing of the individual under news scrutiny (someone well known is of news interest). Noticeably, the news value of *conflict* is high on the list of only one textbook (Itule and Anderson 1991), at the very bottom of another (Bunton et al. 1999), and near the end or absent in the other cases (Hough 1988; Lorenz and Vivian 1996; Mencher 1997 and 2006). Similarly, the news value of *impact* (or *consequence*) is high on two of the lists and in penultimate position on the other two (and absent in Hough 1988).

One explanation for the differences is that textbooks have pedagogical aims that do not necessarily reflect actual news outputs (much as the explanations in grammar guides make language out to be simpler than is found in naturally occurring contexts). However, in the "real world," the omission of *conflict* on the lists is not insignificant, according to editor John Diaz, as "conflict (or the absence of it) can be a huge factor in determining whether something is considered news" (personal communication).[1]

---

[1] John Diaz writes in 2007 (personal communication): "I point no further than the current criticism of mainstream media for failing to sufficiently challenge the basis for the war in Iraq. Why wasn't

Also near the bottom of each list is a category marker for the "unusual" news angle. Each list has some way of accounting for the *unusual* or *novel* (or *deviant*, in the case of Textbook 1; and *rare* in the case of Textbook 5), with the exception of Textbook 3, whose *human interest* listing could conceivably encompass any of those types of story. Perhaps this variation is because "impact" or "unusual" elements can be interpreted more loosely *in situ* than the deictically grounded time, person, or place factors of *timeliness, prominence*, and *proximity*; and a textbook's underlying goal is to create interpretive stability for learners. Other variations in list order can be viewed as pedagogical, depending on how the authors have organized their material for the textbook market they are aiming for (an assumption I base on a global read-through of numerous textbooks).

The differences among the lists are negligible, particularly when the accompanying pedagogical explanations are taken into account, although they point up the fact that there can be variation. For example, within the lists themselves in Table 4.1, Textbook 2 (Mencher 1997, 2006) and Textbook 4 (Lorenz and Vivian 1996) add the news value of *currency*, which can correlate to some degree to concurrently specified *timeliness*; and Textbook 3 (Itule and Anderson 1991) as well as Textbook 5 (Hough 1988) adds *human interest*, which is a more general catch-all category name for a genre of stories that has some element of a currency, novelty, drama, utility, personal, empathy, or prurience angle. In my own personal library of some three dozen textbooks dating from 1913 to 2007, the lists vary in terms of succinctness from Hough's list of five (*timeliness, proximity, prominence, rarity, human interest*), to Lanson and Stephens's list of eleven (not included in Table 4.1), which includes *impact, weight, controversy, emotion, the unusual, prominence, proximity, timeliness, currency, usefulness*, and *educational value* (Lanson and Stephens 1994).

More recent editions of standard textbooks, such as Mencher 2006, include other news-decision factors like "necessity" – the net result of enterprise or investigative reporting. Mencher calls it "journalism of conscience" (undertaken by reporters from any size or type of news media outlet), intended to remedy or expose a dysfunctional element within the social system (Mencher 2006: 63). Brooks *et al.* (2005) mention "relevance" and "usefulness" in relation to their news-value lists, as "guidelines for judging the news value of any event, issue or personality" (Brooks *et al.* 2005: 5). They also emphasize that beyond the facts, a news story

the press (with the very notable exception of the Knight-Ridder Washington Bureau) more skeptical and aggressive in challenging the Bush administration's justifications in the use of force resolution in fall 2002? I would suggest that one of the reasons was the **relative absence of conflict**, both among experts and within the debate on Capitol Hill. At the same time, many stories get elevated way beyond their societal significance simply because of the **intensity of conflict**." He notes prodigious coverage of contested legislative issues in California in 2007 (a spay/neuter bill and a proposal to outlaw spanking) and minimal coverage of issues of great import (the governor and Legislature's consideration of "ideas to overhaul the healthcare system of the nation's largest state and world's fifth largest economy") [emphasis added].

must be well-told, a point that is becoming more relevant in the wake of the Web. In this vein, there is also a shift toward replacing "breaking news" (see Chapter 7) with "contextual stories [which amplify or explain in greater detail a news event] [...] that aren't available on the Web" (John Diaz, personal communication).

4.1.2   "Insider" coverage calculations

News values may be taught in the classroom, but in the newsroom they are not referred to in so many words but become part of the rationales that guide news coverage and story play. "Reporters may not talk about 'proximity' or 'prominence' but they know what gets on Page One" (John Diaz, personal communication).

In the physical newspaper itself, in the actual result of the daily application of these news values and their outcome in story form, it is sometimes the case that a news practitioner will explain to the reader why something is deemed newsworthy in the "insider" sense. This explicitness is generally found in genre forms outside the prototypical news story such as columns, "op-ed" opinion pieces, or ombudsman responses – meta-commentaries – and is another way for an "outsider" to come to understand the underlying decision-making process that determines whether a story is worth covering or noting, as in Examples 4.1 and 4.2.

Example 4.1
That is what makes it newsworthy when a public official, speaking on the record, sets forth a view that is as blunt and uncomfortable as it is politically unpalatable.
(David S. Broder, *Washington Post*, Sunday, May 14, 2006: B7, emphasis added)

Example 4.2
Motorcyclist Joey Dunlop has passed his driving test. What made that a news item was the accompanying information which reminded us that Mr Dunlop was six times world champion and won the Isle of Mann TT on 21 occasions.
(*Irish Emigrant Newsletter*, April 1997, emphasis added)

In Examples 4.1 and 4.2, the individual reported on does something out of the ordinary for conditions with respect to his standing (*prominence*) in the community (*proximity*); the columnist writing on behalf of each community is explicit about that with phrases like "that is what makes it newsworthy" in 4.1, and "What made that a news item" in 4.2.

There are implicit newsworthiness calculations within these meta-commentaries, as well. In Example 4.1, *Washington Post* political columnist Broder acknowledges that public officials as a rule tend to speak according to the coded format of the political context such that when they do not, it makes news, and this is why a particular incident was covered. In 4.2, the Ireland-based editors of a small newsletter sent via email to the Irish diaspora worldwide describe in detail the reason why a routine non-story – passing a driving test – became news: motorcyclists who are fêted racers might already be considered competent to drive a car. In both examples, the news values of *unusualness* or *novelty*, as well as the *prominence* of the person who acted or his particular function within the specific context, contribute to its newsworthiness.

Newspaper columnists also explain to readers why stories are *not* covered, implicitly crediting news values in relation to reader interest for the decisions. In Example 4.3, the implicit news value underlying the coverage decision is on the grounds of *prominence* and in Example 4.4 it is due to *proximity*:

Example 4.3
It's because someone may have decided that a story [...] of a woman nobody has ever heard of, won't have much significance to readers.
                                         (*Washington Post*, February 2006, emphasis added)

Example 4.4
Of what interest would the state of the streets in Battersea be to the people of Barking or Brent?   (*London Evening Standard*, November 2006, emphasis added)

In these examples, the columnists cite as reasons for an absence of coverage a lack of "significance" (in 4.3) or "interest" (in 4.4) that the story would have for readers – the audience which they are addressing in their commentary. Taking readers into account in this way – "Reporters are constantly measuring what effect events have on their readers" (Newsom and Wollert 1988: 11) – is also integral to coverage calculations within the newsroom, more about which will be said in chapters 5 and 6.

4.2   News values govern journalistic practice

4.2.1   Decision-making heuristic

Journalism educators teach students about news values; in turn news values are implemented in practice. On the student level, the explicit objective of practice is learning how to write well-formed news stories. Understanding "newsworthiness," or what counts as news, and selecting appropriate information elements are central to this endeavor. On the newsroom level this understanding is continued daily: the implicit results of daily practice are a reinforced communicative competence within the profession, which management of news values signifies. This occurs in relation to the unmarked – expected – "knocking out" of news stories on deadline in which the news values are embedded. (See Chapter 5 for an illustration of the salience of news values in a newsroom communicative context, and Chapter 7 for examples in news stories themselves.) Memorizing or learning the list of news values, therefore, is barely the first step. Deploying them daily is where they become critical, understood through action in the newsroom and the external environments of reporting and editing, and through being reminded about what counts (as news) in a particular newsroom context. One textbook tells students about the manifestation of news judgment in this way:

STAGES OF THE NEWS STORY PROCESS...	...AND WHO MAKES THE DECISIONS AT EACH STAGE
STORY CONCEPTUALIZATION ⇢ ↓ ↓	REPORTERS (AND EDITORS) NB – all stages can have prior input or end-stage feedback from editor
• Considering what a story is	Reporter-initiated; editor-assigned
• Should something be covered at all	Reporter, in consultation with editor
↓ STORY CONSTRUCTION ⇢ ↓ ↓	REPORTERS NB – editors usually have input, initiated or requested
• Deciding whom to interview, ask questions of	Reporter
• Determining what questions to ask	Reporter
• What information and detail to include	Reporter
• What element to lead off with	Reporter
• How to frame the story (the *news angle*)	Reporter
↓ STORY POSITION ⇢ ↓ ↓	EDITORS NB – with input from reporters; but editors have final decision
• How prominently to play the story	Editor
• Should there be "art" [photo or graphic]?	Editors, with reporter and photographer
• How long to make the story	Editors primarily; with reporter input
• Where to place the story; how big to place it in physical space	Editors
↓ EVALUATION ⇢ ↓ ↓	EDITORS AND REPORTERS (AND PUBLIC) NB – formal "official" discussion and informal workplace chat both relevant
• How we did	Editors to reporters collectively, and vice versa individually; reporters; public input

Figure 4.1 Stages of the news process that lead to the story

Every day, journalists must make [...] choices about what readers want or need to know. In fact, *news judgment* is an indispensable skill at all levels of journalism. Editors need this skill to decide which of the flood of press releases and tips they get every day are worth pursuing, and which stories in each day's paper deserve the most prominence. Reporters need it to help find stories and to determine which aspects of these stories they should focus on.   (Lanson and Stephens 1994: 10)

In the newsroom, via its plethora of newsgathering activities, news values govern each stage of the reporting and editing process by establishing selection criteria. (See Figure 4.1 for a list of the stages.) They work by providing decision-making parameters, justifications of these decisions, and a "hierarchy of importance" in terms of news-story outcomes that allows fast decision-making and swift dispatch when there are many and disparate claims on time. As Mencher (1997: 181) notes, "Too often, the job requires writing on the run, doing a story with facts gathered close to the deadline." Indeed, the deployment of news values, once they are internalized and part of everyday news work, are "rarely challenged in newsrooms, either in meetings among editors or discussions between reporters and editors," according to Diaz. "We often argue like hell about what is a story or what should go on Page One. But it is almost always within the framework of this unwritten but widely accepted set of news values" (John Diaz, personal communication) – a point that is illustrated at length in the examples in chapter 5.

Above anything else, news values function as a *heuristic*, as a guide that is viable at different stages of the news process, and as such, news values afford fundamental decision-making parameters. As previously noted, they are used or cited to answer key questions: "Is it news?" "What is news?" They are also used to determine *what* or *who* gets covered, as well as *how* to cover it. In effect, they provide criteria for the selection of elements from the beginning to end of the reporting and editing process. In other words, they help to determine what to emphasize.[2]

These newsroom decisions extend to the outcomes in the text that bear direct relation to practice involving reporters and editors. For example, section editors – be they in news, features, sports, business, regional, city, local, or metro – will look first at the *lead of a story* to determine whether the reporter has prioritized the most important news element, the most newsworthy information. Even seasoned reporters will "bury the lede" – or fail to determine the most important aspect of the story and bring it as would be expected to the "top" or beginning – for various reasons that have little to do with individual agency or conscious thought. Sometimes this is because the seasoned reporter is on auto-pilot, or because of his or her over-familiarity with the topic or situation, or because the chronology of the often-pedestrian event, like covering a meeting, gets in the way of locating the most important element or the news item with the most impact or relevance. The editor, then, provides a more detached perspective in his or her exchange with a reporter, at the same time providing reinforcement of what news values or newsworthiness means in context. "Each time a

---

[2] What reporters emphasize is not without issue, creating tensions between journalists and the people being covered. John Diaz provides these examples: "A politician may have a 59-minute speech on the future of national security, but the reporter jumps on the brief shot at [the president] in the QandA period. A three-day county fair may have all sorts of wonderful stories of achievement, fun and divergent communities coming together, but the only story out of the annual event is the stabbing of a 17-year-old kid, which colors the perception of readers who did not attend" (personal communication).

city editor reads a story for the first time, these questions [pertaining to news value] and more come up" (Brooks *et al.* 1999: 39).

News-value parameters operate in tandem with other profession-internal values such as those that lead to story well-formedness within the text itself. For example, stories must be comprehensive and complete in terms of detail and source, the absence of which would lead to a "hole in the story." News values help reporters ensure that these details are present in the text, that despite deadline demands they "present a complete and accurate account" within the story (Mencher 1997: 281). (Chapter 7 deals with story well-formedness more explicitly.)

4.2.2   News values and the news process

Figure 4.1 outlines the different stages of the news process involved in reporting and writing a news story, and indicates who makes the news-value-imbued decisions at the different stages. To help the "outsider" get a sense of the multi-dimensionality of the news process and its attendant decisions within the news-room itself, I have subdivided the different stages of the process pertinent to the news story (or news text) according to *story conceptualization*, *story construction*, *story position*, and *evaluation*, as well as according to who makes the decisions at each stage. (As in a textbook rendition of a dynamic that is central to the news process, the figure simplifies the elements to summarize the general applications.)

News values are not only invoked to answer questions at the *conceptualization stage* about **what** to cover or what counts as news, but also to answer other relevant journalistic questions related to the story and *story construction*: **how** to cover it, **what** to emphasize or start off with (the "lede"), **who** to talk to, **when** to proceed or hold back. They are also relevant to the story's placement or *position* in the paper or on the broadcast: **where** to position it physically in time (radio and television) or space (print) and **how** to play it, incorporating non-textual demands pertaining to space and time on any one day (size of "news hole" and the number of stories to choose from and time to "deadline").

The *participant roles* of the reporter and editor in newsroom exchanges about coverage are both rigid and fluid, bound to both newsroom hierarchy as well as to the unpredictable nature of the daily news. Although news values are the common currency, the differences in the reporter and editor roles, and the different news-gathering and production practices endemic to each position, mean different situations and contexts for decisions. For example, at the *conceptualization* stage, stories can be reporter-initiated, the result of the reporter's own "insider" acquaintance and knowledge of the goings-on on his or her "beat" – traditionally public domains like police and fire, business and technology, courts, government, municipal services, and schools. They can also be assigned by the editor, who in effect provides another set of eyes and operates from an awareness of the larger news context within his or her section of the paper.

During story *construction*, reporting decisions involve who to ask questions of and what questions to ask; writing decisions involve determining the news angle, or how to frame the story, what to lead with, and what information and detail to include. Editors, who can have input while the reporter is reporting and writing and influence story construction when needed, in the meantime are determining story *position* (a consequence of the application of news values): where to play the story (see Chapter 5 for examples of these decisions) and how big to place it in physical space; whether there should be a photo or accompanying graphic or map; and how long the story should be. In the end, editors have the final decision as to story length and the cuts made to it, although reporters come to know through practice the "target lengths" of different types or genres of story (see Chapter 7) and to write accordingly. Mencher (1997: 24) also makes this point, citing the role of practice in the integrated decisions made among the participants: "Usually, the [city] desk will tell a reporter how long the [lawsuit] piece should run, but the city editor knows that his courthouse man, an experienced reporter, will hold it to 450 to 500 words."

News values are also used self-reflectively, to critically *evaluate* "how we did" in covering a particular event, often in relation to input from the public (phone calls, emails, letters to the editor, newspaper-instigated focus groups, and the news profession's general awareness of popular opinion and critique). Self-reflective discourse is found routinely in newsroom meetings and memos, trade publications, and at trade conferences. It is thus present in formal, "official" newsroom discussions, generally led by editors, as well as in informal workplace contexts (water-cooler, breakroom, post-work drinks) among reporters and editors. *Timeliness*, for example, is the news value often cited in relation to story-relevance, as when a reporter misses a story or pursues it too late, but it is also cited in relation to the professional value of being first with the story, of being competitive within the professional context ("did we get beat?"). Similarly, *proximity* is viewed to be at issue when a local or locally meaningful story is overlooked, but it also exists in relation to discussion about practitioners' professional responsibility to readers, and the stories that result: "Reporters are constantly measuring what effect events have on their readers. A tiny fly can be more newsworthy than a space-shuttle landing if that fly and its offspring have a taste for fruit and you are writing for a newspaper in a fruit-producing region" (Lanson and Stephens 1994: 11).

At the same time, readers are also measuring the calculations of reporters, often disagreeing with them. "We hear criticism from readers who say we're not emphasizing [the deaths of US soldiers in Iraq] enough and should highlight these deaths, even of relatively small numbers, on Page One; that to accept these casualties as 'routine' news for the inside pages is to play into the hands of the Bush administration. We also hear from readers who blame the mainstream media for underplaying, and thus marginalizing, the efforts to impeach Bush and Cheney. We also hear the mirror of such criticisms from Republicans. I could give a thousand examples" (John Diaz, *San Francisco Chronicle*, personal communication).

4.3   News judgment and "instinct"

Someone who has succeeded in internalizing the meaning of news values – and is performing accordingly in the variety of discursive circumstances to which they must apply – displays "good news judgment," a valued trait in a newsroom employee. Time and experience within the profession are necessary for this practice-oriented awareness to happen: "experienced editors and reporters develop a sense of what readers want," according to Itule and Anderson (1991: 46). News judgments are also exercised along with outside demographic and survey information (generally compiled by marketing people, not editorial staff) that supplement day-to-day reporting and pavement pounding, all of which provide "editors and reporters with background information that can help hone their instincts" (Itule and Anderson 1991: 46).

It is this internalization of news values and the routinization of coverage decisions instigated by them which may be behind the somewhat magical attribution of news decisions to "instinct," the implicit knowledge of what news is, of "knowing it when you see it." Describing a reporter as having "news sense" or a "nose for news" is another way this implicit, internalized knowledge is referred to – in a complimentary manner – within the profession. The public occasionally gets an inside view of this thinking. For example, a newspaper columnist responding to readers' queries as to why certain stories are overlooked makes reference to this "amorphous" journalistic sensibility. He writes: "The decision to go with one story rather than another turns on what we in this business consider 'newsworthy.' It's an amorphous term, but editors <u>claim to know it when they see it</u>" (King 2006, emphasis added, see appendix 1C).

Even textbook authors, who are charged with isolating and articulating the nuances of news practice for newcomers and beginners to learn, describe the end-product of journalistic socialization and learning how to make good reporting and editing decisions by referring to "instinct." Itule and Anderson, in noting other factors besides the listed news values (in Table 4.1) that influence coverage, also include as relevant to making appropriate news judgments the "instincts of editors and reporters ... <u>They know news when they see it</u>" (Itule and Anderson 1991: 40, emphasis added).

4.3.1   "Instinct" critiques

This "instinct" does become scrutinized and deconstructed when there are either insider or outsider critiques of coverage, such as will happen frequently in the

US especially in the aftermath of constant print and broadcast news coverage of a victim of a violent crime like murder, kidnapping, or rape. Often these coverage critiques in the US relate to the race or income of the victims (white, middle-income, taxpayer vs. black, lower-income, welfare recipient), addressing inequities in coverage and providing examples of equally news-deserving victims from the undercovered ethnic groups, communities, or income brackets.[3]

Critiques such as these highlight what news people have called the "disconnect" between news practitioners' interests and the community of coverage (cf. ASNE reports 1999a, 1999b) and often are a call to make coverage decisions more conscious and less routinized, to base news judgments more on mindfulness and less on instinct, as well as to make them more community-relevant. For example, in Example 4.5, *Washington Post* columnist Colbert I. King, responding to a reader question about the limited extent of coverage of a Northeast Washington, DC, (black) woman's disappearance in a February 2006 column (see Appendix 1C for full version), does the columnist-critic's job by essentially problematizing newsworthiness and underscoring the "disconnect." At the same time, he is reflecting the public's view about the limitations of news reporting by saying: "What draws the interest of people in the news business [...] often bears little relationship to what people who live in communities [...] care about." Whether the news practitioners themselves believe they have made responsible, newsworthy decisions and conscientiously follow their respective paper's mission to focus on local news is not really at issue in view of King's account. His point is that internalization of news values and the routinization of news practice may come at the expense of coverage that appears, in the contingent moment of decision-making, to go outside the newsroom newsworthiness "norm" (or what has become, by accumulative circumstance, the newsroom coverage norm such as, the case King writes about, "inner-city events"). What some editors "regard as routine" can be at odds with what people "really care about":

Example 4.5
Sometimes there are legitimate reasons for not publishing a report ... But the fact is that inner-city events that some editors regard as routine – the loss of a young man to gunfire, a mom separated from her children, kids left to fend for themselves – are the kind of issues that people who live in those communities really care about.
(Colbert I. King, *Washington Post*, February 18, 2006: A33, emphasis added)

---

[3] Critiques of coverage on the basis of race appear to be more numerous following high-profile stories in the US media than in the UK, whether these stories then disappear from public view (Polly Klass, Chandra Levy) or become part of cultural myth (JonBenet Ramsey). Even extensive national coverage of a Californian family lost in the mountains of Northern California starting in November 2006, which ended in a death, was used as a point of coverage comparison a few weeks later when an African-American Miami resident went missing.

At the same time, King is also highlighting the actual role of internalized news values in everyday editorial (news-story) decision-making, whether the outcome is desired or not for either insider-journalist or outsider-reader community:

Example 4.6
It's because someone may have decided that a story like hers, of a woman <u>nobody has ever heard of</u>, won't have much <u>significance to readers</u>. It's because someone has concluded that there is <u>nothing out of the ordinary</u> about an adult black single mom walking out on her family. It's because such behavior is considered <u>commonplace</u>, too <u>routine</u> to warrant precious <u>space</u>.   (*ibid.*, emphasis added)

His point that the news subject he is writing about was someone "nobody has ever heard of" and would therefore not have "significance to readers" relates to the news values of *prominence* as well as *impact* on the community of coverage. His critical assumption that an editor determined "nothing out of the ordinary" had happened to warrant coverage, that the subject's behavior was "commonplace" and "routine" is also a way of saying that the news value of *unusualness* or *consequence* was missing. In short, the missing woman's story was not reported because there was nothing "newsworthy" about it, according to reporter and editor determinations in the newsroom or on the beat; it was, as King says, "too routine to warrant precious space."

4.3.2   Discursive outcomes

On the discourse level, King's column also indicates the multiple strands that have to come together to get something in the paper. In his account, there were several occasions that were missed, several *"points of appropriate intercession"* (cf. Cotter and Cotter 1998) – places within a topically limited, profession-specific discourse exchange that create and restrict response options between or among the interlocutors – that were not followed up on. These points of appropriate intercession are places in communicative exchanges between reporter and news source (spoken, written, or observed) where the reporter might have connected with the story differently in some journalistic manner to change the decision not to cover it – to change the *null discursive outcome*. For example, King writes of the initial police press release about the case, and the subsequent Detective of the Year award to the detective who solved it, to indicate that the police did their part in disseminating the information to the media (see Appendix 1C). In this way, he is implicating journalistic practice and decision-making in the no-story outcome.

On the other hand, without speaking to the editor who made the actual decision, there are several journalistic rationalizations for the *null discursive outcome* (based on my own and others' newsroom experience) that can be suggested. Rationalizations for the no-story outcome based on King's account of the coverage events might be that the press release was issued on Christmas Eve (it was) when staffing was low and it was overlooked, or the next morning's paper was ready (or already in its print run) such that only the most newsworthy of events (involving death and disaster on US soil) would warrant a change or press stop. Or that the reporters may not have known about the Detective of the Year award: it may not necessarily have been a regular "beat" story, especially if the reporter's time was spent elsewhere or if other news events took precedence on that day.

In short, journalistic rationalizations such as the ones that I am hypothetically positing here are often on newsworthiness grounds, coupled with other exigencies of practice like time and space (cf. Bell 1995, 1996). The potential opportunities to change a story's discursive outcomes are still worth being aware of, as King makes clear.

There are other factors at play that influence discursive outcomes such as where a story is positioned, whether it is covered, how much to emphasize it through length, layout, headline style, and photos and graphics – also known as "art" (see Chapters 5 and 10). Traditionally, these factors include availability of space, the amount of news occurring on a particular day, a balance or mix of types of news (see Chapter 7), the time to deadline (and its print or Web relationship), day of the week (which affects availability of space and editorial staff), the audience or readership (see Chapters 5 and 6), and the focus or *topical scope* of the news outlet, which can vary tremendously among publications. The individual reporter's journalistic rationalizations, and the editor's calculations of time, space, and content – and the resulting story play, story angle, and discursive outcome – are initiated, executed, and defended on the grounds of newsworthiness.

4.3.3   The scope factor

News judgments also take into account the *scope* of the newspaper as well as its readership, a point that King does not mention. A paper's *scope*, or the *extent of its coverage purview*, might be metro, regional, local, daily, or weekly and thus coverage criteria would vary within the application of news values. Any story, including the ones like the missing-person story King refers to, would have a different "media life" depending on the scope of its local or nearest paper. Depending on the paper's scope and community focus and circulation area, a missing-persons story that does not involve a well-known person (*prominence*), that involves someone ordinary or socially invisible as in King's example, may be published in sections as various as "police blotter" briefs, or on Page One, or in separate community-specific parts of a metro or regional paper. The *Washington Post*, for instance, has a weekly insert that varies according to the circulation or delivery destinations in the District of Columbia, Maryland, and Virginia's "local" coverage areas. While the *Post* and other nationally recognized metropolitan US newspapers like the *New York Times* and *Los Angeles Times* follow the industry standard and have policies in place regarding local news coverage (see also Chapter 6), this does not mean a story that would easily make a more localized or lower-circulation paper, such as the Redding (Calif.) *Record Searchlight* or the Quincy (Mass.) *Patriot-Ledger*, would get in nor would it necessarily have the same amount of detail.

Addressing an entirely different coverage situation, but with the same coverage-field considerations in mind, a London newspaper media columnist responding to a reader's claim that his newspaper covers the mayor at the expense of what "people want to know about locally" writes:

Example 4.7
First, the Standard is a metropolitan paper, not a local borough news sheet. Of what interest would the state of the streets in Battersea be to the people of Barking or Brent?

Second, it is entirely appropriate for the paper of all London to be interested in the Mayor of all London.

(Roy Greenslade, *London Evening Standard*, November 1, 2006: 41, emphasis added)

He establishes the paper's coverage field and pan-London scope (it is a "metropolitan paper … of all London") on the grounds of relevance to readers and the responsibility of the paper. News about one neighborhood's streets would not appeal to another neighborhood; but news made by an official whose actions impact the entire city is of "appropriate" interest for the paper. The news values of *proximity* and *importance* play into these newsworthiness decisions alongside other factors involving story coverage.

The focus or *topical scope* of the news outlet can vary tremendously among publications despite their shared sense of professional perspective, training, and responsibility to community. For example, respected, longstanding publications like the *Wall Street Journal* emphasize business angles; the *Santa Barbara Independent* reports the local community by following the mission of the alternative newsweekly; and local or regional-circulation daily papers, like the Appleton (Wis.) *Post-Crescent* or the Scottsdale (Ariz.) *East Valley Tribune*, respond to reader needs within their locales and deliver a mix of local news and wire-service-provided national and international news. Headlines can give a glimpse into this variation in topical scope (the headlines in Example 4.8 are merely indicative, not predictive):

Example 4.8
- How H-P Reclaimed its PC Lead Over Dell (June 4, 2007) – *WSJ* – a Page One business feature about two major computer corporations.

- Capps Votes No/Opposes War Funding Bill (May 31, 2007) – *SB Independent* – a news story about a Santa Barbara "Congressmember" (to quote local *Indy* style) voting against a federal war appropriation bill.

- Virus a threat to fishing industries/ VHS found in whitefish, a Door County tradition (June 5, 2007) – *Post-Crescent* – a Page One lead story on a deadly virus in Lake Michigan fish.
- Critics claim Scottsdale's purse strings loose (June 5, 2007) – *East Valley Tribune* – a news story about the city's annual budget and finance projections.

The stories are relevant to each paper's coverage scope: big corporations which influence the global economy the focus of the *Wall Street Journal*'s coverage; the liberal actions of a member of Congress who represents the local constituency covered by the alternative paper, the *Independent* (who with similar attention have avoided the more typical gendered forms in their use of "Congressmember"); a deadly fish virus that will impact on local commerce and culture in the Appleton paper; and reactions to decisions about the city budget the focus of the Scottsdale-area paper.

4.4   Similarity and variation

4.4.1   News value universals

As a result of **practice routinization** and **process dynamism**, discussed in earlier sections, there is both similarity and variation across outlets. Because news values are recognized throughout the profession, they function as selection criteria in every newsroom; news values are invoked to make decisions about story play and importance in some 1,700 newsrooms throughout the US, as well as in broadcast studios. In this way, news values engender similarity with respect to practice: Editor A in Texas will think about the same parameters as Editor B in Maine or Editor C in Hawaii (or Editor D in London). The result is outcomes that shape news texts by bringing together rhetorical and ideological practices, through journalistic writing and newsworthiness decisions that routinize story type, story structure, story angle, writing style, source quotation, etc., and are familiar to the practitioner (cf. Chapter 7). As Mencher (1997: 58) notes: "Reporters follow the guidelines of their editors and publishers. Reporters also agree among themselves on what constitutes news. Thus, at any given time, news in the mass media is similar." Mencher's comment speaks to essential conditions that circumscribe the news community ethnographically: professional practice involves participants in the newsroom operating within well-established hierarchies, and reinforcing the meaning of news values through the actions that follow.

The similarity is obvious in papers that share *coverage scope* and a sense of mission to the reader – business papers, newspapers of record, and the like – as well as in papers that share geographical proximity. The four top-story headlines listed in Example 4.8, despite the different coverage communities they represent, are similar in that they all relate to economic or financial concerns of varying order, despite variation in coverage scope.

The similarity is also occasioned from within the news media not merely through shared actions that delineate professional practice but also because of the role key participants within the industry, such as the *Washington Post* and the *New York Times*, play on a daily basis. In terms of non-local coverage, they set the agenda for the rest of country. According to Ben Bradlee, former executive editor of the *Washington Post*, the *Post* and the *Times* are especially influential "because […] they are the main influence on the people who decide television news, decide radio news, and decide so much of the serious agenda" (Ben Bradlee, personal communication). On the West Coast, John Diaz, Editorial Page Editor of the *San Francisco Chronicle*, notes that the *Los Angeles Times* as well as the *New York Times* and *Washington Post* send their next-day story budgets (lists of potential stories) "to newsrooms across the nation every afternoon." He adds: "The *NYT*, in particular, has enormous influence on what other newspapers do. If the *Times* is listing a certain national story as above-the-fold, Page One […] then it takes a pretty self-assured editor at a lesser major metro (i.e., the rest of us) to bury the story inside" (John Diaz, personal communication).

Beyond the influence of participant structures endemic to the profession, news value-engendered similarity exists on the discourse level with respect to coverage topics within news genre forms. One of my earliest unintended lessons about what counts as news, as a restricted genre with limited *topical scope*, was a 1970s-era "Rocky and Bullwinkle" television cartoon. The bad guys, Boris and Natasha, had caused the shut-down of a small-town newspaper, leaving the editor and the townsfolk distraught. Hero Rocky, "the flying squirrel," noticed lots of old editions piled up behind the newspaper building. Holding one in hand he quoted the headlines, "Cat Up a Tree! Man Bites Dog!," noticed similar activities (firefighters rescuing stranded cats, a man getting the better of his canine best friend) occurring around him in the present time, and excitedly saved the day, getting Bullwinkle and the editor to distribute the old copies – with new dates. (Behind the success of well-known newspaper parodies such as *The Onion* (www.onion.com) is mastery of the genre form on multiple discursive and sociolinguistic levels, from lexicon to register, from the specific to the more abstract.)

Equally, the outcome of newsworthiness calculations will vary across outlets and circumstance. News values exist in the abstract to the extent all journalists agree on their meaning, but vary according to the context of each day's paper in each community. One can share agreement about news values, *per se*, but still disagree with their application or weight relative to other stories and values, as in the missing-woman story that King wrote about (Appendix 1C and Examples 4.5 and 4.6, and in newsroom situations described in Chapter 5) – hence, there is variation in output. Part of the knowledge someone acquires through experience is the ability to assess newsworthiness in relation to the context, to gauge the *weight* (to use the journalistic term) of not just one story, but one story in relation to all the news that is occurring around it at that time. Thus, as Lanson and Stephens (1994: 15) write: "It is unlikely that you could program them [news values] into a computer and get the computer to select the correct angle for the story."

My own experiences in the newsroom and the classroom underscore these points. With journalism students' classroom-assigned news stories, written from an identical set of facts, each "practice" story handed in varies according to the student's interpretation of the facts with respect to their understanding of news values, as well as their individual "literacy competencies" (or the ability to synthesize information and write about it), and the extent to which they have internalized notions of newsworthiness and story structure at that point in the semester (see Chapters 7 and 8 for discussion of story structure). My experience in newsrooms indicates a similar process, albeit a less "controlled" one: discussions about stories and their intrinsic newsworthiness among and between reporters and editors are also contingent upon momentary circumstances and assessed in relation to what is occurring on a particular day, determining newsworthiness being a fundamental goal of a great deal of newsroom discourse and interaction (see Chapter 5 for examples). Additionally, reporters and editors bring their personal and professional experience – their own practice history – to bear in arguing for particular stories. (A corollary may then hold that diversity of editorial perspective affects content positively in that greater range and perspective is presented.) News values may be commonly held notions, but they are inevitably *interpreted* variably (see also Beeman and Peterson 2001).

4.4.2   Interpretation and variation: in-group vs. out-group assessments

The interpretation of the effects of news decisions, motivated by news values and newsworthiness rationales, varies from within the profession and outside of it. Simplifying the differences, one could say that the in-group assessment of what counts as news is "textual," and the out-group assessment of what ends up in print or on the air is "ideological." In other words, the news practitioner operates from the principle that news is shaped (reported) to get the most out of a *story* – textual. The lay reader believes that news is shaped (slanted) to sell papers – ideological.

What news practitioners evaluate ultimately in the everyday as they go about their jobs are the textual outcomes: Did a story make it into the paper? Or find its way onto the Evening News? Or appear online? Did we get a quote? A photo? Did we scoop the competition? Is the story complete? Was our decision to publish that photo or name or video appropriate? A reporter's priority is to get the story, to get a byline, to get something good enough to go on Page One, not to sell papers as such. (I am talking about reporters, those with the least interest in or everyday connection to the paper's bottom-line.)

The out-group assessments, on the other hand, are often essentially from ideological positions, attributing a great deal of agency to the reporter's thought processes, assuming that reporting and play decisions derive from the economic priorities of media outlets, and acknowledging the intrinsic persuasive power behind information and those who hold access to framing or presenting it.[4] From that perspective, bias charges are inevitable. The lay assessment reads text (or interprets a news story) from the outsider viewpoint; rightly or wrongly identifies underlying ideological frameworks; and does not incorporate insider routines, values, or processes in their critiques and evaluations. This is one reason many larger US newspapers have outside "ombudsmen" whose charge it is to respond to reader concerns, help clarify journalistic practice, and render it more visible to the public on every level: textual, ideological, grammatical, moral, etc. Some newspapers have also established community advisory boards to comment on coverage.

Of course, any textual–ideological "divide" is something of a false dichotomy, but it is also a device to allow us to isolate and think about the factors that create the variation in interpretation between the community of practice and community of coverage. What is important for the news community to understand is the **public's interpretive position and the logic of its assessment**, how the public's "logic" might be different from its own but just as reasonable. Both insiders and outsiders can consider that many ways of thinking become normative over time and are worthy of scrutiny and problematization.

4.5   Conclusion: the role of news values

4.5.1   News values as "emic" coordinators

News values might be best viewed as "emic coordinators" for the role they play in decision-making and text production: they help to coordinate the "emic" or structurally significant and community-identified patterns of reporting and writing, to restrict the "etic" overload or all that is potentially meaningful within the news process.[5] In this "emic" role, news values provide a **hierarchy of importance** for practitioners as well as a guide for coverage decisions, one that becomes internalized in practice. "Reporters store thousands of facts about people, events, policies and the many incidents of their daily experience" (Mencher 1997: 380). The good reporters, he says, use what he terms a "vast storehouse" in making decisions about what is "important" and newsworthy. Newsworthiness, thus, provides a constraint amidst the myriad facts. Textbooks

---

[4] Numerous reporters I have talked with over the years (most recently at the *Daily Express* in London) unanimously say that the demands of the job leave them with no time to think that way.
[5] I am adapting the *emic/etic* distinction from Pike (1967), as a way to clarify the manner in which reporters understand newsworthiness.

define newsworthiness and provide lists and examples of news values, but actual application in the day-to-day – such as Mencher alludes to – results in a constant exercise in decision-making. As such, attributing outcomes to news values – in relation to temporal and situational demands (deadline, staffing, and news hole factors) – becomes part of normal operating procedure.

For sociolinguistic researchers of news media language, it may be helpful to regard the *emic coordination* operations of news values in the same sense as social variables like age, gender, and occupation – aspects that help to isolate and analyze the features and factors of language use in sociolinguistics (cf. Labov 1972a, etc.). Or to see their operation in relation to ethnolinguistic methodological heuristics like Hymes's "speaking" grid or Agar's "schema" heuristic (Agar 1986; Hymes 1972b, 1974), which helps researchers to isolate and interpret what is often seen at the early stages of ethnographic fieldwork as overwhelming amounts of potentially culturally relevant communicative field data. Or to realize that their formulation and application is culturally constrained – by the news community itself as well as by the larger social context in which it works (cf. Leitner 1980, 1984) – and thus judgments of news texts might be superficial without a more profound cultural understanding of practice and its "insider" entailments (cf. Briggs 1986; Satoh 2001; Van Hout 2008, etc.). Another way to view the operation of news values as *emic coordinators* is to examine them in relation to theoretical concepts like *contextualization*, *indexicality*, and *co-occurrence* – leading to a productive synthesis of the manner in which news values can be described as operational tools that have impact on professional practice and news texts.

For journalism educators, the notion of emic coordination is already *implicit* within descriptions of reporting and editing practices, best seen in newswriting textbooks. It is the seasoning, knowledge, and competence that comes with experience and time on the job, intended to facilitate decision-making under deadline and to produce well-reported and well-written stories (in journalistic terms). Indeed, the most thoughtful journalism educators call for the same skills that linguistic anthropologists expect of themselves and their students: to take nothing for granted, to understand the people who are in essence providing one's story or one's data, to "make strange" (cf. Agar 1980) or go beyond one's comfort zone as a mechanism for understanding.[6] Indeed, Mencher essentially points to participant observation as a "corrective" to journalistic detachment:

---

[6] One year University of California Graduate School of Journalism professor Bill Drummond organized a seminar class of eight graduate students who spent a semester reporting an "under-covered" community in nearby Marin County according to the diversity variables of the students. His objective was that they challenge their own attitudes and unexamined stereotypes from within their own group as well as from the relative "face-safety" and reporter-role distance of covering the actual community.

[It] allows the reporter to step outside routines and familiar environments to achieve new insights and to avoid another trap – the tendency to stereotype. [...] Forgetting that life is endless variety and change, some reporters look at the world through a kaleidoscope that is never turned. As a consequence, their observations reflect only a narrow, static vision.

(Mencher 2006: 266)

4.5.2   Summary: the importance of news values

The news stories we read and hear are the end-product of a series of decisions, practices, and values that are fundamental to the news community yet seldom acknowledged by academics (but see early Verschueren 1985 and Bell 1991, and recent Cotter 1999a, 1999b, 2003, Perrin and Ehrensberger-Dow 2006, Peterson 2001, and Van Hout and Macgilchrist in press). In this chapter, I examined rationales reporters and editors employ to determine "newsworthi-ness" to begin to answer the obvious "outsider" question: Why are certain attributes of an event or situation reported on, and thus **fronted**, and other elements buried or overlooked? These journalistic rationales revolve around "news values," the group-agreed qualities such as *proximity* (local interest or readership relevance) and *prominence* (standing of individual under news scrutiny) that make an item newsworthy and are central to motivating deci-sions about what to cover. News values should be viewed as key elements constituting journalistic discourse and the relation of practitioners to the news, as defined by the news community. They **constitute** newsworthiness or what is news, and are **used** to decide what is news.

News values also play a role in journalistic identity: their competent appli-cation in reporting and writing – learned in the classroom and practiced in the newsroom – is a marker of craft competence and journalistic skill (cf. Chapter 2); as such, they promote and reinforce membership in the community of practice as well as reinforce assessments about what is news. Awareness of their application by reporters and editors helps to make more transparent the role of process in understanding news texts. News values limit the scope of possibility and frame news texts by reinforcing internally held values about what counts as news, results that are implicitly but not obviously part of news stories – until "insider" columnists point out the parameters (as in the King example) and we as "outsider" academics investigate news texts within the context of process to come to understand the decisions that determine whether a story is worth covering. Chapter 5 will provide further insight into decision-making processes inside the newsroom and show that in addition to news values, the relationship with the *community of coverage* predominates in these determinations.

5   The "story meeting": Deciding
       what's fit to print

KEY POINTS

- The story meeting – the regular daily meetings of editors to discuss news and decide story play – is the predominant "speech event" in the news-production process. It serves a gate-keeping function, as well as a place to negotiate and reinforce journalistic identity through discussion of news stories and their placement.
- In the meetings, news values are invoked by different editors to resolve differences of opinion and support positions. Story meeting negotiations of newsworthiness are a more internally situated (and thus not visible) function of a newspaper's priorities and commitments than the editorial pages.
- Issues of craft and community are reified in the story meeting, through explicit reference to them.

Looking at the process of newsgathering requires a focus on the dynamic and emergent, as well as the patterned and habitual. The "story meeting" (or "budget meeting," as it is also known) is one such patterned and dynamic event. Several times a day, editors gather to talk about the major stories that will appear in the coming day's paper, discussing and arguing for stories eligible for Page One. The story meeting, as a recurrent speech event where a great deal of professional activity is performed and decisions are made, is a primary setting for the daily negotiation and reinforcement of professional values. The story meeting, and the discursive activities that comprise the story meeting, predominate in the news process. It is important to keep its inherent multidimensionality in mind, as what ultimately ends up on Page One is the result of the *interplay and negotiation of participants, context, and occasion*. This interplay is what informs editorial decision-making, as will be illustrated.

The story meeting creates the context for negotiation among the editor-participants, which is itself both patterned and fixed, as well as dynamic and emergent. Story meetings can thus be viewed from two perspectives: as a fixed, routinized, or unmarked *setting* for newsroom decision-making whose patterns, goals, and participant relationships formulate a type of predictability and uniformity in the everyday; and as a *context of communicative exchange* that highlights the dynamic and emergent functions of talk and interaction in the newsroom from which actions are taken and meaning emerges within and external to the news community. To best evaluate and understand story-meeting discourse then, it is necessary to be aware of linguistic tools and measures, as well as journalistic constraints and norms of behavior.

Journalistically, story meetings are where editors discuss the day's news with their colleagues, decide what is important, and determine what goes on Page One. In the process, *text values and news values, interactional norms*, and *participant relations* amongst editors are reinforced, and the newspaper's *orientation to the community of coverage* is made explicit. Thus, the analysis and explanation of the data in this chapter will be focused on the activities that constitute the ethos behind journalistic behavior, and that signal the functioning of a communicatively competent member of the journalistic discourse community.

As a case study, I present discourse-level evidence and examples from several months of ethnographic observation of story meetings at a metropolitan daily newspaper in California, informed initially by my own previous career as a daily newspaper reporter and editor, and subsequently by my current career as a linguist. The findings are fourfold: The data illustrate how (1) conflicts about story play (where the story ends up in the paper) are resolved, (2) identities within the group are established, (3) connections to the local community are formed, and (4) the boundaries of the profession are maintained.

Linguistically, story meetings can be seen as speech events with normative routines, participant roles, and objectives – objectives that are social, discursive, structural, and ideological – that influence the shape of news texts. Story meetings are relevant on the sociolinguistic level from different perspectives: as a *speech event* with particular structures and functions, for its key *role* in the news process, and as a *site* of values negotiation and reinforcement. The story meeting has a role in the news process and in the profession: it has a gate-keeping function; it maintains and negotiates journalistic identity; it situates the participants relative to each other, to the news-negotiation process, and to the news itself.

To keep a focus on the setting's multifunctionality, I will discuss what happens at the story meeting, key features of which include: negotiations that involve news values (discussed in Chapter 4) invoked by different editors to support positions and resolve differences of opinion; the co-occurrence of other values, such as rhetorical skill and deadline expedience; and the boundaries or norms of professional behavior and communicative competence and how they are maintained. Relevant to the objectives of the story meeting process but not necessarily visible for non-journalists, are the negotiations among editor-participants, local priority emphasis (the engagement with the *community of coverage*), and the discursive functions and outcomes of the story meeting. Factors such as news values, other professional foci, and the role of the audience, which are often backgrounded in academic discussions, will be at the forefront. Also at the forefront is how the interplay of context and occasion (already discussed in Chapter 4) provides the particular outcome we see on Page One on any one day.

5.1   What happens at a story meeting: *The Oakland Tribune*

The Alameda Newspaper Group (ANG) is a consortium of seven papers in the East and South Bay in Northern California. *The Oakland Tribune* is ANG's flagship paper. (The other papers are the *Tri-Valley Herald*, *San Mateo County Times*, *The Argus*, *The Daily Review*, *Alameda Times-Star*, and the *Marin Independent Journal*.) By virtue of being a consortium and under the same ownership, editors from all the papers participate in story meetings via conference call – a somewhat unusual communicative setup in that usually the majority of a single paper's editors will be on-site and physically available for a story meeting. There is a degree of both resource-sharing and independence among the papers and front pages will reflect this mix. At the same time, the seven papers' editors are all aware of each other's coverage. The objective of the story meetings is to inform the collective and decide on or agree on shared stories for Page One; and to determine or be aware of what will "lead" on individual papers.

The *Tribune* itself is a community-based metro paper with a daily paid circulation of more than 92,000[1] in an ethnically diverse urban area east of San Francisco and north of San Jose/Silicon Valley. It was the first major metropolitan newspaper in the US owned and edited by an African-American, the late Bob Maynard. While there are several nearby newspapers in the Bay Area that carry more national visibility (the *San Francisco Chronicle* and the *San Jose Mercury News*, for instance), it is important to note that these larger-scope papers, despite their geographical proximity to the *Tribune*, are not considered competition *editorially* (in terms of news and feature coverage, as opposed to advertising revenue; to a news professional, "editorial" indicates the news or reporting side and not the ad or commercial side of journalism). The *Trib* serves a different, more community-focused function. Indeed, this was Maynard's objective: "he was the latest in a long line of news pioneers who had

---

[1] The Audit Bureau of Circulations' weekday circulation figure is 92,794 and the Sunday circulation figure is 91,691 (preliminary figures averaged over six months on September 30, 2009). Paid-circulation figures do not necessarily reflect actual readership, which is higher and tracked by other research protocols (Abate 2005).

used every technique possible to create a newspaper that was, as he put it, 'an instrument of community understanding'" (Newton 2006).

I was present at thirty-four story meetings over a two-month period at the *Tribune* and conducted individual interviews with *Trib* editors. My general goal was to begin to ascertain how news values and the connection of news to community are reinforced and negotiated at story meetings. More specifically, I looked for explicit examples of editorial objectives in the discourse that editors produced in exchanges about stories. These explicit examples will support and illuminate the general claims about news discussed in earlier chapters, such as the role of news values in decision-making, the presence of a professional craft ethos, the actual extent of the "community factor," and the daily priorities that news reporters and editors engage with.

5.1.1   How it works

Story meetings are scheduled to occur throughout the day at strategic times before, during, or after publication or press runs. They last from ten to twenty minutes, depending on time constraints, which are always an issue with daily deadlines. The story meeting components at the *Oakland Tribune*'s early afternoon meeting are as follows:

1. Editors from the *Tribune* come into conference room at the main newspaper building in downtown Oakland. They carry "story budgets" – a list of stories for the next day's paper that reporters are working on. The configuration of editors varies, depending on work schedules – usually always the Managing Editor (ME), News Editor, Regional Editor, City Editor, and someone standing in for the Business section.
2. General chitchat while waiting for the meeting to begin, not necessarily related to the news of the day.
3. The phone in the center of the conference table rings. The editor who coordinates the meeting (whom I will refer to generically as the Phone Editor) generally puts the *Tribune* on hold until the other papers' newsrooms are on the line for the conference call.
4. The meeting begins with the Phone Editor asking for contributions from the *Tribune*.
5. The meeting continues with contributions by editors at other papers.
6. It continues with contributions by Sports and Cue (the features and entertainment section) Editors, and the Wire (national and international) Editor.
7. **Discussion about Page One story candidates: the "negotiation segment."**
8. Conclusion of collective meeting: closing statements and phone is deactivated.
9. *Tribune* editors finish deciding on Page One lineup, incorporating their Oakland-interest stories. (Editors from the other papers do the same for their respective locales.)
10. Editors return to work (newsroom).

With or without the conference-call modality, the *Tribune*'s setup follows the basic pattern in newsrooms throughout the US. For example, at the *Washington Post*'s daily 2 p.m. story meeting, the editors of each section present the day's stories and "make tentative decisions about which stories will appear on the front page of the newspaper. At the 6 p.m. story conference, more definitive decisions are debated and made on the placement of stories, although late-breaking news often results in even-later changes" (Washington Post L Street lobby display; field notes). It was similar in form and objective to my own experience at a regional paper, other site visits (to *USA Today* and the *San Francisco Chronicle*), and observations at the *Miami Herald* and Spanish-language *El Nuevo Herald* (Janine Turner, Philip Handmaker, Silvia Arellano, personal communication).

5.1.2   *Participant roles and newsroom hierarchy*

The story meeting, like any speech event, is an activity that has underlying rules and assigned roles and a particular purpose known and fostered by the partic-ipants in the speech event (Hymes 1972b). This knowledge and the practice it entails is also the case with the editors who participate in story meetings. While I will not focus in particular on participant relationships, it is important to mention the *issue of hierarchy*, as many people outside the business believe that news decisions are made by one power-endowed individual – along the order of *The Wizard of Oz* and its "man behind the curtain" prototype. In general, however, while there are hierarchical divisions in newsrooms in terms of job title and expertise based on proven record and on experience, there is no hierarchy as such in the majority of decision-making exchanges at the story-meeting level. In the abstract (as there are certainly exceptions across newsrooms), decisions are not necessarily made according to who says what; instead, they are made according to what gets said about the story, what gets said about the news. It is the news values that predominate and guide decision-making (as discussed in Chapter 4). As the upcoming examples will show, the news is prioritized by the editorial collective (the editors) according to who can argue better on the grounds of news values, or what can be most convincingly said about the value of the news at issue.

Whereas this "flat hierarchy" is not necessarily the case in all newsrooms (editors elsewhere have indicated otherwise to me), it was borne out by the exchanges in the *Tribune* story meetings and in keeping with my own profes-sional experience. Two situations from my *Tribune* field observation indicate the backgrounded role of personal position even when the news-value aspect is clear-cut. One example is "up the chain-of-command," and the other is "down the hierarchy." In the first case, the *Oakland Tribune* Managing Editor – who inhabits the nominally highest position in the story meeting – was arguing for an embassy bombing story on Page One. What was noteworthy was how vociferously he had to argue, which was indicated by the length of time on topic, tone of voice, and markers of frustration that no one understood its import or impact (exhalation of breath, "Come on, people!"). But no one automatically sided with him because he was the "boss" or even because he changed key or tone of voice.

In the second "down the hierarchy" case, an editor on the other end of the teleconference was new to the story-meeting routine, and introduced himself as such for the benefit of the editors at the other locales. The reaction to his contribution by the *Oakland Tribune* editors was not dismissal of his argument for a particular story, but of concealed irritation at how much time he took to present story facts as well as the amount of extraneous detail he provided: in the time-framed deadline context, it was too much irrelevant background. He did not know as a beginner to the meeting context the nuances of what was expected, nor what was communicatively competent within that group or within that type of exchange for this particular group of editors. (The *Tribune* editors were consistent, as was the Managing Editor, in keeping participation competence separate from news content and news decisions.)

5.1.3   Page One and story hierarchy (the news that's fit to print)

More important to the outcome of decisions about story play than the internal newsroom hierarchy is the *story hierarchy*, the ordering of stories in terms of *newsworthiness* and *relevance*. The most visible outcome of the story meeting is on Page One, where the stories deemed most newsworthy and relevant during that day's discussions are placed. Page One reflects what is routinized and normative in terms of form (stories, headlines, photos and graphics, layout and display, and, possibly, advertisements), as well as what is contingent and dynamic in terms of content and story hierarchy; hence the similarity and variation across news outlets. In that way, Page One also reflects various values of the news community and the community of coverage (as was noted in Example 4.1 in Chapter 4). The Page One equivalents on radio or television are the first or "top" news stories broadcast, or the home page of a news website.

5.1.4   Key features and outcome of meetings

Editors negotiate what appears on Page One by appealing to a sense of newsworthiness (discussed previously in Chapter 4 and next in Section 5.2), a perspective that reinforces what is professionally appropriate and what is viewed as significant for the community of coverage, as will be discussed in Section 5.2. Key features of the story-meeting interactions that I witnessed (and earlier in my professional life participated in) are the extent to which *news values are invoked* and the extent to which learned professional *boundaries are maintained*.

Table 5.1 *Journalistic and discursive outcomes*

Outcome of meetings	Discursive points
(1) What goes on Page One decided	Group-specified goal
(2) Group of editors understands what's important	Within *particular and emergent* context
(3) Text values and news values reinforced	Indirectly through talk and interaction
(4) Interactional norms and participant relations reinforced	Macro-praxis result
(5) Relation to community of coverage made explicit	Macro-praxis result

The outcome of the meetings is multifold in terms of journalistic action and discursive result (as illustrated in Table 5.1). First, what goes on Page One is decided, which is the explicit and group-specified goal; and second, the editors as a group understand what is important in the context of that day's news, an outcome that derives from a context that is both *particular to* and *emerges from* that specific day's array of news at that point in time. Additionally, news values and text values are reinforced indirectly through talk and subsequent action – indeed, these embedded professional practice-centered values are the primary currency of exchange. On the macro-praxis level as well as the micro-talk level two things occur: interactional norms and participant relations are reinforced as a result of the exchanges about story play, and the relation to the *community of coverage* is made explicit.

5.2   Role of news values in story meetings

News values, the elements of content that govern each stage of the reporting, editing, and story selection process, underlie all discussion at story meetings. As discussed in Chapter 4, news values function as key elements constituting journalistic discourse and the relation of practitioners to news. News values, defined explicitly by the news community (as opposed to the academic community), concern *proximity, impact, importance, recency, conflict, change*, etc. They constitute newsworthiness or what is news; they are the parameters used to decide what is news. News values in general have a primary role in the structure of news content, and have a role in establishing a profession-specific ideology that governs decisions and perspectives – key factors that come into play in story meetings.

The fact that news value application is context-driven means that it relies fundamentally on relevance (Sperber and Wilson 1985; and see Chapters 6 and 7). Thus I would propose that the "in-group taxonomy" of common news values (*proximity, impact, importance, recency, conflict*, and *change*) be viewed in relation to linguistic insights. A "journo-linguistic taxonomy," useful in a more global analysis of news discourse that involves linking text with practitioner, thus distills news values into a list that includes *importance*, *impact*, **relevance**, *proximity*, and *timeliness*.

As noted in Chapter 4, the role of news values is easy to see in terms of the *text* or story output. A story with impact, like a tax hike or election result, gets "higher" or more prominent coverage than a meeting notice or club event. Less apparent is the role of news values in *practice*, or the multi-stage *process* of reporting and editing that leads to the fully formed story. Even more backgrounded, but essential, is their display in recurrent discursive activities within the newsroom, such as story meetings, where news values are invoked by different editors to resolve differences of opinion and to support positions.

5.2.1   How news values come into play

When editors are presenting their "nominations" for Page One, news values are invoked explicitly whether the context is agreed or conflictual. Example 5.1 [TAX BILL] is an illustration of a neutral, routine, non-conflictual exchange in which the editors are in the middle of determining which stories are salient for that day's paper and invoking news values to help fix significance:

Example 5.1
TAX BILL

STORY MEETING EXCHANGE		NEWS VALUE RELEVANCE
Editor A:	Has he [president] signed it [tax bill] yet?	Query re status: info needed to establish importance of story.
Editor B:	He signed it this morning. It'll be a little old.	Proposition 1: story losing **recency** value.
Editor C:	It's still pretty significant.	Proposition 2: story is **important**.
Editor X:	Mmm-hmm.	Uptake [by unidentifiable editor] is neutral.
Editor C:	It affects everybody.	Proposition 2 is reiterated and made more explicit; **readership** is invoked.

(*Source*: field notes)

Editor A first queries the status of the news event, whether a tax bill had been signed by the president: the information is needed to establish the importance of the story and to determine its position in relation to other stories. Editor B's reply indicates that the story is losing its *recency* value: "He signed it this morning. It'll be a little old." However, Editor C responds with a second news-value-instantiated proposition, that the story is *important* ("It's still pretty significant"). And, after a neutral response cue (cf. Schiffrin 1987) from another editor encouraging him/her to continue propounding his position, Editor C indicates why it is significant – "It affects everybody" – underscoring the story's *importance* and arguing that its *impact* has a wide reach (in effect, invoking the story's *relevance* to the readership as well as the impact of the story itself).

5.2.2   When news values conflict

News values are used not only to establish the rationale for an editorial position with respect to a particular story, as in Example 5.1, but they are also used within the negotiation that occurs when two or more values, such as *importance* and reader *relevance*, "conflict" with each other. In Example 5.2 [PACNET] we see how editors invoke news values to resolve conflicts about *importance* and *relevance*, in other words, values that have salience to both the *news community* and to the *coverage community*:

Example 5.2
PACNET

STORY MEETING EXCHANGE		ARGUMENT STRUCTURE
1. First mention		
Business Ed:	PACNET is a pretty good story.	• **First mention**
	Netscape browser customers are having problems with Windows 98.	
	We were tipped by a caller who couldn't call out.	
	PacBell confirmed it	
	It could go on [Page] One – it's pretty good.	
2. Later in the meeting		
Business Ed:	I'd like to see PACNET [out front]	• **Proposition**
Other editor:	I wasn't too thrilled …	• **Objection**: story lacks
	[doesn't impact enough readers]	*impact, relevance*
	[calculation surmising how many PacNet customers have Netscape Navigator who also have Windows 98]	
Business Ed:	It's the first glitch we know of …	• **Invokes NV ("1st x")** to
	[relates it to Internet Explorer problems]	support proposition
		• Invokes larger context provides background
Other editor:	Let's make that a skybar.	• Solution acknowledges NV
Business Ed:	OK.	• Acceptance/resolution

(*Source*: field notes)

In Example 5.2, the Business Editor brings up PACNET in relation to the business stories on tap for that day. In the first mention, he foregrounds it

("PACNET is a pretty good story"), the hedge ("pretty") indicating to the story-meeting listener that support for positioning the story on Page One may or may not follow. To support his point of view that the story is worth looking at, however, he explains that customers were disadvantaged (news values of *importance, relevance*); the paper was "tipped by a caller" (news values of *proximity* and *impact*, underscored by the borrowed value judgment of the caller, or member of *community of coverage*, whose input is valued – see Section 5.3); the paper investigated the claim ("PacBell confirmed it") so it is independently supported, in this case by the telephone company involved. He then explicitly nominates it for Page One ("It could go on One – it's pretty good"), while simultaneously opening the exchange for disagreement (modal "could" and hedge "pretty") and concludes by briefly summarizing other, unrelated non-Page-One stories, as per the larger story-meeting speech event expectations of providing overall context of the day's news.

Later, when the meeting turns to finalizing the Page One contenders, the Business Editor is more direct about his view that PACNET is Page-One-worthy ("I'd like to see PACNET [out front])." Another editor objects, claiming the story does not impact enough readers (lacks *impact* and *relevance*). The Business Editor counters by invoking a variant of the news value of *importance* ("it's the first glitch we know of ...") and then provides background and context for understanding its significance. The other editor's counter-proposal – to make the story a skybar (which means including it in the skybar headline lineup at the top of Page One) – which the Business Editor agrees with ("OK"), is an acknowledgment of the Business Editor's *newsworthiness* arguments.

The relative simplicity and ease with which agreement is reached indicates: (a) trust in the co-participant's judgment built up over time through multiple shared interactions; (b) acknowledgment of newsworthiness as presented by the respective editor; and (c) the need for swift resolution to make deadline – which was achieved or ultimately justified on newsworthiness grounds.

5.3   Other news-community values

News values co-occur with other values of the news community, particularly those pertaining to *professional practice and professional identity*, as well as to the news community's *relationship to the local community* – as the next two Examples, 5.3 [BELFAST] and 5.4 [ZORRO], show. These "other values," such as rhetorical skills that are prized and local news priorities that privilege proximity to the local community, are not necessarily specific to the story itself or to story positioning in that day's paper but are equally important as they are fundamental to practice and self-identity, and relevant to our academic concerns as discussion and decisions related to them recur daily (evident both in my data and in prior story-meeting experiences I have had).

5.3.1   Text values (rhetorical skill)

In Example 5.3, an aspect of the text itself – irrespective of the newsworthiness of the story – is highlighted by the Wire Editor as meaningful and relevant for possible consideration for Page One:

Example 5.3
BELFAST

Wire Editor:	This is a good story just for its lede:	"Another night, another nightmare for the people of Belfast …"

(*Source*: field notes)

A reporter's rhetorical abilities – writing a good lead or opening paragraph (or "intro" as it is referred to in the UK) – is a fundamental aspect of normative professional practice and communicative competence (see chapter 7), and the Wire Editor's comment reinforces this point. A good "lede" (to use the profession's colloquial spelling) draws in the reader through style, content, and succinctness. The editor does not elaborate or analyze (for example, he does *not* note the poetic alliteration and rhythm of the first four words which also semantically summarize the ongoing and most recent situation in late 1990s Belfast). But he is invoking the larger shared understanding that a good lead, a lead that "performs" well rhetorically and journalistically, has value and thus is worth remarking on.

Also, given the metro-community focus of the *Tribune* and the role of other papers in the region for providing national and international news to area readers (such as the *San Francisco Chronicle, San Jose Mercury News, The Sacramento Bee, Los Angeles Times*, and *The New York Times*), the Wire Editor, who sorts and evaluates thousands of column inches of incoming wire stories per day from multiple wire services (like the Associated Press, Reuters, etc.), often does not have much of significance or relevance to the **local** community to recommend for Page One, and would tend to promote a story on the basis of other news-community values to get something "out there." The **text value** is offered as a position or argument for Page One inclusion when, for instance, the news values of *proximity* (the news is happening in Belfast) and *relevance* (it does not have direct impact on Oakland) do not. That no one thought twice about or challenged this rhetorically based argument on independent newsworthiness grounds indicates its unmarked position as another value in the larger context.

5.3.2   Local priority emphasis (proximity)

That papers prioritize the local is no surprise to American reporters and editors. The extent to which the local priority is held constant *is* a surprise to "outsiders."

The story meetings on a daily basis reflect the local priority emphasis, as we saw in Example 5.1 and will see in Examples 5.4 [ZORRO] and 5.5 [ALASKA OIL]. (I consider the local priority emphasis of the news media in the US from other perspectives in chapters 2 and 6.) In Example 5.4, another key value within American journalism – *local priority emphasis* – is foregrounded. The example illustrates how the *proximity* news value is used to maintain a local priority emphasis:

Example 5.4
ZORRO

a. *Story meeting exchange*	*Proximity indicators*
Editor A: the person who owns the rights to Zorro lives in the East Bay	←
Oakland Ed: Ah, that's good for us.	←
b. *Skybar form*	
Man behind the masked man/	
John Gertz talks about his role as co-producer of "The Mask of Zorro"	←
c. *Subhed atop of story*	
America's favorite swashbuckler returns to the silver	
screen in a film co-produced by John Gertz of Berkeley	←

(*Source*: field notes)

In the story-meeting exchanges about this story, in Example 5.4, Editor A invokes the news value of *proximity* – "the person who owns the rights to Zorro lives in the East Bay." The *Oakland Tribune*'s circulation area is the East Bay. The *Oakland Tribune* Editor's response, "Ah, that's good for us," indicates reception of the point ("Ah") and reinforces the paper's objective to relate the news to the community and the actual relation of the community to the news. "Us" means the East-Bay-situated *Tribune* in relation to the other ANG consortium newspapers in the South Bay participating in the story-meeting conference call.

The local priority emphasis maintained in the story-meeting exchange by mention of the "East Bay," Oakland's geographical location, and reaffirmed by the Oakland Editor's positive comment, is continued in the outcome on Page One of the *Oakland Tribune*: the story was given mention in the *skybar* above the fold (Example 5.4.b). In the *skybar* headlines on Page One ("Man behind the masked man/John Gertz talks about his role as co-producer of 'The Mask of Zorro'"), *proximity* is backgrounded in that there is no explicit mention of John Gertz's East Bay residency. However, the use of his name, particularly in a headline as here, indicates that he is someone that we (the reader) already know or should know: by *journalist-centric* inference he is someone famous and/or local. (And since John Gertz is not a household name, the conclusion that is arrived at according to practice norms, and may or may not be arrived at by readers, is that he is local.) The use of a named individual in any newspaper headline (and in many sorts of leads) happens quite consciously. The extent to which individuals are or are not named is discussed explicitly in textbooks, taught to students as instructors correct and respond to their classroom news-writing assignments, and reinforced in the newsroom by editors.

In the "subhed" or secondary headline above the actual story inside the paper (Example 5.4c), *proximity* is explicitly foregrounded again – "John Gertz of Berkeley" – through use of his name and his residency. The implication of this direct identification – again from the journalist's practice perspective – is that we should know him, and that he is from around here. It is also important to mention that proximity may not be the only reason "Berkeley," as opposed to "East Bay resident," gets mentioned as it does in this headline. The physical space available on the page, as well as headline conventions that prohibit starting a "deck" (line of headline) with a preposition (conventions pertaining to headlines that do vary across news outlets), and the need to flag the story as interesting and relevant despite fairly minimal language output, are intersecting factors. Anyone familiar with the area would know that Berkeley, the city adjacent to Oakland, is in the East Bay, the inference on another level reinforcing the local dimension. (It is worth mentioning that the use of the word "local" in a headline or lead is generally actively prohibited by editors as it is not specific enough. Knowledge of this point can be considered a marker of journalistic communicative competence for a print reporter. The conditions are different for broadcast. Television news conventions rely on phrases like "area man" or "local woman," as do non-insiders pretending to imitate broadcast reporters.)

The ZORRO examples also illustrate how the value of *proximity* mediates throughout the progress of a story in terms of its textual outcomes irrespective of its news-value-instigated placement on Page One. In this case the *proximity* dimension is indicated in the *skybar* headline (Example 5.4.b) and in the story subheadline (Example 5.4.c), as well as in its positioning on Page One.

5.4   Boundaries and norms of professional behavior

5.4.1   Politics

The journalistic practice goals of "objectivity" and detachment, actively perpetu-ated cultural values within the news community, are an aspect of the news person's professional identity (as discussed in Chapters 2 and 7). The extent to which they are embedded becomes visible when certain "boundaries" are breached. During my time in attendance at the *Tribune*, I noted several places where subjective comments – when an editor made a personal as opposed to a journalistic com-ment – were sanctioned, notably when an editor went beyond news-value grounds in arguing for a story's placement. (Example 5.5 will show this.)

Despite surface similarities, it is important to observe that there are cross-cultural differences in evidentiality practice – in the way information is attributed or the voice of the reporter is authorized – that occur in other countries' media (e.g., Cotter 1999c; Love and Morrison 1989; Knight and Nakano 1999; Peterson 1996; Satoh 2001; Scollon 1997; Scollon and Scollon 1997; Waugh 1995).[2] Mainstream American news culture works actively (if not always successfully) on the news-practice level to eliminate personal opinion in its actual news stories. It is a requirement to label anything construed as "subjective" as "analysis" or "opinion." News stories that relate to politics (local or national) or socially divisive issues like abortion are particularly held to scrutiny. Beyond the story and on the institutional level there is also self-monitoring: *Columbia Journalism Review* regularly reprimands specific news organizations for conflicts of interest and advertiser influence on coverage; and progressive "watch" groups such as Fairness and Accuracy in Reporting (FAIR) produce reports outlining where the industry falls short in this way.

During my fieldwork, the salience of these boundaries was made clear when editors transgressed them in some fashion during the story-negotiation exchanges. It was then that the Managing Editor reminded them that I – ratified by the group but nonetheless an outsider – was there, listening, as in Example 5.5.

Example 5.5
ALASKA OIL

STORY MEETING EXCHANGE		> *Negotiation segment*
[...]		
Editor A/fone:	A Alright, well we got two readers [*story type*] now.	
Editor B/Trib:	B Uh IRAQ?	>1
Editor C:	Yeah.	
Editor D:	Wouldn't ALASKA OIL–?	
Editor A/fone:	A Yeah that's a pretty good environmental issue <u>now</u>. Not to mention we have Chevron oil company <u>here</u>.	>2
Editor C:	(laughter)	
Editor A/fone:	A Alright, ALASKA OIL?	>3
Editor B/Trib:	B Instead of what, BEES?	>4
Editor A/fone:	A Uh, instead of IRAQ	>5
→	**[audible side comment about Clinton and political maneuvering]**	>6
Editor B/Trib:	B I don't see how we can keep that [IRAQ] off Page One.	>7
	I agree, ALASKA OIL is good, too.	>8

[2] Linguistic anthropological studies of responsibility and evidentiality (cf. Hill and Irvine 1993) and intertextuality (Hanks 2000) provide insights that are relevant to questions raised by news practice and its effects, such as reported speech (Besnier 1993), intentionality (DuBois 1993), and culturally situated performance boundaries (Bauman 1993).

	I think it's <u>better</u> than KILLER BEES, and we've been knowing about killer bees for the last two years.	>9
Editor E/ME:	*	**Do you know your comments about uh about Clinton and starting the war will be in this national survey –**	**>10**
→		**this person's been with us a month now.**
Trib group:		(laughter)
Editor A/fone:	A	**Oh no, there I go again.**	**>11**
Cotter:		**Better watch out.**	**>12**
Editor A/fone:	A	**(?) killer bee swat team**
Trib group:		(laughter)
Editor B/Trib:	B	I want to make the ALASKA OIL and KILLER BEES optional then.	>13
Editor E/ME:	*	**Yep.**	**>14**
Editor A/fone:	A	So we're talking about IRAQ, INFANT DEATH, and, and, ALASKA OIL?	>15
Editor E/ME:	*	**Or BEES.**	**>16**
Editor A/fone:	A	Or BEES. Alright?	>17
Editor C:		Alright.
Editor B/Trib:	B	OIL and BEES I guess can be optional?	>18
Editor A/fone:	A	Alright? That sounds good. Anything else? OK, thank you very much, bye bye.	>19
(Phone hung up)			>20
Editor B/Trib:	B	**[Editor A] was a little passionate there.**	**>21**

(*Source*: field notes)

Before discussing Example 5.5 in detail, I will summarize the exchange in brief:

Lines 5, *6	Ed A wants IRAQ story off Page One; makes side political comment.
Lines 7, 8	Ed B disagrees.
Line *10	ME interjects with reminder I'm there (re political comment).
Lines 13/18	Ed B's "solution" – making OIL or BEES optional – in effect gets around political opinion associated with the IRAQ story.
Lines 14/16	Solution by Editor B underscored by Managing Ed response.
Line 15	New Page One story lineup confirmed.
Lines 17/19	Ed A aligns with Ed B's solution/and the collective agreement.
Line 20	Collective meeting concludes.
Line *21	Ed B notes Ed A's transgression.

In the *negotiation segment* of the Page One decision exchange in Example 5.5, Editor A (the Phone Editor) indicates that the collective (in a preceding segment not reproduced here) has agreed on two "readers," or feature-type stories for Page One, meaning that three out of four or five other stories still need to be agreed to. Editor B, the *Tribune* Editor, suggests IRAQ (in Line or Segment (1)), which Editor C agrees with ("yeah"). Another Editor, D, suggests ALASKA OIL. Significantly, the Phone Editor A agrees with Editor D and supports the proposition on the grounds of *timeliness* ("*now*") and *proximity* ("*here*") in Line or Segment (2):

Yeah that's a pretty good environmental issue now.
Not to mention we have Chevron oil company here.

The next turn is Editor C's laugh response, possibly at what could be interpreted as a somewhat far-fetched notion of *proximity* in relation to the *importance* of a story about the oil pipeline thousands of miles away in Alaska. The Phone Editor reaffirms ALASKA OIL with a question in Line/Segment (3), allowing a turn in which the *Tribune* Editor in Line/Segment (4) questions: "Instead of what, BEES?" The Phone Editor responds in Line/Segment (5) – "Uh, instead of IRAQ" – the "uh" discourse marker signaling a potentially disfavored response to his stand, which he attempts to buttress by making additional comments about Clinton's political timing (in Line/Segment (6)).

The *Tribune* Editor B disagrees in Line/Segment (7): "I don't see how we can keep that [IRAQ] off Page One." In arguing for IRAQ on Page One, Editor B makes his support of that story clear, while agreeing in Segment (8) that "ALASKA OIL is good, too" and a better option than "old news" KILLER BEES on the grounds of *timeliness* in Line/Segment (9):

I think it's better than KILLER BEES, and
We've been knowing about killer bees for the **last two years**.

In Line/Segment (10), the *Tribune* Managing Editor E interjects with a reminder I am there ("Do you know your comments about uh about Clinton and starting the war will be in this national survey – this person's been with us a month now"). Following that "transgression reminder" are the following turns: a supportive laughter response by the *Tribune* editors to the Managing Editor's "national survey" humor; the Phone Editor's self-deprecating response in Line/Segment (11) – "Oh no, there I go again"; my acknowledgement of my presence to the people on the non-visible end of the teleconference by actually speaking in Line/Segment (12) – "Better watch out" – at the same time underscoring the illocutionary force of the ME's warning; and the Phone Editor's accepting responsibility for the transgression by (humorously) worrying about a "killer bee swat team," simultaneously referring to one of the Page One story contenders on the table, and returning the topic to the purpose at hand.

In Line/Segment (13), the *Tribune* editor provides a "solution" – making OIL or BEES optional ("I want to make the ALASKA OIL and KILLER BEES optional then") – in effect getting around the issue of political opinion and its conflation with a story. His solution is underscored in Line/Segment (14) by the Managing Editor's response ("Yep"). In Line/Segment (15), the new lineup is confirmed by the Phone Editor: "So we're talking about IRAQ, INFANT DEATH, and, and, ALASKA OIL?" In Line/Segment (16), after the Managing Editor responds, "Or BEES," the Phone Editor aligns with the solution and the collective agreement in Line/Segment (17) repeating, "Or BEES. Alright?" The *Tribune* Editor confirms this in Line/Segment (18): "OIL and BEES I guess can be optional?" The Phone Editor allows for feedback, confirms the collective position, and concludes the meeting in Line/Segment (19): "Alright? That sounds good. Anything else? OK, thank you very much, bye-bye." The phone is hung up and the *Tribune* editor's first reaction, in Line/Segment (21), is not to the news, as would be customary, but to the transgression: "[The Phone Editor] was a little passionate there." Although it happened infrequently, this was not the only occasion during my time at the *Tribune* that the Managing Editor reminded the editorial collective on the other end of the phone line that I was there, an issue undoubtedly exacerbated by the teleconference channel we were operating in.

5.4.2   Popular culture

Contrary to political opinion, I noticed consistently that personal "social" opinions related to historically distant and thus neutral pop culture, which reinforced shared intra-generational knowledge through the frame of nostalgia, were not avoided or sanctioned, as in Example 5.6 about the death of Buffalo Bob, a very popular 1950s children's television character:

Example 5.6

BUFFALO BOB

Editor A/fone:	OK, what do we want to do for out front, folks?
	BUFFALO BOB, I don't know,
	he was a big influence in my life.
Many:	YES. Yes.
Editor B/Trib:	[?]
Editor A/fone:	I agree. POWERBALL, BUFFALO BOB, CLINTON

(*Source*: field notes)

In Example 5.6, Editor A (the Phone Editor) introduces the Page One *negotiation segment* of the story meeting by asking for nominations for Page One: "OK, what do we want to do for out front, folks?" He nominates BUFFALO BOB, justifying the choice *not* by establishing its newsworthiness or by citing a news value but by saying "he was a big influence in my life." The agreement by all the editors participating in the call – at the *Tribune* and over the phone – was also atypical: an overlapping chorus of yeses.

In this context, it was interesting to note when personal opinion was licensed: personal "social" opinions connected with the sharing of pop culture and shared intra-generational knowledge went by unremarked. But even then, the digression to the personal was still out of the ordinary: at the start of that meeting, when the *Trib* editors immediately told the Phone Editor (Editor A), in response to his phatic opening "How are you?," that they had been bemoaning the loss of Buffalo Bob of Howdy-Doody cartoon fame, Editor A asked: "Are you covering it?" Editor A's question was a journalistic response; the inference in the story-meeting context is that any mention of an event equals coverage in some capacity and that its mention here meant it had been part of a coverage decision discussed ahead of time by the *Tribune* editors to be introduced at the story meeting.

5.4.3   The Managing Editor as arbiter

Example 5.5 (ALASKA OIL) is just one of several instances over time that show the Managing Editor (ME), the one responsible for my being there as a researcher, as an arbiter monitoring the extent of what counts as a transgression – personal political opinions – and providing the explicit verbal sanctions or norm-reminders that result.[3] Deadline expedience ruled out any other consideration. In a memo to the *Oakland Tribune* editors after I concluded my fieldwork, I wrote:

I've appreciated [the Managing Editor's] "watch-dog" role [...]. His interjections when an outlying [non-*Tribune*, phone-based] editor gets too political or opinionated are a valuable indicator of the limited extent to which news people are supposed to get involved with the news.

The Managing Editor's interjections were good reminders of the complexity of the issues of bias in relation to the internalized professional beliefs of news practitioners, and demonstrate as positive evidence the norms that are fundamental to a practice-socialized, communicatively competent news professional. (Whether they are upheld and to what degree is another discussion.) There were enough instances of the ME functioning as arbiter, reminding the editorial collective on phone and in person in the *Oakland Tribune* conference room that there was an interpreter for the "outside world" present. The ME's comments showed the extent to which editors work or are meant to work to keep personal opinion out of the equation; or how they are able to build around personal values by focusing on journalistic ones. (This *objectivity value*, an important point with respect to a reporter's identity, will be discussed in greater detail in Chapter 7.)

---

[3] His occasional reminders of my presence to the editors on the other end of the line who did not see me daily did not appear to influence their interactional behavior – as there was no change in the editors' interactional style – which was my initial sociolinguistic researcher concern.

Consistently, in the story meeting setting, the boundaries established professionally indicated that personal opinion related to politics was a violation of professional norms, whereas social evaluations of a particular sort, such as nostalgia relating to popular culture (as in Example 5.6), were permitted. This was opposite to when I met with them privately to ask about the Oakland news context, during which time humorous comments about local politicians were sometimes made in passing. The speech event of a one-to-one interview was different than that of a story meeting, which is a professional situation that demonstrated group collective interactions, not only in terms of structure and expectation but in harnesses on personal comment. Still, it is relevant that the comments in the one-on-one context of an interview were humorous, within the joke genre, and that the Managing Editor was not there to sanction them or to remind them of the boundary between the insider community to which they are responsible and the academic interloper that was me.

5.5   Conclusion: news priorities in relation to practice

5.5.1   Co-occurring variables and boundaries

Story-meeting interactions, negotiations, and decision-making processes are the result of co-occurring variables involving Page One presentation and deadline demands, *newsworthiness*, and *local priority emphasis* – all of which are situated as primary processes within journalistic production, are recurrent features of everyday action and decision-making, or have priority within journalistic practice. These co-occurring elements react variably and interdependently depending on circumstance, situation, and context. Indications of this variability are internal disagreements among editors within a single news outlet, as illustrated in the *Oakland Tribune* meetings, and the differences in Page One story play across all news outlets, as a quick view of a row of newsstands on any one day shows. It is instructive to see what is similar and dissimilar across publications even on a superficial comparative-content basis. Table 6.2 only minimally illustrates this observation.

Concurrently, the three elements that constitute the dynamic process of news production – text (or news story), values (professional norms), and relationship (participant structure) – operate alongside the story-meeting-relevant variables. These process elements are made visible within Page One and its textual outcome; through notions of *newsworthiness* and its ratification of journalistic values and news ideologies; and via *local priority emphases* that speak to the relationship and the active engagement the news community has with its community of coverage (readers, listeners, watchers, newsmakers, critics, audience, etc.). The internal (or professional-specific) and external (or community-specific) orientations of the story meetings co-occur, allowing for a complex integration of meaning within the news community.

As has been noted, news-value assessments and story-placement decisions undertaken by editors in story meetings are always considered in relation to the *community of coverage*. For example, the news values of *significance* and *proximity* – which underlie key questions "Is this story significant? Does it take place or affect us around here?" make consideration of the *community of coverage* inherent to the process. However, the *local priority emphasis* and focus on readers (or audience, media interlocutors, community of coverage) only goes so far. Other journalistic practice-justifications such as the **right to know** and the **need to know**, discussed at length in trade journals and ethics forums, and relevant to any society's news culture (e.g., the British media dictum to "inform and delight" which has its roots in Renaissance ideology), supersede. One conclusion that can be drawn is that news values provide an override that licenses the authority of the journalistic community over the concerns of the coverage community, particularly when a situation is contentious or skirts wider social ethical codes and culture-specific notions of responsibility, as routinely occurs. It is a different conclusion about news decisions than the one usually drawn by the public, where coverage actions are attributed to "selling papers" (i.e., corporate profit) or rampant journalistic unscrupulousness. Not that these explanations are not valid; just that there are discursive and interactional norms and routines that news practitioners also follow and adhere to.

5.5.2   Locating news priorities

A profession-specific speech event like the story meeting can encompass and motivate our understanding of both the ideological and the linguistic. Linguistically, the story meeting affords a focus on both the structural and functional features of news production (identifying the speech events and discourse forms characteristic of the news media) as well as allowing us to consider the professional ideologies that constrain journalistic practice and which inform and are informed by the larger cultural context. From this perspective, it is relevant to examine the multi-dimensionality of the story meeting theoretically and functionally, and articulate the different elements that come into play. In that light, this chapter highlights the following discursive elements that characterize a story meeting:

- Story meetings as a speech event.
- News values as central to decision-making and ultimately text or story shape.
- News values integrated with attention to "community of coverage" and influence on story frame or angle.
- Story meetings as a locus for the reinforcement of communicative norms in the news community.
- The alignment of news community to (non-neutral) events and social positions.

Table 5.2 *News story example summary*

Story slugs (identifiers)	Discursive illustration
(1) TAX BILL	How news values come into play
(2) PACNET	When news values conflict
(3) BELFAST	Story well-formedness and rhetorical skill
(4) ZORRO	Local priority emphasis
(5) ALASKA OIL	Managing Editor as boundary monitor
(6) BUFFALO BOB	Social opinion (vs. political opinion)

The six story-meeting examples (5.1–5.6 above) discussed in this chapter were selected to give a comprehensive look at a "prototypical" story meeting, to cover the primary elements of its discursive multi-dimensionality. Thus, the examples (as summarized in Table 5.2), were selected to illustrate: how news values come into play (1); when news values conflict (2); other values such as story well-formedness (3) and local priority emphasis (4); an exchange in which the Managing Editor functions as "boundary monitor" sanctioning political opinion (5); and an exchange in which social opinion is licensed (6).

The examples can also be viewed in terms of how news values co-occur with other values internal to the news community: text values, as in BELFAST (Example 5.3); shared social experience, as in BUFFALO BOB (Example 5.6); and local priority emphasis, as in ZORRO (5.4), PACNET (5.2), and ALASKA OIL (5.5).

Ideologically, the story meeting can be seen as a site of cultural production, embodying specified openings for evaluation. Talk and interaction are framed by the worldview of editors (and their collocation of professional and personal experiences), who use news values (as do reporters for stories) as pivot points for discussion and decisions. Most non-journalists (academics included) cite a newspaper's editorial page stances, the points of view of columnists engaged by editors to deliver opinion, or a context-limited "folk content analysis" as evidence of its bias (and untrustworthiness). I argue instead that it behooves us to look at the story meeting, where stance and position are recurrent in **negotiations of newsworthiness**. Negotiations of newsworthiness inevitably lead to decisions of inclusion and exclusion, and can be demonstrated to be a more internally or cross-professionally situated function – and marker – of a newspaper's priorities and commitments.

The "op-ed pages" in actuality and by design reflect only a tiny amount of the news text that comes at us in print. Op-ed or "analysis" journalism is consciously segregated by mainstream reporters and editors from news reporting processes and the "news pages" in physical placement, genre form, and lexical choice. (In that way, explicit personal opinion is professionally constrained.)

Thus, looking for ideology in news texts alone delivers only a partial account (but see Santa Ana 2002 for a discussion of *Los Angeles Times* coverage of immigration; and Lakoff 2000b for compelling critiques of news media sallies into creating, not reporting, our political culture, and through instigating the actions that follow). As such, an "insider" discursive process or speech event, such as the story meeting, is a more interesting sector for ideological analysis than the more explicitly positioned editorial or opinion pages, particularly as the extent to which personal subjectivity can be subsumed to professional objectivity is a contested one inside and outside of journalism.

5.5.3   Summary: speech events in the newsroom

Story meetings comprise a speech activity that occurs daily in all news organizations; it is the predominant speech event in the news-production process. As a speech activity, we look at *rules* that govern its process and outcome; *roles* undertaken by participants; and the *relation* of setting, participants, and norms of interaction. In this chapter, I have discussed what happens at a story meeting, the role of news values in determining story placement, and the profession-specific boundaries that circumscribe the activity. I discussed factors intrinsic to story meetings, such as what values internal to the news community are reinforced and how relations to the larger community are made explicit, and noted *co-occurrences* with other values (both procedural and ideological) that function variably (and event-dependently).

Story meetings serve a gate-keeping function within the profession, as well as a place to negotiate and reinforce journalistic identity through discussion of news stories and their placement. They are a crucial site for the emergence of values that pertain to the news media context. They also point to the importance of practice-based ethnographic research, and the insights which can better inform our analyses and understanding of news processes and outputs. My attendance at the *Oakland Tribune* budget meetings confirmed what I knew from past experience and what journalists know from everyday practice: that *news values undergird decision-making* and that local knowledge and awareness of the *community always affect story play.* The community- and interaction-based dimensions of news practice, about which the story meeting provides some insight, will be the topic of Chapter 6.

6   The interaction-based nature of journalism

KEY POINTS

- To explore the interaction-based nature of journalism is to challenge some fundamental models of mass communication and assumptions about the way journalists relate to each other, assuming a *reciprocal transmission* at the heart of the enterprise rather than a one-to-many schema.
- The "supremacy of the local" in American journalism means that local news is privileged. This internal value becomes externally manifested, and is then critiqued differently by insiders and outsiders.
- Interaction is located in many of the activities that reporters engage in to gather the news and can be identified in a number of ways: in the number of sources required for stories; in attribution practices; and in various forms of outreach to the community.
- The notion of *pseudo-relationship* (building on Boorstin's notion of "pseudo-event," a constructed vs. real event) helps to characterize the dynamic that exists between the practitioner and the community of coverage, as one that is situational and partial.

News stories are seldom written as an introspective exercise, but are produced with a group of listeners or readers outside the newsroom in mind. Perhaps opaque to the layperson is the fact that mainstream journalism, despite its technical (mass-media) constraints and one-to-many paradigm, has as its goal a responsiveness and interaction with an audience (or what I call the *community of coverage* (see Chapter 2)). To explore the interaction-based nature of journalism is to challenge some fundamental models of mass communication and assumptions about the way journalists relate to each other. Examining the interaction-based processes of daily journalism provides another way to look at the relation of the journalist to the **audience** as well as the dynamic of that relationship to news **texts** and to journalistic **practice**.

The interaction-based nature of journalism involves processes as diverse as keeping the reader – and the community – in mind while reporting and writing; developing reporter–source relationships; maintaining language policies and "community standards"; and publishing letters to the editor, blog URLs, and reporter email addresses. These are all measures that sustain the *pseudo-dyad* and foster *reciprocal transmission* between the news community and coverage community (Cotter 1999b), more of which will be said in this chapter. To fully characterize what counts as interaction-based, and which in entirety I only describe in overview, includes the ways journalists think of the relationship; the way it is manifested through practice, performance, and language; how it can be defined in the news context; the way linguists can regard it; and what evidence is available to make interaction-based sociolinguistic claims.

Looking at the **relation** of news to community, which I do here, means examining the participant structure or discourse relationship behind it. I introduce the notion of the ***pseudo-relationship*** (extending Daniel Boorstin's 1961 notion of "pseudo-event," or a constructed, non-organic circumstance like a press conference which is reported on by the media) to characterize the relationship between the media and the public. Linguistically, I discuss how this relationship is embedded in professional identity and practice and results in pragmatic motivations for particular ways of using language that are identifiable to the news genre (e.g., sentence-initial connectives, Cotter 2001). I also discuss the multiple ways in which "interaction" can be identified in the journalistic context, and how the Web makes more transparent this interactive relationship.

Thus, this chapter will cover fairly broadly what constitutes interaction; the motivating forces of "the local"; and where interaction occurs in news practice and where it occurs in news texts – all factors that underpin the "pseudo-relationship" between news practitioners and the people they report on and for.

6.1   Interaction through practice

6.1.1   Characterizing interaction

Interaction in the news media context is constituted through **practice**, and thus can be examined, studied, and analyzed according to a range of sociocultural, linguistic anthropological, sociolinguistic, socio-interactional, and ethnolinguistic approaches and analytical frameworks that attempt to shed light on issues of performance, practice, and community and the communicative patterns that emerge (Morgan 2006 summarizes a range of points about speech community; also Bauman 1977, 1986; Bourdieu 1977 [1972]; Goodwin 1990; Labov 1972a; Lave and Wenger 1991; Ochs and Schieffelin 1983; Rampton 1995; Wenger 1998, etc.). Practice elements vary with respect to internal and external (or professional and community) **relationships**, as well as with the text itself. For example, getting the necessary *fresh quotes* for a news story – through interaction with a source – has a direct outcome in shaping a news **text**. So does the practice of working in a newsroom: stories are *not a single-author outcome*, but the result of a varied configuration of reporters and editors, whose work-task objectives derive from different requirements of the news story production process, alongside the information from sources. News practice also involves a conscious *attention to* ***audience***, community standards reminders to news staff, coverage policies, and language policies (avoiding offensive language, for instance).

The material selected and presented in the news media as a result of this practice reflects a **participant relationship** – between the media cohort and its audience or community interlocutors – such as one would characterize in any speech community, community of practice, or discourse community. One way to describe the news- and coverage-community relationship is as a type of dyad, such as exists when two people communicate or interact. In the news media case, given the constraints and complexities of the channels of transmission (print, broadcast, or Internet), and the roles that are assumed (by both news practitioners and the coverage or local community), we can view the news and community participants as comprising a ***pseudo-dyad***. From the news profession's perspective, given its interaction-centric focus, the communicative exchanges between both communicators in the dyad can be seen as ***reciprocal transmission*** (a counter-perspective to the one-to-many mass communication model).

Reciprocal transmission is the operation behind the interplay of texts, news practitioners, and audience (or *community of coverage*) and is what allows the media to: (1) engage with the community on professional and personal levels; as well as to (2) provide content that captures facts or perspectives about the social worlds in which media and community reside (cf. Cotter 1999b, 1999c). Obvious practice-based examples of reciprocal transmission that help to build the interactional elements on which a participant relationship is based and develops range from letters to the editor to reporter–source relationships, reporter–community relationships, and editor–community relationships, to the activities that are removed from the day-to-day business of reporting and editing. These more consciously abstracted news-community activities include meetings that news practitioners have with community leaders or focus groups, as well as readership surveys. From a news-ideology point of view, *reciprocal transmission* also operates within the professional injunctions to focus on the local (mentioned in Chapters 4, 5, and 7).

Irrespective of journalistic communicative goals, the news media select information and topics to present based on the same principles used by interlocutors in conversation: communication, persuasion, connection, and articulation of identity. As with a conversation, the "news interlocutors" make assessments about shared or prior knowledge, what might be of interest, what would be offensive or proper, what information is wanted or needed. An editor's recollection of this type of exchange appears in Example 6.1:

Example 6.1
[...] the [email and text] traffic coming in from viewers did help to inform both the tone of our coverage and also the direction it took. We had a sense of [...] some of the questions our viewers wanted answered [...] and also heard from people caught up in the chaos.
(David Kermode, editor BBC *Breakfast*, "Getting the tone right," August 10, 2006, emphasis added)

In Example 6.1, the editor of a morning radio news program relates input from viewers (during a breaking-news event) as guiding their coverage, as well as providing a specific focus for the journalists' information-gathering process through the "questions our viewers wanted answered."

Any conversation can also be constituted and interpreted in the context of the participant relationship, and thus elements of symmetry, hierarchy, power, ideology, and institution influence the interaction; hence the notion of the *pseudo-dyad*. (Given the limitations of space, I will not address interactional asymmetries that exist within the news-community relationship explicitly; merely point out the areas where they can be addressed.) Similarly, the range of links in the larger community network also has a bearing on the news-community relationship. As noted in Chapter 2, reporters in a small town may function within the *community of coverage* in many and different, or "dense" and "multiplex," ways (cf. Milroy 1987): e.g., as parents of school-age children, members of civic, church, or volunteer groups, neighbors, etc. Reporters in larger-circulation areas might not have as many, or would have different or more attenuated, social network ties alongside their separate priorities as reporters in that community.

6.1.2   Attention to audience

There has always been an awareness, even by solitary, garret-living writers, of the reader: an awareness of the reader as respondent, hearer, communicative participant, dumping ground, or interested party. Readers, as is conventional in a wide range of novels, are often addressed in a deferential, symmetrical way as "gentle reader" (Quirk 1986). "Reader, I married him" is a classic example of the asynchronous interaction-based authorial connection (as in the Charlotte Brontë novel *Jane Eyre*).

In the news realm, the reader (or listener or viewer) has a similar valued albeit distal position. Instead of the explicit vocative utterance, the news practitioner attempts to make a connection by other language-based, rhetorical, or topic-focused means – and does so through garnering *attention* and maintaining *relevance*. Equally important is the fact that the "news-community relationship" is not just a single operation but is manifested in different domains in different ways, e.g., reporter to individual reader or source, editorial groups to community groups, news organization to community, the profession more generally to the community in the abstract. (Discussion in Chapter 3 further illustrates this point, as does Example 6.1 above.)

The "gentle reader" trope conveys an aspect of the individual writer's relationship to his or her audience, made up of a single individual who is being addressed, a one-to-one dyadic relationship. The journalistic relationship, however, is somewhat more interconnected in that the journalist communicates as a socialized member of his or her profession, not as a solitary writer. Reporters also communicate incorporating their pre-existing knowledge of a particular community (as do ethnographers). And while news practitioners are taught to respond and write with the individual "reader" in mind, particularly when writing the story, the larger generic *community* of which the reader is part is more consciously considered when making more general editor-level decisions about coverage that would be relevant to this community.

In Example 6.2, a weekly London magazine's editor recollects how his team responded journalistically to the July 7, 2005 terrorist attack on London transport routes. It clearly shows the editorial process involved ("we knew we had to pull it [the magazine's front cover for that week] and run with a new image"), the thinking behind their decisions, and the publication's overt connection with people and place:

Example 6.2
On the tatty whiteboard that hangs in my office I can still make out the words we wrote that summer's morning, as *Time Out*'s senior editors and I tried to make sense of the worst ever terrorist attack on the capital [...] We had already sent our summer preview cover [...] to the printers. We knew we had to pull it and run with a new image. But what could it say? 'Resolute', 'courageous', 'tenacious', 'tough', 'defiant'. The words we scrawled felt clichéd and insensitive. In the end we ran with the simple legend: 'Our City'. I'm not even sure we knew what it meant, but instinctively it felt right. And as the capital prepares itself for Friday's anniversary, it still feels like the right thing, the only thing, to say.
(Gordon Thomson, Editor, *Time Out* London (No. 1872), July 5–12, 2006: 5, emphasis added)

The editors' decision to use a vocative phrase, "Our City," calls attention to the community connection, speaks to a pre-existing or ongoing relationship, and is both "attention-getting" and relevant on the personal, community-inclusive level. It includes all residents of London. Adjectives (such as the ones they discounted for being too "clichéd and insensitive") did not communicate this relational message and objective of connection.

Reporters as individuals also consider the readers, as we saw in Chapter 2, but often from a more practice-internal or hands-on perspective, as a response to individuals they have encountered on their beats and through their reporting experiences. For example, when technology reporter and columnist Declan McCullagh left Wired News for a position elsewhere, he included an excerpt from his farewell column in his politics and technology mailing list (June 14, 2002), in which he acknowledges his editors, fellow reporters, and, significantly, readers:

Example 6.3
I owe my readers an equal debt for their commitment to keeping journalists in line: It's humbling to know that readers often know far more about a subject than the writer. (emphasis added)

McCullagh is not only acknowledging the expertise, approbation, and aid of "his" readers, but is reinforcing the point by repeating it amongst a different, more personal and non-journalistic community (the politics and technology mailing list, of which he was moderator). The "equal debt" he is attempting to discharge puts readers on par with his professional peers (a counter-example to the misguided generalization in academia that reporters only write for each other).

In a different way, but characterizing the same reporter–reader/viewer relationship awareness, British Channel 4 broadcast reporter Jon Snow in Example 6.4 repeats the practitioner's professional belief that the audience is not an abstract assemblage, but a single individual, which enables the reporter to make a visceral connection, to operate as if they are "only ever talking to one person."

Example 6.4
The moment a human being is able to go and connect with some of the human beings on the ground, and then connect back home again with some of the human beings who are watching on a one-to-one basis – that's the beauty of television; you're only ever talking to one person.
(Jon Snow, January 13, 2006, Bagehot Lecture, Queen Mary University of London, emphasis added)

By "on the ground" he means connecting with people in actuality and in-person, not virtually, and on their home turf, not his. His comment conveys the professional understanding of the reporter as mediator on the "human being" level, not just the conveyor of information, but as the element that facilitates connection of disparate and different communities and individuals. The single "human being," the reporter, speaks with a small subset of human beings, i.e., the person (or persons) affected by or involved in the news, and in turn shares this "connection" with a similar small subset of human beings "back home" whose participation from within their domestic space organizes it on a "one-to-one basis." Snow's use of the phrase "human being" to refer to the reporter, the reported on, and the news consumer makes this interpersonal and interactive journalistic connection in his view personal, symmetrical, and jointly constituted.

Editors and editorial groups also consider the readers but more actively as a particular group constituted within the community with a voice and influence (financial, political, social). From an *institutional* perspective (further up the news-culture hierarchy than McCullagh's reporter's-view example) are the comments of William Mock, former managing editor of *The Beaumont (*Texas*) Enterprise*:

Example 6.5
"We have to second-guess what our readers really want to know [...] Experienced editors and reporters develop a sense of what readers want."
                                              (quoted in Itule and Anderson 1991: 46, emphasis added)

Mock's comments were included in a newswriting textbook, through which novices begin to become socialized in the communicative norms and ideologies of the profession as they concurrently learn how to write news stories. Explicitly stated is that readers are part of the equation, and that reporters have a duty and must take action – in Mock's words through "second-guessing" or considering what readers want to know. This activity is part of what constitutes becoming journalistically "experienced." He goes on to mention that other tools, such as surveys and demographic studies, give other sorts of information that also become part of the action process that influences reporting:

Example 6.6
"Readership surveys and demographic breakdowns, of course, provide editors and reporters with background information that can help hone their instincts."
                                              (quoted in Itule and Anderson 1991: 46, emphasis added)

The word "instinct" is a salient one for news people. The term, when used, summarizes one's news sense, one's news judgment, one's "nose for news." If a reporter or editor has a good instinct for news – good antennae for recognizing news and its relevance to the community – he or she is a good reporter or editor (cf. Chapter 4). News judgments and news practice, then, are fundamentally connected to being relevant to the reader. (The *Time Out* editor's use of the word "instinctively" in Example 6.2 refers to a collocation of understanding and experience which journalists draw from, not necessarily to a logical-propositional chain of reasoning.)

Editors also acknowledge their sense of journalistic purpose with respect to the community, particularly when the situation is culturally complex, as in Example 6.7, which refers to a shooting in the Amish community in Pennsylvania. When the community affected by the news event is one whose values diverge from journalistic ones, it calls into question the role of the reporter or photographer on site.

Example 6.7
    The horror of the Oct. 2 schoolhouse shooting that left five Amish girls dead and five more critically wounded brought into vivid conflict the journalistic value of bringing the news to readers and the human value of wanting privacy in grief.
    Add to this Amish feelings about being photographed, and the event presented a situation of great sensitivity to Post editors and the photographers […] on the scene […].
                        (Deborah Howell, *Washington Post*, Sunday, October 15, 2006: B6)

The newspaper's ombudsperson is responding in her column to comments and criticisms from the paper's readership about the intrusion of news coverage into a community that, as is commonly known, values its separateness from the outside or Westernized "English" world and for whom photographs carry diametrically opposed cultural value. Howell quotes the photographers whom the local non-Amish community instructed in Amish cultural norms, a consequence being that they primarily shot from public spaces, with telephoto lenses, did not "hover" from above in helicopters, and asked for permissions before publishing. (She also quotes a professor of American religious history affiliated with a college near the Amish community who provides more cultural context that amplifies the complexities of the reporting process in relation to that event in that community.) The often overriding "journalistic value of bringing the news to readers" and its potential intrusive impacts in this case are more consciously considered because of the competing values of the community being reported on, values which the news practitioners are trying to respect.

    To summarize, the "gentle reader" leitmotif reminds us of the long-acknowledged relationship (in Western culture) of the writer to the reader. Example 6.3 shows the reporter relationship with the reader, and Example 6.4 the reporter relationship with the viewer, one that exists, to quote Snow, "on a one-to-one basis." Example 6.2 shows the news organization's relationship (and sense of editorial responsibility) with the community of which the reader and writer are part, in this case making a literal connection through the use of the first-person plural "our" that establishes a shared place, space, and cultural understanding (as opposed to the distancing editorial "we"). Example 6.5 keeps the connection separate, but shows how the priorities within the local-community and news-organization relationship (as with *Time Out*'s editorial decision-making) are made through a practice-instantiated connection that is ongoing. Example 6.7 provides a different view, in which the values within a community being reported on have an effect on journalistic practice. Finally, Example 6.1 illustrates the extent to which viewers and readers participate in and contribute to the shape of news, "inform[ing] both the tone of […] coverage and also the direction it [can take]."

6.1.3   Addressee-oriented goals of newswriting and reporting

As well as honing an *instinct* for news, by determining what is *relevant* to the reader, there are also goals within the actual act of writing up the news, of producing the stories. Here we come to the *text* or news story itself. Example 6.5 above illustrates the fundamental rule of journalism: that reporters should *take their readers into account* when they write or report. This is made clear in journalism textbooks, trade publications, and innumerable newsroom inter-actions – in short, in all the official and unofficial channels that circumscribe the journalist's professional identity. Journalism textbooks all discuss news-writing and its goals *in terms of the addressee*, and reporting in terms of the community, and their injunctions to "make it easy" or interesting for the reader are surprisingly consistent over time. For example, the *news values* mentioned in Chapter 4 – news is unusual, timely, surprising, local, about change and conflict, evokes human interest (which can be boiled down to whether a reader would care to hear about it or not) – are standard ones that are found through-out a range of textbooks I consulted (and indeed, have used), despite nearly a century between the oldest in my corpus (1913) and the most recent (2007).

Besides correlating newsworthiness and story value in relation to the reader or viewer, textbooks discuss newswriting itself in terms of the reader, instruct-ing reporters to strive for *ease of comprehension* for the addressee and the resultant need for *simplicity in writing style* (points made in chapters 7 and 8). The 1913 textbook says effective newswriting "enables the reader to get the meaning with the least effort and the greatest interest" (Bleyer 1913: 62, emphasis added). Similarly, a 1988 textbook reminds the reporter that: "The media writer must make the audience's task as easy as possible" (Newsom and Wollert 1988: 55). More recently, novice journalists are told that "unless their stories are clear, interesting and well written their readers, viewers and listeners will move on to something else" (Mencher 2006: 135). "If it is interesting, they will pay attention. Otherwise, they turn elsewhere. People are too busy to tarry without reward" (*ibid.*: 126). The same conditions apply to younger and computer-literate readers and viewers who "want to know the day's events, and when they turn to their computer screens – as many of them do – they want the information straight and to the point" (*ibid.*: 129). Bleyer refers to the "reader," Newsom and Wollert to the "audience," and Mencher to the "reader, viewer, and listener," reflecting the fact that "the media" now includes tele-vision, radio, and the Web.

Addressee-oriented goals exist on more macro-levels; there are additional ways that news organizations orient their production to specific audiences or communities, particularly in terms of discourse-level topic and informa-tional focus. "Zoned editions," which contain news stories that have more restricted "local" scope, are produced by metropolitan newspapers to be

Table 6.1 *How "the local" is manifested*

Profession-specific emphases	Linguistic categories	Outcomes in practice
• Relation of news to community • Profession's reinforcement of local focus • Localizing the news	• Journalistic IDEOLOGY • Professional IDENTITY • News TEXT	• **Decisions** – norms of practice • **Socialization** – positioning • **Discourse** – story specifics

distributed to – and relevant to – the different communities and neighborhoods comprising the larger circulation area. (Zoned editions and the demographic realities they embody also provide focus for advertisers.) Technologies such as the Web also help news organizations further segment their audience, both commercially and editorially. For example, visitors to the BBC News website have the option of selecting a UK version, which gives "prominence to the breadth and depth of BBC content in the UK including news, sport and weather [...] You may prefer this version if you live in the UK," or the International version, which "gives prominence to world news, sport and weather [...] You may prefer this version if you live outside the UK" (source: www.bbc.co.uk, emphasis added).

6.2   The supremacy of the local

What maintains the foundation of interaction within the news community is the industry's constant reference to the *community of coverage*. "Readers" or "viewers" are frequently cited, as noted in Examples 6.5 and 6.6 above, within newsrooms and industry discussions. These discussions reinforce and make explicit the role of the reader/audience/community in the journalistic enterprise, and the need for local news coverage (a particular feature of US journalism). The supremacy of the local results in the news text outcomes we read and hear and download. In the news practitioner sense, "local" means *relevant*.

The significance or supremacy of "the local" can be examined through the three main analytical routes underpinning this book that, taken together, comprehensively characterize the practice-based elements that come into play in the news process: journalistic **ideology**, professional **identity**, and news **text**. That *news is related to the community* underpins journalistic ideology; the profession's *reinforcement of "the local"* relates to a primary marker of professional identity; and the story shape that results from *localizing the news* is reflected in the news text outcome itself. (Table 6.1 summarizes these points.)

The profession's emphases in relation to the local have multiple outcomes in practice which have been mentioned in other chapters, e.g., *decisions* in relation to norms of practice (Chapter 5), and *socialization* within the profession (Chapter 3). Heeding the professional objective to "localize the news" influences the shape of the news text and results in specific discourse outcomes that become generic types familiar to news narratives: for example, the *local angle* in a story or the use of the *illustrative individual* in a lead, who stands in for an abstract concept or general policy, as in Example 6.8:

Example 6.8
ATLANTA – Vince Marzula started his trip to Las Vegas by losing money at the security checkpoint at the Atlanta airport.
    "I threw about $100 of stuff in the garbage – hair care products of my wife," the 35-year-old from suburban Atlanta said Thursday.
    A month after the federal Transportation Security Administration announced rules permitting only limited amounts of liquids on board airplanes, confusion over the regulations has led to longer waits at security checkpoints around the country.
                            (Daniel Yee, Associated Press, Friday November 3, 2006)

In Example 6.8, the story is about new Transportation Security Administration rules described in paragraph 3. But the news element is introduced by an "illustrative individual," someone who has been affected and can thus illustrate what some of the implications of the policy change are.

6.2.1   News values and "the local"

The supremacy of the local relates to larger-issue inclusion or exclusion decisions that are news-value-justified; the news value of *proximity* often trumps the news value of *importance* (cf. examples in Chapter 4). Textbook authors remind would-be reporters of the need to pay heed to the local in Example 6.9:

Example 6.9
Would inner-city residents of Los Angeles, for example, be interested in the death of a former governor of North Carolina?   (Itule and Anderson 1991: 43)

Their point is relevant to novices, who are generally instructed that news that involves a death, no matter how seemingly insignificant, is more important than property damage or political decisions, no matter how extensive or far-reaching. (This point is emphasized in sayings like "if it bleeds, it leads.") In Example 6.9, the implied answer to the question posed is that "inner-city residents of Los Angeles" (likely urban, potentially non-English-speaking people of color living in Southern California, or whatever demographic or stereotype the reporter/editor is basing his/her decision on) would not be interested in the demise of a politician on the other side of the country whose career actions had no impact at all on their lives (as a state, North Carolina does not have the cultural or urban resonance for Californians that, for instance, New York or even Florida might). The example also shows that

Table 6.2 *Stories above the fold on May 4, 1998*

	Washington Post	Washington Times	Baltimore Sun	NY Times	USA Today
Story type					
● **Local**	*Whitbread*	*Whitbread* 1	*Whitbread* 1		
● **National**	Burton	Burton		Burton 2	
● **International**	*Japan/econ*	*China/tech*		*Paris/art theft* 1	
National	Politicians	Politicians			
Local			*Hopkins* 2		
● General					Car safety
General					Cancer help
General					Teen smoke

learning a rule is one thing: putting it into practice involves interpretive judgments based on other values within the community that are integrated in complex ways.

6.2.2 *"Local" news in relation to news organization "scope"*

While the news media emphasize and work towards the local, that does not mean that national and international stories are overlooked. Indeed, it is expected that major non-local news will be reported, the extent of which will depend on the paper's *scope*. Table 6.2 lists one day's worth of headlines "above the fold" (headlines that can be read through a news-stand window) for five newspapers that are readily available wherever newsboxes are congregated around Washington, DC: outside of hotels, metro stops, shopping centers, grocery stores, businesses, etc. They are: *The Washington Post*, *The Washington Times*, *The Baltimore Sun*, *The New York Times*, and *USA Today*. The headlines were chosen from a day in which no wide-impact breaking news is occurring (and are taken randomly from 1998 in my archive). Monday editions also tend to be smaller and to reflect local events that occurred over the weekend.

The New York Times and *The Washington Post* have national scope and distribution, with the *Post* in this market having more local relevance. *The Washington Times* and *The Baltimore Sun* have narrower regional or area scope. (Baltimore is a city in Maryland forty miles from Washington, DC.) *USA Today* is distributed nationally, with headquarters in the DC metro area. Besides local stories, the **scope** of each paper and its community range and relationship also reflect what is chosen for Page One (as previously discussed in Chapter 3).

For the purposes of discussing *scope*, I categorize the news stories into four types (roughly following newsroom parameters): local, national, international, and general.

Local stories   *The Washington Post, The Washington Times* and *The Baltimore Sun* to different degrees have overlapping local readership. All three featured the Whitbread Round-the-World sailing race restart in nearby coastal Annapolis in tandem with the annual Chesapeake Bay Bridge Walk, either with a photo or story or both. It was the lead story in *The Washington Times* and *The Baltimore Sun*. It was a "local" event and relevant to the area's readership sphere, particularly to Marylanders in the Baltimore-area and nearby Chesapeake Bay communities. *The Baltimore Sun*'s second lead story concerned a fund-raiser for The Johns Hopkins University which is located (locally) in Baltimore. As it was a local story, despite the national reputation of the university, it was not featured in *The New York Times* or *USA Today*.

National stories   The Burton story (about a congressman's actions as Chair of the House Government Reform and Oversight Committee) was national news: it was the second story in *The New York Times* as well as the two Washington papers, where, coincidentally, the business of the region is often the nation's. Because the "local industry" is the federal government, both Washington papers also featured stories involving other politicians in, roughly, fourth-story position.

International stories   *The New York Times*'s lead story was international: a Corot painting stolen from the Louvre in Paris. The Washington papers also had Page One stories that concerned international issues: the economic crisis in Japan in *The Washington Post* and US technology in China in *The Washington Times*. (The choice variation between the Washington papers, in the absence of additional contextual information, is likely arbitrary.)

General news   *USA Today*, which is distributed nationally and is not meant to be aligned with any one part of the country, functions somewhat as a control. Its main stories were on topics with broad appeal: car safety, a cancer "weapon," and teens and tobacco, nothing that would restrict the news to a particular locality. Of course these stories could be adapted by other media outlets elsewhere; they could be "localized."

6.2.3   *Scope and variation*

The news organization's *scope*, which operates on the local level of coverage, also manifests itself in terms of its relational and informational purpose – its

1. *The Wall Street Journal* is read by the people **who run** the country.
2. *The New York Times* is read by people **who think they run** the country.
3. *The Washington Post* is read by people **who think they should run** the country.
4. *USA TODAY* is read by people **who think they ought to run the country but don't really understand the *Washington Post*.** They do, however, like their smog statistics shown in **pie charts.**
5. *The Los Angeles Times* is read by people **who wouldn't mind running** the country...
6. [etc.]

Source: author unknown; February 6, 2002 version, sent by a linguist

Figure 6.1 US papers and people who read them (email forward)

ideology and identity or "philosophy of the medium" – as well as outcomes in coverage or in the type of news text. "The business-oriented *Wall Street Journal*, for example, selects stories on the basis of criteria different from those of a metropolitan arts and entertainment publication" (Itule and Anderson 1991: 45).

Figure 6.1 shows a somewhat facetiously compiled list of US papers and the type of people who read them. The list comes from an Internet "humor" post, which I include for reasons I outline below. The post (which gets amended and added to and is still making the rounds of the Internet as recently as late 2008) characterizes what is distinctive about each paper as well as its community of readers, making the relationship inseparable as well as demonstrating the interconnectedness of news to community. It also shows the variations that occur within and between communities (media and reader) under an overarching umbrella of professional and cultural norms and patterns (our quest for understanding this "umbrella" is an objective behind ethnographic research).

The post's author has honed in on the "philosophy of the medium" which illustrates how it instigates variation within the profession in terms of readership. The variation within the list comes from the different community-based relationships and how they are perceived or fare within the larger US culture. Each paper comes with its own cultural stereotypes, a mindset about it, an assumed readership, and descriptive focal points. The post reflects this. It is general knowledge that *The Wall Street Journal's* (*WSJ*) focal point is business (more specifically, capitalism – the mechanism upon which the country operates). *The New York Times* (*NYT*) possesses a New York centrism (implicating Wall Street, the center of finance, hence readers "think they run the country"). Washington, DC, does not have the fiscal or cultural relevance of New York City, and the humor post implies that for *The Washington Post* (*WP*) politics might be important but it is not the same as capitalism. *USA Today* is depicted in terms of their graphics ("pie charts") and their short, non-jumped stories, both of which are signature features of the publication, suggesting an in-kind super-ficiality of the readers. Similarly, the *Los Angeles Times* (*LAT*), which is way over on the "Left Coast" and whose national scope tends to be minimized by power-brokers east of the Mississippi, is characterized by the "laid-back" stereotype of the Southern Californian who is reading it.

I received this email twice at an interval of nearly six months apart, first from a journalism department colleague at a West Coast university and then from a linguist at an East Coast university, neither of whom knows each other. There were small but interesting differences in the language of the two near-identical posts that reflect potential differences in the journalist and layperson relation-ships to news texts. The version from the linguist was longer – eleven news-papers mentioned – and entitled, "*Who reads what and when*" (evoking the basic who-what-when-where-why reporting questions, the "Five W's"). The journalist's version was edited down to ten newspapers and was entitled "*Newspaper Hierarchy*" (complementing Top Ten lists, a familiar media genre form, and news-community-internal hierarchies of importance).

Both senders understood the forward as something meant to be amusing, as something within the genre of humor. The linguist's forward came with the personal note: "Foreigners find this **funny**. Cheers from Barcelona." The linguist is not a US native, and situated herself as an outsider – a member of the group of "foreigners" – a discourse-level mitigation in case we recipient "insiders" included in the forward did not find it humorous. We might, after all, be avid *USA Today* or *LA Times* readers. The journalist's forward came with the personal note: "Some journalism nerd **humor**." The sender situated it as journalist-oriented, marking it as somewhat unusual but still praiseworthy through use of the semi-marked (and ironically chic) term "nerd."

The journalist sender's edited and shortened version was forwarded to my US university email inbox on August 29, 2001; the linguist's was sent nearly six months later on February 6, 2002. This suggests a possible scenario: the linguist's version was more likely the original version, authored by a news practitioner (inferred by the sender's knowledge of the Five W's in the title: *Who reads what and when*). It was subsequently edited by an e-peer who retitled it, made it a typical Top Ten list (changing it from eleven), and tightened up the language. The two versions got transmitted through different channels. (Multiple versions, with alterations to fit the circumstance, are now available on the Web.)

It is important to note that the post lists "household name" papers, ones that most educated and aware US residents – "lay people" as well as journalists – would have knowledge of (whether or not they had physically ever seen or handled them is another matter). However, anyone with an insider connection with the news profession would find the list a bit clichéd, or obvious, and not particularly relevant to everyday news work or even accurate. My point is the newspaper names in the US can be "read" like city names, which come with stereotypes and assumptions (as well as exclusions) that history, familiarity, and lack of insider knowledge can entail. A generic city list would have the familiar big names (San Francisco, New York, Chicago, Washington, DC, etc.) and the familiar regional cities (St. Louis, Seattle, New Orleans, Dallas, etc.). Other US cities (a city is defined variously by state according to population and governance structure) are less familiar (Bloomington, Shreveport, Louisville, Alexandria, Boise, etc.) as well as potentially unknown to all but those in the geographic area (Rockport, Yakima, Columbia, Newport Beach, Appleton, Red Bluff, etc.).

The post (and its subsequently adapted versions) thus replicates larger, socially salient stereotypes about a news organization's scope and its *community of coverage* relevance, drawing from general stereotypical knowledge about these cities. (For example, *"The Chatham-Harwich Chronicle* is read by people who believe the other 13 towns are non-U [non-upper-class] and probably vote Democrat anyway."[1]) It also reinforces and iconizes the familiar and restricts understanding of the actual reach of the news media. Most reporters are employed by one of the 1,400-plus "non-big-name" papers in the US (as well as non-dailies). Some time spent with an "insider" institution, such as the Poynter Institute's online "Webfront," would show how lots of "little" non-"name" newspapers are embedded within normal, mainstream, unmarked, and unnoticed news culture. These papers serve large swathes of America that are often overlooked, short-sightedly, by national or metro media.

6.3   Loci of interaction

Interaction is located in many of the activities that reporters engage in to gather the news: interpersonally, institutionally, internally, externally, and through the medium itself. On a textual level, interaction can be identified in a number of ways from within the news stories themselves: in the number of *sources* required for stories; in *attribution* practices (cf. Chapter 7); in the decisions (and language use) that go into reporting, writing, and editing the stories. In addition to the reporter/source and reporter/reported-on participant structure that derives from news reporting, the news organization/community relationship itself is reinforced by various forms of *outreach* to the community. The goal of these outreach activities is the relationship, not the actual news product. Example 6.10 shows how viewers and listeners are invited to participate in a public online forum to "engage [...] as much as the medium allows."

---

[1] www.capecodtoday.com. Posted April 11, 2008.

Example 6.10

The BBC wants to be open and accountable, and so this site is a <u>public space</u> where you can <u>engage with us</u> as much as the medium allows. We're happy for you to criticise the BBC in your e-mails and comments, and to ask serious, probing questions of us – we'll do our best to respond to them. […] We can't promise to respond to every e-mail, but we'll do our best to read them all.   ("Welcome to The Editors," May 12, 2006, emphasis added)

A news organization's activities within the community on behalf of community service operate simultaneously with the interactions that derive from reporting. However, the news organization's support of a community endeavor, such as literacy or the arts or sports, tends to be news outlet- or institution-based, not individual news practitioner-oriented. Reporters themselves do not necessarily involve themselves in their employer-sponsored community service activities as it would be seen to compromise objectivity (and thus mitigate against credibility, cf. Chapter 2). Community outreach generally comes from the business, not editorial, side. Examples of these efforts can be seen very visibly in a range of community activity, including sponsorships of community events, public-service announcements about local issues, and advertisements in theatre and concert programs. *The Fresno Bee*, for instance, associates itself and its arts support with the local community's regionally vaunted orchestra with advertisements in the Fresno Philharmonic concert program. A recent ad read, "In tune with your community," reflecting the news community's profession-determined position – as responsive and relevant – within the larger community.

6.3.1   Interactivity vs. interaction

As noted earlier, there is a difference between journalistic "interactivity" and linguistic "interaction." This is a relevant, subtle, and important point. Linguistic *interaction* means the evolving, emergent, community-based activities and exchanges between and amongst participants that reflect and reinforce social organization. Interaction creates our social world. Journalistic *interactivity* means the use of technologies like the Web to achieve information exchange, and in the process establish positions of professional identity and interaction (in the linguistic sense).

There has always been interaction and interactivity in the news media-coverage community worlds: visible are the letters-to-the-editor which get printed, and internally are the complaints, telephone queries, story tips, and canceled subscriptions and advertising which are responded to. The Web has made journalistic "interactivity" like letters-to-the-editor writ large, as it were, as noted in Example 6.11:

Example 6.11

<u>Interactivity</u> isn't new of course. […] people have been writing to us here at Breakfast for years. It's just much easier now, with modern communication. So is

there any point in e-mailing, texting or calling us? You bet. And, yes, every little
helps.
        (David Kermode, "In the bag," August 4, 2006, www.bbc.org, emphasis added)

The editor in Example 6.11 tries to encourage participation, especially as "interactivity" is made "much easier now" with "modern communication," confirming
that the effort is worthwhile. In Example 6.12, however, he notes a downside to
"interactivity" but then dismisses it more or less on the grounds of "taste".

Example 6.12
Interactivity isn't to everyone's tastes of course. Some people tell me they turn off when
we read out viewer's e-mails.
    [...] a show like Breakfast has to be in tune with its audience to be a success. What
better way could there be of knowing whether or not you're connecting with the people
watching?   (*ibid.*)

He also uses the same metaphor – the news organization or its output being "in
tune with" its audience/community – as *The Fresno Bee*.
    As the benefits of online-instigated "interactivity" are so universally hyped to
news consumers by editors, it is somewhat refreshing to observe when a news
practitioner critiques it, as in Example 6.13.

Example 6.13
[...] it marks the end of a silly pretense about interactive media: We give you our e-mail
addresses and then, in theory, we have this nice chat. Forget about it. Not only is e-mail
too often a kind of epistolary spitball, but there's no way I can even read the 3,506
e-mails now backed up in my queue – seven more since I started writing this column.
        (Richard Cohen, *Washington Post*, May 9, 2006: A23, emphasis added)

Cohen's critique points out the reality versus the ideal – "in theory, we have
this nice chat" – noting that it is not necessarily possible to engage with emails
from readers which are "too often a kind of epistolary spitball" as well as which
arrive in overwhelming volume. The BBC journalist in the more encouraging
Examples 6.11 and 6.12 also acknowledges, in Example 6.14, the sheer numbers mentioned by Cohen:

Example 6.14
When I tell people what I do, there are a few questions I always face [...] 'And does
anyone really bother to e-mail, text or call you?' is also a regular question. The answer
to that one is yes, thousands. And do we pay any attention? Yes, we'd be mad not to.
        (David Kermode, "In the bag," August 4, 2006, www.bbc.co.uk, emphasis added)

Kermode nonetheless encourages listeners to respond, saying on behalf of the
news institution that they would "be mad not to" pay attention to "thousands" of
emails, texts, and phone calls. Cohen refers more personally – with specifics
(3,506 emails in his queue) and with exasperation – to the "silly pretense" of
interactivity. Both journalists, through positive and negative example, make

clear the interactional objective behind "interactivity," whether it succeeds or not. On a more abstract level, the pro and con professional opinions about interactivity might have something to do with the inherent nature of the news media-coverage community relationship, as discussed in section 6.4.

6.4   The pseudo-relationship between news media and community

I have already spoken of the *pseudo-dyad* to characterize the relationship of participants in the communicative news "conversation" between journalist and audience, between the news community and the community of coverage. I would like to take that further and situate the *pseudo-dyad* in what I refer to as a ***pseudo-relationship*** with the objective of observing where interaction resides in action, text, practice, and process, and at the same time affording an alternative to the prevailing one-to-many mass-communication model.

The *pseudo-relationship* follows from social theorist and historian Daniel Boorstin's seminal articulation in 1961 of the *pseudo-event*, which he characterized as a "synthetic," managed, or constructed happening, as opposed to a spontaneous event like a train wreck or earthquake. He used the evolution of the *pseudo-event* to clarify how technological, historical, and communicative-norm changes in news reporting can be addressed to understand aspects of the news reporting and publication process and its consequent impacts on social – and media – life.

Boorstin's *pseudo-event* concept, which essentially problematizes reporting processes, has long been viewed as a key way to look at *what* reporters have been reporting on and how to examine the process and their coverage choices critically. In Boorstin's eyes, a *pseudo-event* is not naturally occurring news, but something that is planned, designed, organized, and managed with a news coverage outcome in mind. Press conferences and interviews, for example, fall under the aegis of a *pseudo-event*. Boorstin at the time was responding in part to a change in coverage circumstances and social expectation, to what in more recent times has become known as "info-tainment," the blending of information and entertainment, and "spin." (Spin, I would propose, may be considered a maturation or rhetorical offshoot of the pseudo-event process and what Orwell in 1949's *Nineteen Eighty-Four* referred to as "Newspeak.") More recently, former *Washington Post* Watergate reporter Carl Bernstein echoed Boorstin's concerns when speaking at a school in Greenwich, Connecticut. He was quoted in a November 2, 2007, Associated Press story: "The ideal of providing the best available version of the truth is being affected by the dominance of a journalistic culture that has less and less to do with reality and context."

6.4.1   The pseudo-event (Boorstin) and the pseudo-relationship (Cotter)

A **pseudo-event** is an event that is "created to be reported" (Boorstin 1987 [1961]: 42). It has the following features:

1. It is planned, not spontaneous.
2. It is scheduled for the "convenience of the reporting or reproducing media."
3. Its relation to reality is ambiguous.
4. It augurs reality: it becomes what it reports.

In other words, the pseudo-event is not spontaneously occurring, but "comes about because someone has planned ... it" (Boorstin 1987[1961]: 11). As it is "created to be reported," it is scheduled for the convenience of media deadlines. Boorstin argues that it is predicated on an ambiguity in meaning, situating what someone has said against what might have happened, in the process gathering audience interest. As a public relations or persuasion tool, its realities can become "self-fulfilling" (*ibid.*). It becomes real by virtue of its dissemination, evoking the aphorism of "where there's smoke there's fire."

The *pseudo-relationship* shares integral principles or features with Boorstin's pseudo-event. It is an evolving relationship, as in a family or even a workplace, but one that comes from a particular set of circumstances. It is planned or constructed in the sense that it derives from the necessities of news production, and equally, the objectives of those who rely on the media coverage. The interactions are constrained by the fact that the relationship is necessary for the media, or the newsmaker, to operate or to even exist. Irrespective of the putative power differential within the news-community relationship, it lacks "reality" in the one-to-one, interpersonal, real-time interactional sense; the relationship is ambiguous. The relationships become "real" because people talk of them as real, act according to their realities, and respond to consequences for the actions of the participants.

As an "interactional event" or process, the *pseudo-relationship* has the following features (that derive from the pseudo-event hypothesis):

1. It is *situational* and *contiguous* (to the meanings of place, time, salience of identity, embedded social contexts).
2. Relations to "real *time*" vary. Unlike the pseudo-event, where the question becomes, "Is it real?," the operative question in the pseudo-relationship is, with respect to temporality, "Is it relevant?"
3. The relation to a prototypical relationship (face-to-face, not channeled through media) is *partial*.

In addition, beyond the Boorstin framework, the pseudo-relationship has a role in the **news-practice-audience dynamic**. Thus I propose that it also contains these features:

4. It is both an explicit and implicit *factor in news decisions*.

5. It is *emergent*. It depends on prior discourse, shared sociocultural meaning, and co-constructed interaction.
6. It is *constructed* through an interweaving of language, cultural norms, and medium-specific routines.
7. The *recipient is implied* (i.e., implicated in all editorial actions and decisions)

The *pseudo-relationship* can be viewed more precisely along sociolinguistic lines, which can specify the components that create its *situational* and *partial* nature. The simulated aspect of the relationship is evident in discourse elements such as **reported speech** (which in the case of the news story genre can also be considered "constructed dialogue," cf. Tannen 1989), **narrative reshaping** (motivated by profession-specific text norms and the implied recipient, cf. chapter 7), **stylistic accommodation** (cf. Bell 2001; Gonzalez 1991), and an **asynchrony of time** – the interactions and their framing of them within the news narrative do not necessarily occur in real time nor are they reported in the order experienced (Bell 1991; Schudson 1986). Additionally, there is the backgrounded **power asymmetry** inherent in the news media-coverage community relationship, bolstered and sustained by the proximity of media to "axes/access of power" (access to information and to individuals in power), and the rules of production that in the US relate to the First Amendment.

6.4.2   The pseudo-dyad and news language

Interlinked with the simulated or pseudo aspects of the news–community relationship are several attributes in common with participant relationships comprising the "normal" or "real life" dyad:

- Communication is based on relevance (cf. Grice 1975; Sperber and Wilson 1985).
- Interlocutor considerations (taking the audience into account) are part of the exchange.
- Talk is a basis (e.g., interviews, reported speech are fundamental to news practice and story production).
- The necessity of renewal (e.g., quotes, "freshness," even news itself) motivates and furthers interactions and relationships.
- Embedded phatic elements (from informal language to story relevance to "fresh talk" to calls for "interactivity" noted in Examples 6.11 and 6.14 above) speak to a role that goes beyond information delivery.

The "pseudo-dyad" itself, based as it is on the reporter–audience relationship (which influences reporting and editing decisions that have outcomes in text), nonetheless lacks the possibility of immediate feedback between interlocutors, as one finds in a "normal" dyad. Despite the Web, it lacks what Robin Lakoff (1982) terms "visibility." Yet both interactional objectives and technology-modality limitations motivate the particular uses of language in journalistic texts to satisfy the unique requirements of the "pseudo-dyadic" genre as well as to maintain the news–community relationship. For example, the insertion of discourse devices generally attributed to casual speech is one strategy to facilitate the pseudo-dyadic relationship. Thus we find spoken-mode devices – beginning an utterance with a connective, or using coordination rather than subordination to structure the utterance string – in print, or repetition or prosodic emphasis in broadcast (cf. Cotter 2003). These devices structure the text as well, facilitating reception of the message as much as a medium lacking "visibility" or immediate feedback can allow. Beaman (1984: 61), for instance, notes the functionally heavy role of *and* in spoken narrative, in which it is used in part "as an introducer of clauses, and as an indicator of the sequential ordering of events in a narrative" – much as it is likewise used in newspaper texts (see examples in Chapter 9).

6.5   Conclusion: identifying interaction in the journalistic context

As a researcher, there are different ways to focus on the issue and question of the interaction-based nature of journalism that range from the theoretical to the functional, and involve an awareness of newsroom contexts, reporting and newswriting practice norms, journalistic identity, local community relationships, and news-story outcomes. I have attempted to touch on them in this chapter and argue on behalf of an analytical orientation to the role of interaction in the journalism enterprise.

There are benefits to this approach. On the *theoretical* level, an interactional focus challenges traditional one-to-many mass communication models, affording the potential for more nuanced insights into society's primary infrastructures of communication and information transmission, particularly in the "interactive" Internet Age. On the *discourse* level, we can evaluate the evidence or presence of an interactional dynamic in news talk and text to better understand its role and to understand what is patterned and rule-governed about news language. On the *practice* level, we can identify the explicit *functions* of "interaction" within both the newsroom and the community and the communicative *contexts* in which it evolves.

I have introduced the concept of *reciprocal transmission* to characterize the dynamic flow of interaction and obligation between the people who report and the people who are reported on, among the reporters, editors, photographers, sources, local community, and news profession. Interaction in the news context derives from social, relational, and textual actions that circumscribe news practice, and relationships derive from the evolving community-based activities and exchanges between and amongst participants that reflect and reinforce social organization. From the journalistic perspective, alignments and identities are expressed through language, decisions about the relation of news to the community, and community outreach activities. The supremacy of the local, relevance of the news to the coverage community, and attention to audience guide reporting, editing, and presentation decisions. The Web makes this interactive relationship, which has been fundamental to Anglo-American journalism for centuries and understood within the profession, more transparent.

As with other ongoing interactional processes between the news media and the local community, the news-and-community relationship shares features with the prototypical one-to-one or locally situated kind – even those relationships that entail power asymmetries. But at the same time it operates differently, hence my development of the notion of the *pseudo-dyad*, and the *pseudo-relationship* (building on Boorstin's notion of the pseudo-event), one that is partial, constructed, and contingent. What is distinctive about the news community's communicative goals is both familiar and unfamiliar, constrained by the objectives of the news profession. Procuring live or fresh quotes, not working alone within the newsroom's physical space and boundaries, and attention to audience by individual reporters and editorial groups all relate to the addressee-oriented goals in newswriting that are particular to the news media–coverage community relationship. Our main objective as researchers in understanding the news–practice–audience dynamic is to better understand the relation of news to the community in which it transpires and is reported on. This relationship is behind what gets reported on and what becomes the news story. Chapter 7 will detail what happens next.

Part III

Constructing the story: texts and contexts

7   Story design and the dictates of the "lead"

KEY POINTS

- Well-formed news stories follow strict guidelines, but everything follows from the lead. Its setup dictates the order and focus of the rest of the elements of the story.
- The lead is of paramount importance in the construction of the news story. A "good lead" is evaluated for its craft value as well as for its putative purpose of getting the attention of readers.
- The deceptive simplicity of a news story, given its underlying complexity and story-formation rules, means the reporter who can produce them has mastered the requisite verbal and interactional skills of the news community and can be deemed communicatively competent – or "a good reporter."

In a news story, unlike a joke, the "punchline" comes first. The structure of news stories follows a particular order, influenced by what reporters identify as the most important or newsworthy element. This element is emphasized in a variety of ways in the "lead," or first paragraph or beginning of a story, from the strategic use of passive voice in print to vocal emphasis in radio to the use of visuals in television. More than any other textual demand, writing a good lead is the most advanced of skills, generally acquired last by learners who have already mastered other aspects of good story design: organization, placement of attribution and quotation, and insertion of background and context. News stories have never traditionally been held as exemplars of prestige writing, and are not often described in terms of their textual complexity. But like a medieval musical motet, with its polyphonic lines and rigid harmonic prohibitions, seemingly simple rules of craft are manifested in ways that are structurally complex.

In Chapter 7, I focus on news story design and its most important component, the lead. Story design involves the interrelation of both text and content components, by which I mean that news stories are distinguished by the structures of the text and by the kinds of information (or news dimension) that are borne by the text. Both components are fairly tightly circumscribed by journalistic rules of practice, which I will detail. Thus, I look at *story design* and what components are required; focus at length on the lead and its importance in text and content; and examine the *principles of newswriting* that support practice (points that come up again in Chapter 8). From the linguistic perspective, we can see that the elements of story design work in tandem with other factors and constraints generated within the journalism profession as the filters, or *discourse parameters*, that help to produce "news language."

7.1   Principles of newswriting

The principles of newswriting are no mystery to reporters who have been instructed in their elements from day one at J-School and are available and codified, in some semblance of similarity, in all newswriting textbooks. Behind news stories are a fairly predictable set of rules that affect both **text** and **practice**. These rules manifest themselves in story-internal newswriting strictures as well as in genres and subgenres (the weather story, the day-after-Thanksgiving shopping story, the bank holiday travel story, and so on), and in modes of practice relevant to reporting and editing (whom to call, dealing with deadlines, and what to do when). On the language level, reporters are taught to write in simple, short, "straightforward" sentences and short paragraphs; to use "strong" or active verbs; to eliminate the passive voice; to avoid clichés; etc. The fact is that closer linguistic examination of news stories reveals more complex sentence structures, what amounts to a restricted lexicon in all grammatical categories, frequent appearance of passive voice constructions, and a prodigious display of clichés suggesting that other communicative and journalistic issues work alongside codified newswriting rules (cf. Cotter 1999b).

All reporters are essentially taught to strive to write and report with two kinds of goals in mind: goals that relate to the content of the news story and goals that relate to the shape of the text or story design, goals that are intrinsically interconnected. From the journalistic perspective, once the *newsworthy* element has been decided (cf. Chapter 4), reporting-driven "content goals" include *complete information, balance of sources*, and *accuracy*. Newswriting "text goals" involve all the elements of story *organization*, as well as a good *lead*, appropriate *sentence structure, attribution* and *quotes*, and *Associated Press style*[1] (which will be discussed in later sections of this chapter).

Separate but related to these story objectives are the rhetorical goals of discursive *brevity*, lexical *precision*, factual *accuracy*, and content *balance*. Rhetorical goals in newswriting are familiar to any journalist, as learning about these objectives is part of training (although they are not referred to as

---

[1]   In the UK, *The Times, Guardian*, and *The Economist*, for example, have style guides that fulfill the same objectives as *The Associated Press Stylebook*.

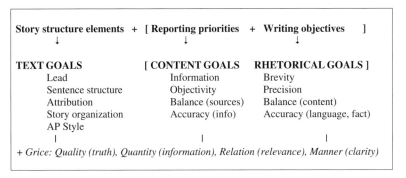

Story structure elements + [Reporting priorities + Writing objectives]
　　　　↓　　　　　　　　　　↓　　　　　　　　↓

TEXT GOALS　　　　**[CONTENT GOALS**　　**RHETORICAL GOALS]**
　Lead　　　　　　　　　　Information　　　　　Brevity
　Sentence structure　　　　Objectivity　　　　　Precision
　Attribution　　　　　　　Balance (sources)　　Balance (content)
　Story organization　　　　Accuracy (info)　　　Accuracy (language, fact)
　AP Style
　　|　　　　　　　　　　　|　　　　　　　　　|
+ Grice: Quality (truth), Quantity (information), Relation (relevance), Manner (clarity)

Figure 7.1 Composite story goals

"rhetorical goals" as such). The reporter learns, via different channels within day-to-day practice, to achieve them and is told: eliminate unnecessary words, find the most precise word to say what you mean, double-check facts because accuracy means *credibility* (cf. Chapter 2), and strive for a *balance* of sides or positions when covering a story, to "get both sides" (cf. Chapter 6). Indeed, the most perspicuous newswriting short-course would revolve around philosopher H. Paul Grice's conversational maxims of Quantity, Quality, Manner, and Relation: Say only what needs to be said for the situation, be truthful, be brief and clear, be relevant (Grice 1975). This "Gricean connection" is a factor that I will mention but not belabor at this point.

There is not necessarily a simple or one-to-one correlation between rhetorical (or text or content) goals and their manifestation in the news story. *Brevity*, for instance, relates to *words* and *form*: minimize word use; keep sentences and paragraphs short. *Precision* relates to *words* and *language*: choose the word that best conveys the meaning; follow prescriptive rules of usage (cf. Chapter 9). *Accuracy* relates to *facts* and *content*: facts, and language use, must be correct; information must be vetted. *Balance* relates to *content* and *participants*: both or more sides of a story must be included to achieve "balance"; sources must reflect more than one viewpoint. *Balance* and *accuracy* are profession-specific terms that are used explicitly, frequently, and every day by journalism educators and news practitioners to describe craft-based reporting objectives. *Precision* and *brevity* are more general terms that meta-discursively summarize two components within the news practitioner's underlying writing objectives.

The news story can be seen as the outcome of writing and reporting actions, as illustrated in Figure 7.1. Figure 7.1 summarizes the necessary elements of *story structure*, which involve *text goals*; *reporting* priorities that revolve around *content goals*; and *writing* objectives that achieve *rhetorical goals* necessary to produce a well-formed news story. Collectively, they work to build the writing and reporting *conventions* behind the writing and reporting of news stories, which a news practitioner fluent in his or her craft follows. The figure also illustrates how the "Gricean connection" relates to story composition.

7.1.1   Performance factors

Most journalism educators break down the elements of the story, in similar fashion to Figure 7.1, as a way to teach students how to write news stories and then to evaluate the stories that they write. Initially, they start by evaluating students or novices on how well they can write a news story, on how well they can achieve "text goals" involving the lead or first paragraph, sentence structure, story organization, attribution, and appropriate style (cf. Figure 7.1), the elements that structure the story. Beyond meeting "text goals" necessary to produce a well-wrought news story, there are additional performance factors. The story structure elements, with the addition of a nuanced understanding of reporting and writing conventions, can produce "flow," or a sense of effortless-ness in the way the story "reads." The notion of "flow" in essence is a marker of communicative competence, an indication that socialization and integration of appropriate craft skill valued within the community of practice has occurred. "Flow" is not a journalistic concept, as such, nor specified as a shared textual value in journalism education (although see the reference to "momentum" in Mencher 2006: 159). But it is one way of telling students (as I did in the journalism classroom before becoming aware of its position as a theoretical concept in anthropology, cf. Beeman 2007) that following the newswriting precepts and strictures alone – ticking the boxes – does not necessarily make what the community would consider to be a good story.

Cognitively, too, learning the various reporting and writing conventions helps the production of news stories. It is easier to write a story that follows, to some degree, a pre-existing form. It allows rapid reproduction, rapid turn-around, the time-sensitive knocking-out of stories. A reporter is not inventing the form every time he or she has a story to write; innovation in that regard is not encouraged. Readers and listeners learn the conventions, as well, but from the recipient end. From this, they construct a plausible and even logical "story" or account about what goes into news practice based on the output they read, which does not necessarily match the thought and action processes that the reporter has followed in writing the news story. As they do not actually know what has been involved to produce the story, often their assessments or surmises come across to journalists in the same way that folk etymologies come across to linguists: a perspective not based on empirical knowledge. Nonetheless, the conventionalized patterns that are observable in news discourse across time help to maintain what can be identified as a news story for both readers and reporters. (See Appendix 1.)

7.2   Story design

The news story is composed according to a *hierarchy of importance*: the most important detail or element comes first; the others follow in descending order. This creates the "inverted pyramid" shape of the conventional story. Other key composition rules that fulfill both content and design objectives involve providing *attribution* of information (a rule that varies cross-culturally), sufficient *context* to understand why the story is important as news, and enough *background* information to understand the story's relevance and news position over time.

7.2.1   Goals of design – attention and apprehension

As noted in earlier chapters (particularly Chapters 2 and 6), print and broadcast stories are designed as they are for reasons that are very much audience-driven and relate to two coexisting and interdependent goals for the recipient: getting the reader's and listener's **attention**, and quick **apprehension** by the reader or listener. "Grabbing" the reader is the province of content-related decisions, particularly manifested in the lead; and quick apprehension of the story is the functional charge of the text or story design. These two concurrent objectives run through many different types of stories and across media modalities. The news profession invariably observes that there are many claims on readers' or listeners' time, and it is incumbent on reporters to make it easy to get the news. Example 7.1 from a textbook reinforces this point:

Example 7.1
Many [readers] have time to read only a few paragraphs of most stories. If a reporter were to write an account of a car accident by starting when the driver left the house, many readers would never read far enough to find out that the driver was killed. Instead, such a story starts with its climax:
> Two people died Thursday when a backhoe fell off a truck's flatbed and sliced the top off an oncoming vehicle near Fairchild Air Force Base.
>
> (Brooks *et al.* 1999: 123, emphasis added)

In Example 7.1, beginning the story "with its climax" – note the focus on the lead – will catch and sustain the readers' attention. Similarly, radio stories are constructed to "allow the listener to stay with the reporter through the entire report. The writing can't be so brilliant that the listener stops listening in mid-report to mull over a cleverly crafted bit of writing" (Dvorkin 2001).

The need to attract and hold the reader's attention are communicative goals that are supported by text-dependent story design factors as *information-driven* as the lead paragraph and as *comprehension-friendly* as the length of journalistic utterance (as in size of *sentence, paragraph*, or *story*). On the radio, this awareness of gaining and holding attention is manifested both structurally and functionally through the use of "accents of interest" (cf. Bolinger 1982, 1989) within news-typical intonational contours (cf. Cotter 1993; Van de Velde 1996), as well as consciously "writing for the ear" (cf. Newsom and Wollert 1988: 54).

7.2.2   The inverted pyramid

The *hierarchy of importance* that governs the ordering of information elements in a news story has a very iconic manifestation. Stories are organized in the shape of the *inverted pyramid* in which the most important elements are placed highest, with news elements of lesser importance following. The "top" of the news is the most important in both print and broadcast modalities and includes the first paragraph or "lead" (or "intro" in British journalism), the first page of the newspaper or the first link to a Web page, and the very first story presented in real or recorded time in a broadcast medium.

The inverted pyramid also reminds reporters of the pre-eminence of *news values*, and the need to sort or prioritize them accordingly within a hierarchical relationship. What drives these information hierarchy decisions is "newsworthiness" (see Chapter 4). As always, the notion of what *counts* as news influences the set of structural and informational elements that comprise what becomes characteristic of news (cf. Cotter 1999b).

The inverted pyramid shape, which functions iconically to represent the hierarchy of elements, is the primary and prototypical point of reference. For all news stories it governs the interlocking relationships of form and content. It allows for spatial organization on the page: stories that run too long are cut from the bottom (in pre-pagination days, they were literally cut from the bottom by X-ACTO-knife-wielding editors and production staff). It focuses attention for the reader and the reporter, bringing the most attention-grabbing element to the fore. It is a story design concept that is taught first in newswriting classes to illustrate how the content and structure of a news story have limited discursive manifestations.

7.2.3   Background and context

The insertion of explanatory material – information that clarifies the newsworthiness of the story – is also integral to story design (from the linguistic perspective it can be viewed as an explicit element of news discourse). Journalists know that "background and context" convey understanding of the news focus and know how to employ it to produce a well-formed story. Journalistically, in the day-to-day story-production sense, "background" is differentiated from "context": *background* can be deleted; *context* is considered essential. *Background* is generally inserted at the bottom of the story or below where a story could be reasonably cut without losing the newsworthiness aspect, whereas *context* is information that allows apprehension of the story and is thus filtered or sprinkled in throughout. Example 7.2 illustrates this. It is taken from a twelve-paragraph Associated Press story about the US university named the no. 1 "party school" for 2007 by a national college test preparation company.

Example 7.2
[*Paragraph 2 – context*]:
  The school has made the list seven times in the past 15 years, despite efforts to curb underage drinking and rowdy behavior.
[*Paragraph 12 – background*]:
  The Princeton Review, which is not affiliated with Princeton University, is a New York company known for test preparation courses, educational services and books. It published its first survey findings in August 1992.
                                        (Vicki Smith, Associated Press, August 21, 2007)

In paragraph 2, the information provides context with which to evaluate the news; in paragraph 12, which could be deleted in the interest of space, background is given about the company. Other contextual information in later paragraphs mentions the university's position the previous year and its prior No. 1 "party school" status in 1997.

Physically and conceptually *background* is also differentiated from *context*. As background material is (typically) inserted at the bottom of a story, its placement follows the provisions of the inverted pyramid. In those terms, it makes it expendable, and by extension, the least important. Conceptually, *context* provides information that is necessary to understand the story, particularly with respect to its newsworthiness. It is considered *background* when it is "not essential to [the story's] meaning" (Lanson and Stephens 1994: 161). Determining what is "essential" is another area where journalistic interpretation is called upon, and where the multiple newsroom producers of the story work together. An editor will query and provide backup for a reporter's interpretation, ensuring the story reads clearly and the primary news element is in focus. ("Boilerplate" is a type of background which is repetitive, unattributed, and a discursive element particular to ongoing stories, as we will see in Chapter 8. It is in evidence in the second paragraph of Example 7.3.)

Differences in contextual and background detail are evident in Examples 7.3 and 7.4, taken from two stories about the same event. In Example 7.3 the *San Francisco Chronicle* reporter doing a story about wildfires in Southern California refers to the Santa Ana winds, which Southern Californians in particular are familiar with because of their annual role in major regional wildfires. His story, a wrap-up of the fire thus far, with a "local angle" reporting that San Francisco Bay Area firefighters were heading south to help, provides more background detail (highlighted in *italics*) compared to the Associated Press reporter's version in Example 7.4, which provides more context.

Example 7.3
The conflagrations, which one firefighter likened to Armageddon, are being fed by the desert gales <u>known as</u> **Santa Ana winds**. *Almost all of the great Southern California fires of the past have been fed by* **Santa Anas**, *which typically blow in early spring and fall.*

The result of air pressure buildup in the Great Basin between the Sierra Nevada and Rocky Mountains, **Santa Ana winds** *sweep from the mountains through the lowlands toward the sea.*

(Peter Fimrite, *San Francisco Chronicle*, October 23, 2007: A1, emphasis and italics added)

Example 7.4
Unless the <u>shrieking</u> **Santa Ana winds** subside, and that's not expected for at least another day, fire crews say they can do little more than try to wait it out and react – tamping out spot fires and chasing ribbons of airborne embers to keep new fires from flaring.
[…]
The <u>ferocity</u> of the **Santa Ana winds** in 2003 forced crews to discard their traditional strategy and focus on keeping up with the fire and putting out spot blazes that threatened homes.

(Gillian Flaccus, Associated Press, in San Diego, linked on www.sfgate.com, October 24, 2007, emphasis added)

Fimrite's story provided meteorological detail as well as didactic indicators ("known as" and "which typically") that suggested that not all his Northern California readers would know what the Santa Ana winds were or did (given the cultural, if not actual, boundary between Northern and Southern California and the Northern California geographical positioning and readership of the *Chron*). Flaccus's story, reported on the scene and contributed to by eleven other AP writers in five Southern California locations for nationwide distribution, did not spend time talking about Santa Ana winds generically, but in referential and descriptive terms ("shrieking," "ferocity") to situate the reader in relation to the impacts of the fire itself. Her second paragraph in Example 7.4 illustrates *context* with which to understand the current situation; Fimrite's illustrates *background*, which is expendable.

7.2.4   Types of news stories

News stories[2] as a rule follow similar story-design precepts (as noted in Figure 7.1) no matter their subject matter or genre type. That said, news stories

---

[2] I am not including editorials or opinion columns as a "type of news story." Columns provide opportunities for alterations in register and authorial voice, essentially supporting a level of individuality in newswriting style that tends to be avoided in "typical" news stories. Columnists often have a regular coterie of readers with whom they interact personally in print, which also alters the discourse parameters.

Basic types	→
	Police and fire (including crime, accident, disaster)
	Courts
	Meetings
	Speeches/ Press conferences
	Obits
Sections	→
	Sports
	Business
	Community/Local
	Lifestyle [Food, Automobile, Home, etc.]
Beats	→
	Schools/Education
	Government [City/County/Fed]
	Police
	Business
	Sports
	Religion/Food/Medicine/etc.
Typical genre forms	→
	Advance
	Folo
	Brief
	Rewrite
	Breaking news
	Enterprise
	Investigative
	"Brite"
	Sidebar
Across all sections and types	→
	News
	Features
Restricted to page; named	→
	Opinion
	Columns

Figure 7.2 Story types and genre forms

come in different "prototypes" based on topical focus, subject matter, or communicative goal. The story types are familiar to both readers and reporters, although reporters are familiar with them from the process and production end – from reporting and writing them – and readers via the final outcome in print or on the air. (See Figure 7.2 for a representative list of story types.)

The **basic types** of stories include Police and Fire (including crime, accident, disaster), Courts, Meetings, Speeches and Press conferences, and Obits. These story types are explicitly taught to student reporters and form the basis of textbooks, as they are the basic news stories that reporters at any level are expected to be able to cover. Each type has slightly different conventions of reporting and writing (*crime stories* requiring more "facts" and attributed detail and *speech stories* requiring "good quotes" and witnessed detail, for example).

Types of stories also vary according to the separate **sections** of the paper, such as Sports, Business, and Lifestyle, which require more specialized reporting. Stories on Page One or on news, international, and local or community pages or sections also vary in terms of type. In these cases, stories are written (or chosen from wire transmissions) specifically for the overarching content-orientation of these pages or sections. These pages have a stable physical position in the newspaper where they can always be found. A story about an upcoming community event like a school concert, for example, would not be placed in the international news section or pages. Types of stories also follow from **beats** which reporters cover, such as Schools/Education, Government (city, county, regional, federal), Police, Business, Sports, Religion, Food, Arts, etc. These stories derive from reporter activity primarily (even in the rewriting of press releases); where they end up in the paper is dependent on their news relevance.

Within different story types and sections of the paper there are identifiable **genre forms**. An *advance* is a story written in advance of an event. A *folo* (follow) is a story written about the event after the event. A *brief* is a story that deserves mention but is not so newsworthy as to require great length. A *rewrite* is a reformulation of a press release (or a reworking of a story someone else has provided). *Breaking news* is news that is happening in real time, that is "breaking" and underway. *Enterprise* stories are ones that require more in-depth reporting, take more time to compile, help to provide insights (into an issue, place, institution, social or political dynamic, etc.), and involve the original, lateral thinking and pavement-pounding of the reporter. They are stories that would not have occurred without reporter initiative. *Investigative stories* are ones that deliberately investigate the power realms of society – governments, institutions, individuals, legal and illegal enterprises, etc. A *brite* is a story that is not necessarily serious news, but whose intrinsic merit will (the reporter hopes) create a smile or doubletake. A *sidebar* is a story that accompanies a main story and sheds additional light on it, often explaining something of relevance that helps to contribute to the main story. (See appendix 1 for representative story types.)

News and *features* are genre forms that exist across all newspaper sections and story types. *Opinion* pieces, commentaries, and editorials[3] are usually restricted to the Editorial (Op-Ed) page and named as such. When they appear elsewhere in

---

[3] "Editorials" are "leaders" in the UK.

the paper, they must be named as "opinion" or "analysis." This is a consequence of the *objectivity* value that constrains media discourse (cf. Chapters 2 and 3).

The emphasis in *news stories* is "just the facts." The emphasis in *feature stories* is a focus on elements of broader interest, e.g., human-interest, some quirky dimension of the story, or fronting a small point amongst many to differentiate the story from hundreds of others on the topic, as well as the discursive creativity of the reporter, which is required more often in feature stories. *News-feature stories* embody aspects of both prototypical genre forms, utilizing the *timeliness* of a news event in addition to its impacts on people or community, e.g., stories on people housed in the sports stadium during Hurricane Katrina, or the emotional fallout from school shootings. *Feature stories* alone often lack the *timeliness* dimension in the direct sense, but are presented for other reasons that are fundamentally newsworthy or in the news-you-can-use realm: for example, an interesting person in the community (e.g., someone who has an urban garden or unusual hobby), an ongoing or one-off activity (e.g., a family reunion), business and finance features, and relevance to sections like Food, Recreation, Automobile, Home and Garden, or beats like Education, Police and Fire, Arts, etc.

All news and feature story types and genre forms share similarities in that reporting and newswriting rules are followed throughout, even in opinion pieces, columns, and editorials. That means the lead is important, attribution and length conventions are followed, and reporting has occurred. Figure 7.2 summarizes how reporters and editors often delineate story types and genre forms (it is a representative, not an exhaustive, list).

7.2.5   Attribution

Attribution of information – whether it be attributing a direct or indirect quotation from an interviewed source, or information from a press release, another news organization's story, a website, a report, or other resource – is a key value of US news practice. It is a practice that is particular to US journalism and not necessarily similar in other cultures, English-speaking or not (for instance, see Satoh 2001 for Japanese).

The salient dimensions through which attribution operates can be characterized on the journalistic (or news-culture-based) and the text (or news-story-based) levels.

These levels operate together and have relevance in terms of both the news practitioner's reporting, writing, and editing actions and the news story's final shape (cf. Figure 7.3). The journalistic requirements that reporters must follow to attribute information and quotations from sources have particular *rationales and purposes* endemic to the news community at the same time fulfilling the rules of story design.

Design requirements	Production requirements	Support role
→	→	
• Placement	Within story (physically)	text form
	Support news angle (conceptually)	content
• Occurrence	Sufficient number of sources	form/content
• Quote type variations	Direct, indirect, paraphrase	text form
• Quote length	"Brief"; generally 1 paragraph	text form
• Quote type expectation	Direct, fresh, "good"	content

Figure 7.3 Attribution design

The journalistic rationales behind the conscious and craft-centered use of attribution are based on the discursive "work" it does to support foundational ideals in newswriting, such as *objectivity.* Quoting someone or using another's words allows a distant or "distal" positioning of the reporter with respect to the content and the sources of information. (Responsible reporters are explicitly taught to verify speakers' claims before publishing them, to not take them at face value.) The discursive purpose of attributing a source from the news community's point of view is to render the reporter's voice neutral, to position the reporter as a conduit, or an objective party that is not taking a stance about the topic being covered but is merely conveying a range of views. Thus attribution and quotes themselves, whether direct or indirect, are important to front the speaker or source and his or her stance and to take the opinion of the reporter out of the equation. (Whether this is true or not is irrelevant at this point. It is also important to point out the following: my journalistically situated focus on "reported speech" is different from but does not contradict "constructed dialogue" research (e.g., Tannen 1989 and others); stance, footing, and positioning (cf. Goffman 1959, 1981; and Davies and Harré 1990) are other relevant elements to consider further; and there are additional objectivity questions to pursue and understand through cross-disciplinary academic research in journalism, sociology, media studies, and linguistics.)

At the same time, attribution can also be seen as a mechanism for *story design,* as the placement of quotes and the attribution of information influence the shape of the news narrative. As indicated in Figure 7.3, the requirements of attribution involve several components related to both text design (i.e., story form) and journalistic content expectations (i.e., relevant to the news or information aspect), demarcating some of the news community's practice-based production expectations for what counts as good reporting and writing. Concurrently, attribution has a "support role" in achieving well-formed text and content goals in news reporting and writing.

Placement of quotes within the story is conventionalized to some degree – for example, if a quote or attributed information does not appear within the first several paragraphs, the copy will be rearranged to accommodate this

Table 7.1 *Attribution interrelationships*

Levels of salience	Journalistic outcomes
PRACTICE level	
● Journalistic rationales	● Journalistic rationales have <u>practice</u> entailments
● Discursive purpose	● Discursive purpose follows journalistic <u>ideals</u>, communicative <u>norms</u>
TEXT level	
● Story design	● Story design influences shape/ discourse <u>structure</u>
● (Textual) requirements	● (Textual) requirements necessary to <u>well-formed</u> story

expectation. (For instance, Examples 7.6 and 7.19 in this chapter have first quotes appearing in paragraphs 3 and 2, respectively.) Equally importantly, well-written stories do not generally begin with quotes, except in rare circumstances when the source's words are newsworthy in and of themselves or when they encapsulate the news angle better than anything a reporter could write (see numerous textbooks, such as Newsom and Wollert 1988, for warnings about starting stories with quotes, often a beginner's mistake). Throughout the story, the quotes are positioned to ***support the news angle*** and to support the lead; and a *sufficient number* of attributed quotes or sources is expected (depending on the story type this will be a minimum of two or three sources). *Attribution design* requirements also have a support role with respect to content and text form.

Another area which is attribution-related and thus reflects the incorporation of news cultural knowledge are the explicit situations when one does *not* need attribution. When a fact is "common knowledge" one does not need to attribute the source, as when gathering general or public information from a phonebook or reference book or public record, unless one is specifically quoting from it. Attribution is yet another discourse-level skill that reporters learn. Learning how to differentiate what kinds of information require attribution and what do not is another level of awareness that indicates competence within the profession.

To summarize (see also Table 7.1):

● There are *journalistic rationales* behind attribution, which have **practice entailments** in reporting, newswriting, and editing activities.
● There is a *discursive purpose*, to attribute information to a source, which follows and supports **journalistic ideals** and **communicative norms**.
● Attribution is an integral part of *story design*, and thus influences the shape or **discourse structure** of the news story.
● There are particular attribution *requirements* within the story that must be followed to produce a **well-formed news story** in terms of text and content.

Practice and **text** are the primary levels of profession-specific salience through which attribution operates, which have follow-on journalistic outcomes. Table 7.1 provides a schema of these interrelationships.

7.2.6   Quotes

Beyond attribution, **quotes** as discourse entities themselves are important to understand within the journalistic frame.[4] We can examine them with respect to journalistic ideals and communicative norms; note how they help to construct the well-formed news story; and see how they figure into *story design*. Quotes are information dependent – they are either a **summary** or **illustrative**. They summarize the news at hand, as in Example 7.5, or they illustrate some dimension of it, as in example Example 7.6.

Example 7.5
"For safe food handling, temperature is key. Cold food should be stored under 35 or 40 degrees Fahrenheit and hot foot above 140 degrees. The range in-between is where bacteria grow," noted food-science professor Michael Johnson in a prepared statement.
(*HealthDay*, July 15, 2006)

Example 7.6
Sam LeBlanc tried to cushion the blow when he gave his wife, Karyn, the bad news. He told her to take a breath and think it over, because he knew that what he was telling her would hurt.
Her condominium isn't worth nearly as much as she thought.
"I was a little crushed," Karyn recalled.
(Kirstin Downey, *Washington Post*, November 4, 2006: F1)

In Example 7.5, the quote from a story in the "news-you-can-use" category about food safety during summer picnics summarizes information that the story is conveying (in attribution terms "in a prepared statement" indicates that the information likely came from a press release)[5]. In Example 7.6 the quote illustrates an individual's personal response to the actual, not hoped for, value of her home, developing the general point or newsworthiness angle of the story that falling house prices have consequence for individuals.

In American news practice, quotes *cannot be fabricated*. They must be actual words as recorded by the reporter (well-publicized incidents where they were fabricated or plagiarized by reporters at august places like *The Washington Post, USA Today*, and *The New York Times* are held up as object lessons within the industry). *Quotation marks go around utterances* that have been spoken. To the reporter, quotation marks signify an empirical, actual outcome – something someone has actually said that has been recorded or heard. Often *partial quotes* help fulfill the direct-quote-needed directive when the reporter's handwriting skills (in person) or typing skills (over the phone)

---

[4] See also Zelizer 1995.
[5] See Jacobs 1999 for a discussion of the role of the press release in shaping news discourse.

do not capture the entire utterance or when the quote in entirety is too unfocused or verbose. Even *paraphrases* must be attributed.

The *quoting verb*, because of its purported neutrality, with very few exceptions is "said" (and the somewhat lesser-used "says," found more often in feature stories or press releases). "Added" and "according to" are used stylistically (to help avoid over-repetition of "said" within a single paragraph). Any other verbs like "claimed," "insisted," "opined," "refuted," "declared," "stated," etc. are disfavored and suggest a deviation from the norm. When they are used in mainstream journalism in hard news stories they either indicate a lack of experience or a confident application of experience, or are used for stylistic or legitimate meaning-related reasons. In Example 7.5 above, the use of "noted" as a reporting verb leads me to hypothesize that the story comes from a press release; "said" cannot be used because the reporter did not hear it being said. In Example 7.6 the use of "recalled" evokes the narrative approach of the story's lead; in this case it is used for stylistic reasons befitting a feature or news-feature story.

Direct quotes are considered essential to a well-formed news story; they are needed at some point earlier rather than later in the typical story. Direct quotes from sources bring other voices to the fore. From the profession's perspective, they are avidly sought to add "color," freshness, and immediacy to news stories (Mencher 1997). *"Fresh" quotes* are sought when a reporter is using "canned" pre-packaged information from a press release or when he or she is following a story that other people are pursuing, to either update (enhancing the value of *newness*) or singularize (make particular or newsworthy) the "source voice" in that reporter's story. "It's not your story unless you [as reporter] provide a fresh quote" (Phil Murray, personal communication). A fresh quote will differentiate one reporter's story from another's as well as help to update the story, enhancing the news value of *recency*. A *"good quote"* helps to make a good story better.

"Good" quotes are value-added in terms of rhetorical craft and story design. Journalistically, one objective of reporting – when one is interviewing a source – is to get the "good quote." The examples in 7.7 can be considered "good quotes" from the story development point of view, either because they are vividly phrased (7.7a), witness- or scene-specific (7.7b), or illustrative and personal (7.7c).

Example 7.7

(a) *A source talking about ways to get children to eat more nutritious food:*

[…] adding bean paste to the tomato sauce on a pizza can be an incremental step toward better nutrition "without having the vegetables dance on the top," says David Ludwig, director of the Optimal Weight for Life program at Children's Hospital in Boston.
(Sally Squires, *Washington Post*, October 16, 2007: HE1, emphasis added)

(b) *A Colorado resident talking about the aftermath of a fatal tornado:*

"They're mostly hugging one another, asking, 'Is your house standing, is your family OK?'" said Betty Vipman, who manages JR's Country Store and Video.

(Colleen Slevin, Associated Press, March 30, 2007, emphasis added)

(c) *A classmate talking about the student who killed 32 people on the Virginia Tech campus:*

"We always joked we were just waiting for him to do something, waiting to hear about something he did," said another classmate, Stephanie Derry. "But when I got the call it was Cho who had done this, I started crying, bawling."

(Adam Geller, Associated Press, April 18, 2007, emphasis added)

As well as attending to the content-based requirements of attribution and quotes, as Examples 7(a–c) do, there are also the text-based or rhetorical requirements that demonstrate understanding of the craft of newswriting and understanding of the news story form. The *type* of quote that is attributed – direct quote, partial quote, indirect quote, or paraphrase – is deliberately *varied* (often for stylistic reasons), as is the placement of the attributory phrase (*X said* or *according to Z*). For example, "Smith said" (noun + verb order is preferred) is placed at the end or beginning of a direct or indirect quote; "according to Smith, who said" is used to conjoin two utterances. Or the attribution breaks up a long turn at talk as in Example 7.7(c). Quote *length* is also expected to be short – to accommodate to and achieve balance within the generally short story length overall. (This is why linguists and other academics are bemused when they are quoted so succinctly after a long interview: the information-sharing objectives of academics and journalists, on the propositional and textual levels, are somewhat at odds.)

Something as seemingly straightforward as a quote from a person is of course rife with both journalistic and linguistic issues, questions, and concerns. Quotes, given the importance placed on their authenticity, are not subject to the stylistic constraints that govern news stories. Yet quotes are not verbatim depositions or transcripts: reporters are taught to be selective in which elements of an utterance to use as a quote. This of course raises important linguistic questions for journalists which have socially meaningful implications: When does a reporter "clean up" the grammar of an interviewee? A linguist might also ask what elements of the spoken utterance – the word-searching, the fillers, the self-corrections, the colloquialism or non-standard grammatical form that comes with the territory of unplanned speech – can be eliminated in a "correct" quote that appears in print form? When is someone who is not a transcriber but a news reporter going over the line?[6] Mainstream news editors, as well as journalism educators, speak openly about the

---

[6] Or when do these actions perpetuate negative social and political attitudes (cf. Bucholtz 2000)?

inappropriateness of reporters replicating a speaker's "incorrect" usage or using "eye dialect" to suggest non-standard accent, grammar, or dialect – in large part because it is considered either patronizing or potentially puts the news source in a one-down position by marking the non-standard form in print. Either way, it has the potential to work against neutrality in the journalistic sense; in the linguistic sense, it is another reminder of the complex interrelationship between language and social value.

7.3   The lead

The purpose of the lead[7] is multifaceted. Its explicit discourse or interactional purpose is to attract the reader. Its textual purpose is to set up the story structurally – all composite story elements follow from the lead. More abstractly, it also conveys practice-based craft values and relies on the craft competence of its author, through both writing and reporting decisions and selections.

7.3.1   Importance and purpose of the lead

The lead is of paramount importance in the construction of the news story. While well-formed news stories follow strict guidelines throughout, everything follows from the lead. The lead encapsulates the story, highlighting or *fronting* what is most interesting, relevant, or new. The two most important tasks for a reporter are to convey the *importance of the story* instantaneously and to *provide all the information* possible within the time and space allotted. Not only does the most important information generally come first, but accompanying information must support its importance. Thus the lead's setup, and the information element selected, dictates the order and focus of the rest of the elements of the story. This outcome is the result of newsworthiness decisions: a key feature of leads is that *news values* are embedded in them (cf. Chapter 4).

Another key feature is that the lead relies on language – in all its presuppositional and stylistic manifestations – to accomplish this (as the examples in this section illustrate). The lead is the most important aspect of the story on several levels beyond literal language *per se*. On the discourse level, the focus, approach, and writing must all be integrated. From a journalistic perspective, the focus of the lead is either *reader-* or *story-centered* or both; the approach taken to execute it is *news-element-based* (reporterly); and the writing is *task-specific* – pragmatic in the functional, non-technical sense. From a linguist's perspective, the focus of the lead, whether reader- or story-centered, is a *discursive* and *interactional* enterprise; the approach which takes into account insider routines, objectives, and means is *practice-based*; and the writing is specialized or *genre-specific*.

---

[7] In the UK, it is known as an "intro."

A lead's primary functional goal is to "draw in the reader." This is done in two complementary ways: (1) through *language* – through rhetorical or craft skill; and (2) by *framing* the most reader-relevant element: what is interesting, relevant, or new. It is achieved through *attention* and *relevance* (cf. chapter 6). This functional goal distinguishes the news lead from other genre forms and from other writing tasks such as academic writing, for instance, in which articulation of the scholarly argument is paramount.

At the same time, composing a well-formed lead requires a high level of interactional, professional, and rhetorical skill, which is reliant on a reporter's knowledge of the community, the wider culture, and the profession. These skills reflect both the expectation within the "community of practice" and the sense of practitioner responsibility to the "community of coverage." Thinking about interlocutors (interviewees) or the community of coverage (readers and listeners) introduces the *interactional* dimension. Knowing what acts and decisions are appropriate or communicatively competent is the mark of *professional* acumen. And working within the bounds of space, time, and form – particularly in the constrained dimension of the lead – is the province of the *rhetorical*.

Leads are short, generally, and function as a mini-précis or abstract of the story. Each word counts – nothing is extraneous. The writing is very "tight" – the term that reporters themselves use to characterize the compactness of expression. Writing and reporting priorities both predominate. Writing priorities are clarity and appropriate length. Reporting priorities are fronting the right (newsworthy) element, and providing sufficient detail for conditions of space, time, and form.

In this way, a "good lead" is evaluated for its craft value as well as for its functional purpose of getting the attention of readers and highlighting the newsworthiness or relevance of the story. It is considered the most difficult part of the story to write, and thus writing a good lead means a reporter is a good craftsperson, a good journalist. On the textual level, it is the most difficult newswriting (as opposed to reporting) skill to learn, and thus it is usually the first newswriting component taught. Ultimately, a seasoned professional has no trouble "knocking out" an acceptable lead, so it is a skill that has conventions and expectations, and attributes that can be defined or described. The supremacy of the lead extends to broadcast modalities, as well; for example, the intonation contours of radio news stories emphasize "accents of interest" (Bolinger 1982) within the parts of the utterance that relate to the lead or main point of the story (cf. Cotter 1993).

7.3.2   Types of lead

The purpose of the lead is to accomplish many informational and interactional tasks. It is designed to *attract* the reader, present *new* material, set up the story *structurally*, and to reflect a *competence* of craft on the writing and reporting levels – a variety of functions that lead to variations in approach. Thus there are different types of leads based on content and genre as well as on interactional demands. As different stories require different types of treatment, so leads vary according to essential aspects of stories, resulting in different lead shapes.

The simplest distinction is a binary one: a distinction between *news* and *feature* leads. (Some journalists refer to this distinction in lead approach as *direct* and *delayed* leads (Mencher 2006).) This derives from the simplest distinction of story type, *hard news* and *soft news*. In genre terms, this is roughly comparable to *news* stories and *features*, although there can be variation, as discussed in section 7.2.4. *News-feature* stories embody aspects of both proto-typical genre forms in terms of both the news (primarily through *timeliness* relevance) and human interest or feature angles.

Traditional hard news (or direct) leads are the most proscribed and tend to follow fairly conventionalized formats, following rules on length (keep it short, generally no more than twenty-five to thirty-five words), comprehensiveness (simpler is better, thus one news element or idea is preferred), sentence structure (one or at most two sentences), and the "straightforward recountings of the facts" (Lanson and Stephens 1994: 339). Traditional or direct leads are the "workhorse of journalism, the lead that is used on most stories" (Mencher 1997: 135). Well-crafted traditional leads function as "concise summaries of the most newsworthy information in the story, the most compelling hard fact" (Lanson and Stephens 1994: 61). Conciseness is a stylistic attribute and objective: "The first paragraph is the last place a reporter would want a wasted word or redundancy" (Lanson and Stephens 1994: 61). The craft focus is integral to the lead: "The surest way to test a reporter's competence, editors say, is to see whether his or her leads on spot news events move directly to the point and are **succinct** and **readable**" (Mencher 1997: 135, emphasis added). Examples 7.8 and 7.9 are leads that deliver succinctness and readability.

Example 7.8
Virginia Tech students and supporters lifted thousands of candles to a sapphire sky to remember the 32 people killed by a campus gunman.
(Adam Geller, Associated Press, April 18, 2007)

Example 7.9
Musicians and singers work for years to develop their sense of pitch but few can name a musical note without a reference tone. US researchers on Monday said one gene may be the key to that coveted ability.   (Julie Steenhuysen, Reuters, August 27, 2007)

Feature or soft news leads also use language consciously but to set the tone (or key) of the story. They "not only allow but demand greater freedom of style" (Lanson and Stephens 1994: 84). Example 7.10 is a feature lead on a story about how Washington, DC, compares with twenty-four other US cities in a consumer poll.

Example 7.10
What a worldly bunch we are – and so unfriendly.
(Joe Holley, *Washington Post*, October 23, 2007)

It is short (nine words), provocative ("so unfriendly") as opposed to informational, and positions the reporter who is delivering evaluative information as a member of the same community as the readers ("we"). But it follows the objectives of a good lead in that it also sets up the rest of the story about DC's rankings in a national magazine, in which the city ranks no. 1 on worldliness and no. 23 (out of 25) on unfriendliness. Example 7.11 does the same:

Example 7.11
Miss America 1944 has a talent that likely has never appeared on a beauty pageant stage: She fired a handgun to shoot out a vehicle's tires and stop an intruder.
(Associated Press, April 20, 2007)

Its light tone, Miss America pageant reference, and historical inference make a potential non-story a story. The juxtaposition of a gendered cultural reference with something criminal and potentially fatal at the same time indicates that there will be no surprise tragedy conclusion. Example 7.10 is a nine-word lead; Example 7.11 is a more typical thirty-word lead. In both cases each word counts. In both cases, the reporter is building on shared cultural knowledge assumed of readers, in sentence structure uses a pairing of these elements to set up a contrast of sorts (cf. Atkinson 1984 on rhetorical devices in public speeches), and balances word frequency within each pair component – a metrical pattern to garner attention.

Other types of feature leads such as the **delayed lead** tend to postpone the newsworthy element, relying instead on language alongside the observational powers of the reporter to set the scene or entice the reader over the course of three or four opening paragraphs. The point or newsworthiness dimension is presented after the more rhetorically interesting setup has been constructed, as in Example 7.12. "The delayed lead does not reveal essential information to the reader. That is one of its attractions" (Mencher 1997: 137, emphasis added).

Example 7.12
EINSIEDELN, Switzerland – A librarian at this 10th century monastery leads a visitor beneath the vaulted ceilings of the archive past the skulls of two former abbots. He pushes aside medieval ledgers of indulgences and absolutions, pulls out one of 13 bound diaries inscribed from 1671 to 1704 and starts to read about the weather.
"Jan. 11 was so frightfully cold that all of the communion wine froze," says an entry from 1684 by Brother Josef Dietrich, governor and "weatherman" of the once-powerful Einsiedeln Monastery. "Since I've been an ordained priest, the sacrament has never frozen in the chalice."
"But on Jan. 13 it got even worse and one could say it has never been so cold in human memory," he adds.

[4]→ Diaries of day-to-day weather details from the age before 19th-century standardized thermometers are proving of great value to scientists who study today's climate. Historical accounts were once largely ignored, as they were thought to be fraught with inaccuracy or were simply inaccessible or illegible. But the booming interest in climate change has transformed the study of ancient weather records from what was once a "wallflower science," says Christian Pfister, a climate historian at the University of Bern.
                    (Bradley S. Klapper, Associated Press, September 16, 2007)

In Example 7.12 it is not until paragraph 4 that we know what the story is really about: new interest in old weather records to learn about climate change.

While there are structural and stylistic elements that comprise hard and soft approaches, or news or feature treatments, these are not necessarily fixed. There is not a lead template, *per se*. The hard vs. soft distinction can be a fuzzy one, as in Examples 7.10, 7.11, and 7.12. Once again, the judgments that determine a "hard" or "soft" approach to covering a story and to writing a lead indicate that the process is an *interpretive* one, one dealt with in (and through) *context*, an important point that has been mentioned throughout the book (cf. Chapter 4). Similarly, naming or listing different types of leads (as I did for story types in Figure 7.2) is an exercise in taxonomy more than it is a reflection of what actually occurs in the newsroom, of what a lead type actually can be in its final discursive form. Textbook lists of lead types are a partially comprehensive *emic* rendering of the *etic* possibility (see Chapter 4 for discussion of *emic* and *etic* as concepts that help to characterize cultural patterns).

"Types" of leads are not necessarily specified or part of the discussion in the newsroom, where instead a reporter would be asked by an editor to "feature-ize" a lead, give it a soft-news treatment, give it a feature lead, or do a straight news lead, put on a news lead, etc. However, textbooks, as well as journalism educators and industry publications, do present different types to learners and novices to get them to see the potential variation on the writing-composition level, such as the *narrative* lead, the *anecdote* lead, and the *zinger* or *bright*. The *zinger* or *bright* (also *brite*) is characterized by word play and by "highlighting the unlikely or seemingly absurd" (Lanson and Stephens 1994: 80; see Appendix 1B). The *anecdote* or *narrative* lead types rely on anecdotes as illustration of a larger issue, or narrative or descriptive elements to set the scene or establish the tone or feel of a situation or event, as in Examples 7.12 above and Example 7.13. This lead starts with an anecdote about a lucky homeowner who is the exception rather than the rule:

Example 7.13
    While his flooded neighbors faced an uncertain future, homeowner Bob Foust was already well under way this week repairing the water damage to his house upstream of the refinery's oil spill.

Not only did his house escape the oily gunk carried by floodwaters, but Foust had a very rare commodity in this southeast Kansas city – flood insurance.
(Roxana Hegeman, Associated Press, July 15, 2007)

The lead in Example 7.14, as well as Example 7.11 above, fits the "zinger" or "bright" category.

Example 7.14
Nobody puts Lionsgate in a corner.
That's the message of a trademark infringement lawsuit the studio behind "Dirty Dancing" [has] filed […] against several companies selling merchandise featuring the phrase "Nobody puts Baby in a corner" from the hit film.
(Leslie Simmons, *The Hollywood Reporter*, August 17, 2007)

In Example 7.14, the "zinger" is the use of the phrase, "Nobody puts Lionsgate in a corner." The phrase is not only culturally resonant, clever in its obvious relationship to the source phrase ("Nobody puts Baby in a corner"), and echoes the combativeness of the source phrase's use in the movie, but also encapsulates and suits what is actually newsworthy about the story: that there is a conflict in which our beseiged protagonist will not back down.

The "creative" opportunities these types of leads afford, contravening the premises of the traditional news lead, cause some concern to the extent that beginning reporters are warned that these leads not be used "as opportunities for verbosity and affectation" (Lanson and Stephens 1994: 82). Mencher also reminds novices that a narrative or non-traditional lead must conform to the stylistic and informational expectations of the news genre. He is highlighting the journalistic craft dimension to emphasize to students that a reporter "is just as scrupulous in the choice of material for the beginning of the piece as is the user of the traditional form. Both forms require the writer to identify the major theme and to make it clear at the outset that the story will be concerned with that theme" (Mencher 1997: 125). Example 7.15 is a good illustration of Mencher's points:

Example 7.15
When 100 farm-raised elk fled his private hunting reserve through a bear-dug hole under the fence, owner Rex Rammell – a man with a long history of locking antlers with the state – didn't realize he'd wind up in the governor's crosshairs.
(Jesse Harlan Alderman, Associated Press, September 24, 2006)

Craft is being deployed: every word counts (hence the use of compound adjectives in noun phrases like "farm-raised elk" and "bear-dug hole"), and language is being used performatively on behalf of the news elements. There are a number of news and information elements condensed into the fewest words to tell us, as swiftly as possible, the news: that 100 domestic elk – farm-raised – have escaped through a hole in a fence dug by a bear, that the elk's owner comes with a prior history of action against the state of Montana, and that there is some significant issue related to the missing elk, the owner, and the governor of the state. The phrase "locking antlers" is akin to "locking horns" (altered, no doubt, because elk have antlers, not horns) and suggests through conceptual metaphor the elk owner's combative nature. That he is caught in the "governor's crosshairs" – a reference to the sight on a rifle, one in this case wielded by an official in power – indicates the extent of the conflict, and thus its newsworthiness. It also echoes literal aspects of the story made clear further down: that Rammell's elk are being shot as they wander across federal land.

"Second-day leads" and breaking news   "Second-day leads" occur in two primary instances. The first is when a reporter is following a story that has not "concluded," one that is ongoing, as in Examples 7.16 and 7.17.

Example 7.16
MINNEAPOLIS – Divers found another body in the Mississippi River on Sunday, 11 days after a highway bridge collapsed into the fast-flowing water, raising the official death toll to nine.   (Martiga Lohn, Associated Press, August 13, 2007)

Example 7.17
SAN DIEGO – Wildfires blown by fierce desert winds Monday reduced hundreds of Southern California homes to ashes, forced hundreds of thousands of people to flee and laid a hellish, spidery pattern of luminous orange over the drought-stricken region.

Firefighters described desperate conditions that were sure to get worse in the days ahead, with hotter temperatures and high winds forecast for Tuesday. At least 16 firefighters and 25 others were reported injured since the blazes began Sunday, and one person was killed.

(Allison Hoffman and Gillian Flaccus, Associated Press, October 22, 2007)

In these examples, the time elements are included with the latest developments. The second situation is more complex. If a reporter missed the news on the day it was relevant, but every other news outlet in the area has it, or the event happened past deadline or is still occurring and in flux, then the second-day lead has to convey the importance of the first-day (as it is, ostensibly, the first time readers will see it), without suggesting that it *is* the first day (or else it would be misleading), incorporating what is *new* about the second-day with the *relevance* dimension of the first-day. The story has to "read" like it was never missed in the first place, or is just as important as it was on the first day. It cannot be "read" as old news.

Stories that are written for weekly papers essentially have to be engaged in this practice all the time, to put on a "second-day" lead even when there was an online version immediately after the event (the Web is changing this process, even for daily papers). Say, for example, a weekly paper comes out on Wednesday. On Thursday, a Huge Event happens. By the following Wednesday, the Huge Event is either (1) irrelevant, in which case the item would be short in length, placed on an inside page, and not particularly noticeable; or (2) still relevant, in which case the lead would incorporate the newest aspect of the saga in tandem with reporting the main thrust of the Huge Event (as the reporter did in Example 7.16). It does not necessarily suggest that the story happened yesterday, as it were – just that it is freshly reported and up-to-the-minute. The same rationales apply when the story is missed. The writing challenge is that it is assumed by the reporter that everyone knows about the Huge Event *and at the same time* it is written as if a reader might have missed the story and is not informed – it should contain all the elements of a "first-time" story.

It is equally complex when the story is both ongoing and breaking news, as in Example 7.17. The lead captures the important elements: what is new on Monday, the day of publication, is in paragraph 1. The news angle of the ongoing story is also emphasized by reference to the future, Tuesday and "the days ahead." The day the fires started, Sunday, is, relatively speaking, deep within the second paragraph. (Each iteration of the story that was transmitted that day provided updates that incorporated what was new in the context of prior information.) Example 7.16 shows how a reporter handles an ongoing and important, but not as rapidly evolving, story that in news-practice terms is "old." In Example 7.16, the time element in the first paragraph provides context – a time perspective for readers reminding them of the bridge collapse nearly a fortnight prior, implicating the ongoing recovery efforts as well as the difficulties behind recovery ("fast-flowing water"). As befits a well-crafted lead it draws attention to what is new, presenting the "compelling hard fact" (Lanson and Stephens 1994: 61) – another body recovered.

Ongoing news is in contrast with "breaking news," in which an event is happening in real-time, not on a particular deadline schedule. Reporters scramble to get the facts and write the story, which is continually updated as the event unfolds, as in Example 7.17, and as did occur in the first hours and days after the bridge collapse referred to in Example 7.16. With breaking news, reporters are often challenged or deterred by too many information elements to select from (a plethora of facts, opinions, and judgments) or not enough, as well as access to official sources, who themselves are in a similar, information-gathering phase. Breaking news examples that caught international attention include, in recent history, the Challenger shuttle disaster in 1986, the 9/11 suicide bombings in 2001, the tsunami in 2004, the economic downturns of 2008, etc. On the local level, breaking news is the bank robbery, forest fire, major accident, chemical spill, hostage situation, tornado, court decision, found body, etc.

Breaking news requires a consequent physical change or action on the production end, from updates on websites and between editions, remaking the front page, and producing new editions (typified in popular culture through the pre-broadcast image of a newsboy at an urban street corner shouting, "Extra! Extra!

Read all about it!"). The changes that occur to the text itself involve rewriting the lead (to incorporate the newest and most important information elements) and deleting or amending information within the story that has been rendered factually inaccurate or no longer relevant. Other genre forms, notably the *correction*, are displayed at this time, too. Web transmission of news stories allows greater transparency in this process, as evidenced by notes at the bottom of Associated Press stories, as in these separate parenthetical examples from 2007:

"(This version CORRECTS that search of dorms was Saturday, not Saturday night, and ADDS that search was for fingerprints and other evidence.)"
"(A previous version of this story had the word 'are' in a quote from Rutgers' basketball coach. It should have been 'were.')"

These corrections also reflect the information and style objectives reporters and editors are taught to follow: accuracy in factual detail and in the quotes of sources. They are similar in function to traditional corrections in the newspaper, which repair omissions and errors, as in these examples from *The Washington Post* (July 6, 2002: A2, reproduced in full, emphasis added):

The Phoenix Theater is performing "Independence" through Aug. 3 at the D.C. Arts Center at 2438 18th St. NW. A calendar item in the July 5 Weekend section incorrectly reported the location.
A July 3 Federal Page article failed to mention the last Justice Department job that Andrew Frey held. He was deputy solicitor general from July 1973 to April 1986.
A July 1 Style article about the tabletop game Warhammer 40,000 incorrectly spelled names of game pieces. Nurgling, Tyranid and Dark Eldar are the correct spellings.

Like the AP Web corrections, the details relate to accuracy such as location and spelling, as well as the inclusion of contextual detail that is relevant to a story (following the Gricean Maxim of Quality). The corrections also indicate the range of news that comes under the newswriting protocols.

Complex leads   Traditional leads are generally considered to be the first paragraph, although in more complex cases – when multiple information strands are relevant, or for stylistic reasons in the case of the **delayed lead** – they are spaced out over a couple of paragraphs as seen in Example 7.12 above. A variant of the traditional lead is the **summary lead**, which includes multiple story strands in the opening paragraph. The *summary* lead is used when the multiple story strands together are a primary factor in newsworthiness, as in Examples 7.18(a) and 7.18(b).

Example 7.18

(a) MALIBU, Calif. – Nearly a dozen wildfires driven by powerful Santa Ana winds spread across Southern California on Sunday, killing one person near San Diego, destroying several homes and a church in celebrity-laden Malibu, and forcing an entire community to evacuate. (Noaki Schwartz, Associated Press, October 22, 2007)

(b) WASHINGTON – Protesters blocked traffic and government buildings in Washington, acted out a Baghdad street scene in Syracuse, N.Y., and banged drums in a parade through San Francisco on Wednesday to mark the fifth anniversary of the U.S. invasion of Iraq. (Sarah Karush, Associated Press, March 19, 2008)

In Example 7.18(a), the lead summarizes a number of fire-related events: the quantity of wildfires, a death, destruction of homes and a church, and the evacuation of a community. In Example 7.18(b), the lead in its summary projects the transnational scope of war protest in the US, drawing together contributions from nine other reporters in other locations.

Lead "extensions" Beyond the traditional lead, there have been other techniques presented by newsroom editors and journalism educators interested in pushing the boundaries of the craft in new directions (motivated by an interest in grabbing the reader). The "nut graf" is one such element. The *nut graf* (a compendiary or synopsis paragraph) sums up the story, tells what it is about. It is much like the brief summary that reporters are trained to give editors, both verbally and written on a daily story log. Because the nut graf distils the primary news element as a traditional lead will do, it allows for a "soft" lead treatment – for a more delayed lead approach. It thus appears early in the story, but not in first-paragraph (lead) position. Nor does it rely on the use of language stylistically. In Example 7.19, the nut graf is in paragraph 3.

Example 7.19
When Margaret Chau has a bad night's sleep, she knows to steer clear of loved ones the next day – she's cranky and impatient, and she tends to take it out on others.
"I don't want to deal with things because I'm afraid of not being able to do it rationally or logically," said the Millbrae woman, who suffers from chronic insomnia due to back pain. "I know myself, and I don't want to react badly or do something I might regret."
[3]→ It's no secret that the sleep-deprived are usually grumpy, miserable and not much fun to be around, but new research from UC Berkeley using brain-scanning equipment helps explain why. The study, which was published Monday in the journal Current Biology, was the first to use MRI technology to show exactly what areas of the brain are affected by sleep deprivation.
(Erin Allday, *San Francisco Chronicle*, October 23, 2007)

The *nut graf* points to the fact that there are other elements that come into play besides comprehensiveness or succinctness when the lead is written. The delayed lead allows for stylistic invention; the nut graf brings the news element back to the fore. In Example 7.19, the delayed lead allows for the introduction of the "illustrative individual" (typified in Example 6.8).

It could be argued on linguistic grounds that lead "extensions" such as the *nut graf* also include the *headline* or *pull-quote*, the words that are extracted from within the story and increased in font size to enhance graphic-informational display. This would not necessarily be how journalists would characterize it, as they see these different textual components as having different purposes and different roles in the news setup, as well as being produced and organized by different actors. For instance, a *headline* or *pull-quote* is written or chosen by the copy editor or news editor, not the reporter generally. (Reporters dislike it when copy editors spoil the lead by reprising it in the headline.) However, linguists examining how leads function as the first filter of information presentation could point out that *heds*, *pull-quotes*, *nut grafs*, and *leads* are all discourse-level units of analysis that comprise mechanisms through which salience – or newsworthiness – can be presented, through which **maximal relevance**, a blend of the most important news element plus the "hook" or angle of the story, can be supported (see further explanation in Section 8.3.3).

7.3.3   The well-formed lead

The requirements of a well-formed lead fulfill rhetorical/discursive goals involving *form* – putting the story within a limited physical space; *reader connection*; and *ordering* of elements such that the key or most newsworthy element is fronted. Figure 7.4 summarizes the characteristics, discussed in earlier sections (and depicted in terms of communicative goals in Figure 7.1), that a well-formed lead displays.

The news lead relies on newness, and the best leads reflect what is the newest element of the story, irrespective of other points of interest. Thus, the fronted element in most leads is the news value of *newness*, or by extension, any of the *most, oldest, worst, richest* "superlative" news values (cf. Chapter 4). The *singularity of the superlative*, as it occurs, allows *newness* to be read as *unique-ness*, and vice versa. *Newness* is an especially prominent feature in continuing stories like the Minneapolis bridge collapse in Example 7.16, when people are familiar with the main story thread, wanting to know the latest development whether or not one exists.

When it is not about actual "newness" then the component that has been separated out – as in the WHO or WHAT of the "Five W's" – is fronted. A routine speech by a president is news, in that it is worthy of coverage, because of the WHO: the president does it. A routine or recurring event that a newspaper of record would report on, such as reminders of fire safety at Christmas, a town budget passed without incident, the first day of school, fronts the WHAT. The three leads in Example 7.20 illustrate well-formed leads on stories that one expects to find in (and are in a sense predictable for) newspapers of record and that are relevant to the local *community of coverage*.

Infrastructure Components	Requirements	Mechanics	Grice
Form	Short Tightly written	*proscribed word number* *no "extraneous" words*	*Quantity* *Manner*
Reader	Draw in reader/relevance	*language choice/style*	*Relation* *Quality*
Ordering	Convey newness/ **Maximal relevance**	*newsworthy element/* *fronted element*	*Quantity* *Relation*

Grice (cf. Figure 7.1): Quantity (information), Quality (truth), Manner (clarity), Relation (relevance)

Figure 7.4 The well-formed lead: optimal components

Example 7.20
(a) SHIOCTON – Veteran hunters say dry, cool temperatures and a light blanket of snow for tracking make the best conditions for a successful gun deer hunting season. (J. E. Espino, *The Post-Crescent* (Appleton, WI), Sunday, November 25, 2007: A2)
(b) After every fatal fire in Baltimore, including a blaze that took the lives of three children Friday, fire officials remind neighbors of the importance of smoke alarms. (Frank D. Roylance, *The Baltimore* (MD) *Sun*, Tuesday, March 4, 2008: A1)
(c) Grafton – A joint hearing of the Grafton Village Board and Plan Commission will be held at 5 p.m. Tuesday at the Grafton High School auditorium, 1950 Washington St., to review plans for an 89-bed hospital that Aurora Health Care plans to build. (*Milwaukee* (WI) *Journal Sentinel*, Monday, November 26, 2007: B2)

In these leads for relatively "small" stories, the WHAT component has been fronted: what makes "successful gun deer hunting," the "importance of smoke alarms," and a public meeting about a proposed hospital.

Maximal Relevance   Of all the component parts of the news story, the lead is distinguished by *Maximal Relevance*, by the reporter's selection of the most important news element of the story in addition to the choice of angle or "hook," or approach to the subject. This process can be simplified as a rule:

Primary news element + hook/angle → MAXIMAL RELEVANCE

"Burying" a lead, or inadvertently putting the most important element further down into the story, typifies one of the most common potential errors, in which an aspect of the story that does not best carry the story is selected, in which *Maximal Relevance* is missed.

At the same time, there is no single right way to begin a lead, which is evident in the variation of approach when different reporters cover the same story or even when they choose the same news element to lead with. It is also evidence of the interpretive nature of news. Example 7.21 shows *The Fresno Bee*'s lead on a story about a major California highway crash involving more than 100 vehicles near the city of Fresno in contrast with the Associated Press version, intended for wider distribution.

Example 7.21

(a) In a horrific matter of minutes along a fog-swathed stretch of Highway 99 south of Fresno, two people were killed and 41 others injured Saturday morning in one of the worst pileups in central San Joaquin Valley history.
   It involved 108 vehicles – and, investigators said, a man suspected of driving while drunk.
                                    (Louis Galvan, Tim Sheehan and Felicia Cousart Matlosz, *The Fresno Bee*,
                                                                                    November 3, 2007)

(b) FRESNO, Calif. – More than 100 cars and trucks crashed on a fog-shrouded freeway Saturday, killing at least two people and injuring dozens more, the California Highway Patrol said.
   Eighteen big rigs were involved in the massive pileup on Highway 99 just south of Fresno as patches of dense fog obscured visibility on the heavily traveled roadway, CHP officials said.   (Garance Burke, Associated Press, November 3, 2007)

The "local example" (7.21(a)) specified the location, information relevant to people living nearby or who know the area, and exemplified the extent of the accident by use of the marked non-journalistic word "horrific" and providing historic context with respect to the central San Joaquin Valley. The national version was less specific with local detail.

   Order   Writing a good lead often means forsaking what one automatically assumes about chronological structure, avoiding "And then this happened ... and then that happened ..." constructions, which students frequently fall into. Similarly, late twentieth-century *New Yorker* magazine "leads," or lengthy opening paragraphs which tend toward the digressive in keeping with their literary publication style, are counter-examples of what a well-formed news lead should be. The distribution of information elements instantiated by the lead is predicated on *newsworthiness*, so a reporter will seldom start at the very beginning of the event or incident they are covering (as textbook Example 7.1 makes explicit). Because the lead contains the news element of most importance, and stories thus are generally not necessarily written in chronological order, news stories often alter the temporal order found in the prototypical narrative (as also noted by Bell 1991, evaluating news stories in terms of Labov's (1972b) narrative framework).

   Good leads   Writing a good lead, in the well-formed sense, is considered essential to a good news story. What counts as "good" can be further differentiated. Amongst news practitioners, a "good" lead incorporates all the characteristics and optimal components (noted in Figure 7.4) of a well-formed lead but goes a step further. A good lead has an element of inventiveness, style, freshness, newness of expression. **A good lead reflects the particularity of the reporter's eye**. A good lead, especially, draws the reader in – with language. It thus carries with it a display of craft, on both the *journalistic-functional* and *rhetorical-stylistic* levels. It has "punch" or something salient (as Examples 7.10 and 7.11 show), and enables the story to have "flow" or pacing, an optimum and appropriate distribution of elements (as in Examples 7.9 and 7.12).

For example, a story about Bigfoot, the North American equivalent of the Loch Ness Monster known also by his Native American name, Sasquatch, is so often in the news when something happens with respect to a "sighting" such that when he is not it is worthy of a story. Reported Bigfoot sightings, and documentaries and movies about them, happened frequently in the rural mountain counties of far Northern California in the 1970s. By the early 1980s, they had fallen off, leading regional reporter Garth Sanders to start a story with:

Example 7.22
> Bigfoot, you hairy son-of-a-myth, where have you been hiding?
> (Garth Sanders, *Record Searchlight*, Redding, CA, n.d.)

In his twelve-word lead, not only did Sanders make it clear that this was a story about the recent dearth of Bigfoot sightings and expeditions in his coverage area (cinematic or "actual"), fulfilling the *journalistic-functional* dimension, but he also sets the *stylistic* tone by companionably and somewhat pointedly addressing Bigfoot as one might a long-lost friend. The pseudo-epithet, direct question, and second-person address suggest they are good buddies. The implication, as he is writing for his newspaper's readers, is also that Bigfoot is relevant to the audience; we, too, might be wondering what Sasquatch has been up to. Or why his recent fame has waned. Through his word choice, Sanders captures the figure's mythic and pop-culture resonances, and allows the reader to appreciate his verbal artistry with the near-rhyme (or near-minimal-pair) *son-of-a-myth*. "You son-of-a-bitch" in far Northern California, as in many other places, would not necessarily be taken as an insult, but as an example of backslapping bonhomie. In this way Sanders is evoking the interactional and address norms of his community of coverage.

7.3.4   Mastering techniques of lead writing

The techniques of lead-writing require skills that involve *clarity* and appropriate *detail*, *ordering* of information and *fronting* of newsworthy elements, as well as *length* of sentences and paragraphs and deployment of *AP style*. These skills cover both the *journalistic-functional* and the *rhetorical-stylistic* expectations necessary to produce a well-written news story, with *newsworthiness* the guiding impetus. Reporting skills are also fundamental. The time devoted to the story, or actual reporter effort involved, cannot necessarily be viewed as a **salience contributor**. Equally, the most important news item can come up in a little package, such as an overheard comment, a press release, and the like, or it is hustled through – decisions at civic or government meetings, for instance – or comes crackling on the police radio. The physical time devoted to its access may be very slight, not commensurate with the ultimate importance or newsworthiness of the actual news item.

Clarity and detail   ***Clarity*** is the macro-element upon which intelligible lead-writing and newswriting rests. Clarity is predicated on relevant detail. Details have different relative "value" and operate within the news profession's implicit relative hierarchy of information (as well as codified practices of accuracy and reliability). The information hierarchy promotes the conventionalized ordering of elements in news stories; it helps speedy organization of information when time is at issue, as noted in Section 7.1.

Failures of clarity can occur at different levels of information. In many journalism educators' experience, the failures occur with identification – when to name the person in the first paragraph and when to not – and with context – when to include details to make the story relevance apparent to the reader or not. For example, an unknown person is generally not named in a lead on the premise that as no one knows him or her, the interest or reader relevance is not there. WHAT they did or what happened to them is more newsworthy than WHO they are.

Clarity failures occur also when novices try to cram too much information in the lead, when too many details obscure the clarity of the fronted or primary news element. Students who fear leaving out something essential actually try to include the entire story in the lead. They might operate within the lead-length minimums, but the information load is too high. Including all "Five W's" is three to four too many. A reporter who is communicatively competent will be able to make this call, to select the appropriate element. Most seasoned reporters will confidently choose one or two elements to include in the lead, comfortable that the rest will be coming shortly. Students, however, have not yet developed or internalized a **relative hierarchy** of news elements and often overload the lead with details they are afraid are necessary. They overlearn the Gricean Quantity rule (say what needs to be said).

Insufficient detail occurs when students or novice reporters make too many assumptions, or do not question their own assumptions, about (1) what the reader needs to know and in what order, and (2) what the story requires to be presented as well-formed news discourse. Detail of lesser informational order, such as correct stylistic rendering of times, dates, and places are also part of acquired journalistic communicative competence. Following appropriate news style (e.g., Associated Press style) works on behalf of a pan-professional clarity and uniformity of lexical, orthographic, and sociocultural presentation (see also chapter 9).

Ordering conventions   Besides learning what elements to select, and that relative values accrue to news elements, the novice reporter has to learn the ordering conventions, based on newsworthiness, clarity, and simplicity objectives. Without that knowledge, a lead comes across as disorganized and unfocused, or oversaturated with detail, or uninteresting. As mentioned earlier, it is often the case that the error is one of chronology, in which the reporter writes about the first, but not most important, element of an event being covered. From an editor's perspective, their "stage setting" is easily deletable. (University-level teachers also notice the same irrelevant "stage setting" in inexperienced student papers and essays on academic topics.) When novices approach the challenge of writing up disparate notes from disparate sources in a non-newsworthy chronological manner, it gives what in the journalistic context is unnecessary background, and puts information in the wrong place with respect to story form. The reader, expecting the conventional news story, is likely to move on as there is nothing of interest in the first paragraph. (The punchline has not come first.)

Another complicating factor for learners is that the *relative hierarchy* shifts depending on what is chosen as the primary news element. There is not just one way to go about ordering elements: the news story template, despite its routines (and often cookie-cutter-like outcomes), is interpretive, and varies according to the individual and circumstance, with different emphases on different aspects of the story. Each variation in approach means a variation in element ordering.

Other conditions that influence the lead include occasions when stories are written when there is not much news content, as when reporters must file routine stories while following a candidate on an election campaign or an Olympic athlete through a training regimen. Starting with what can be construed as new, or more unusual, or more prominent (or more visual, as in television) conditions how the story begins and that which follows (cf. Cotter 1999b).

Length   Sentence and paragraph length is a more visible competence marker. Leads written by beginners are often simply too long. (As a guide, news-writing textbooks variously suggest leads with a maximum of 25–35 words.) Or, less commonly, they are too short. Neither is optimum, as Mencher notes:

When a reporter writes a lead, he or she navigates between divergent currents. One pull is toward writing a longer-than-average sentence, as the lead must offer significant information. The other is toward a short sentence, since short sentences are more readable than long ones. The long sentence may be difficult to grasp; the short sentence may be uninformative or misleading.   (Mencher 1997: 147)

In my experience, it takes a half-semester's worth of newswriting practice for students to begin to see how appropriate length becomes part of the defining rhythm and shape of a news story. Even though they have read news stories, and may have latent discourse analyst tendencies, they cannot consistently replicate well-formed leads without training or mentoring in the classroom or in the newsroom. There is a learning correlation in radio, too. The "wild accents" or "overuse" of pitch accents to emphasize information elements in radio news stories (cf. Bolinger 1982) function aurally in the same way as the visually iconic inverted pyramid does for print – to focus on what is most newsworthy, what underlies the lead. Someone trained as a radio reporter is more aware and accomplished in terms of discourse-specific prosodic conventions and their journalistic information-based rationales than someone with a good ear but who is untrained, who relies on receiver-end stereotypes of what news sounds like (cf. Cotter 1993).

"Bad ledes"   In the experience of journalism educators, beginning reporters exhibit problems that relate to their lack of familiarity with journalistic norms (as outlined in Figures 7.1, 7.3, and 7.4). Like mastering any discourse or genre form, e.g., academic writing, it takes a certain amount of practice to get the hang of writing a lead. Students usually find leads are harder to write than they had expected, often "burying" the lead, a characteristic of academic writing with which they are more familiar. It appears easy to sit down to write a story about "the most important thing." It is more difficult to realize there are so many options and that selection finesse is ultimately a key skill to acquire. Novices will front the wrong element or miss the lead, include too much or too little detail, write overlong sentences and paragraphs, and miss or be unaware of the prescriptions of AP style. Even seasoned reporters have lapses.

It is very easy to consider what goes into the craft components and discursive challenges of the lead when it is done wrong. Erving Goffman mined this insight in his 1981 essay, "Radio Talk," an early analysis of media language. He used radio bloopers as his database to show deviations from the news frame and to better understand what comprises the news frame (although he analyzed mistakes on the air from the sociologist's and not the news person's point of view, cf. Cotter 1996a). I will not use examples from my own database of "bloopers," or ineffective newswriting, except to point out that the problems that beginning reporters have in constructing a good lead point to the very priorities that exist: clarity, length, order, and detail (cf. Section 7.3.3).

Irrespective of too much detail, not enough detail, or length or chronology or ordering issues, there are within the profession approaches that are specifically typified as "bad ledes" – no matter the competence, experience, or fame of the reporter. *Cliché leads*, for instance, can range from the overuse of a "typical example" or "affected person example" to introduce discussion of more abstract policy issues or law changes to an over-reliance on specific phrases that have become clichés. "*Christmas came early for …*" is one of the latter. If, between Thanksgiving and December 24 some unexpected benefit or surprise or happy ending comes to a person who might have expected otherwise, then a reporter might connect this event to the holiday season and begin the story with: "*Christmas came early for X when Y happened last night ...*"

Other leads that students and novices (and freelance writers) often over-rely on – until they acquire more communicative competence, news sense, and rhetorical skill – are "*you" leads*, "*imagine" leads*, and *question leads*. These leads, which tend to occur with feature stories, are an over-application of the rules (similar to the *hypercorrection* typical of any learner of a language variety with standards different from one's own). In this case, the lead-writing rules that are being over-applied are to connect with the reader (the "you" address form as well as initiating an interlocutorial turn with a question), to be creative or enterprising in approach ("imagine"), and focus the story in terms of a single theme or angle (by imagining or questioning a particular scenario).

The limitations of these lead types become apparent not only because they are the easy choice and occur regularly, but because they limit the **relevance to the reader**. If a reader has not imagined the specific scenario nor sees a personal connection of any sort with the query the reporter poses, the reader will not be "engaged." For example: "*Imagine you have just graduated from college and don't have a job.*" Or "*Ever wonder why most students move back home with Mom and Dad when they graduate?*" The direct-appeal approach restricts the story to a small set of readers who are in a similar situation as the ones in the hypothetical scenario.

Label leads, which label or say that something happened without concurrently fronting the most newsworthy element, are also a common mistake, more typical of routine news stories. A label lead is a competence miscalculation related to simultaneously trying to provide the context of the story but missing the news angle. A label lead like Example 7.23(a) does not provide much time, impact, or circumstance relevance that a well-formed lead requires:

Example 7.23

(a) "The Anytown Planning Commission met today to discuss the proposed budget for the upcoming fiscal year."

With a news angle, the lead could look like this:

(b) "A proposed 2.6 percent increase in fees for sewage services is being considered by the Anytown Planning Commission, which met today to discuss the preliminary budget for the upcoming fiscal year."

The 7.23(b) version directs attention to something specific and relevant to the circumstance.

And as a reminder that newswriting rules are context-sensitive and subject to alteration, depending on a host of discursive and meta-textual circumstances, the Sanders "good lead" Example 7.22 is a case in point. He used "you" and formulated it as a question, but, as previously discussed, he also met the larger discourse objectives of a well-formed lead. In his case, he broke the "rules" but stayed within the larger communicative objective of engaging his readers – evidence of his professional acumen and communicative competence.

7.4   Conclusion: the importance of craft

This chapter about "story design" is intended to bring to the fore the parameters of news discourse that most broadly concern story structure and narrative order (what story elements in what order), as well as the motivations behind story design that involve topic (or news story) selection; interactional relationship (with reader, colleague, and source); genre form (or story type); communicative competence (or reporting and newswriting craft skill); and the rules of practice that underpin them. More theoretically, it is a discursive companion to Bell's audience design framework and another in a long line of productive applications of Grice's principles. As a newswriting short-course, Gricean conversational principles, dealing as they do with information, truth, clarity, and relation, most succinctly and directly encapsulate the goals behind story structure, reporting priorities, and writing objectives. The journalistic focus on newsworthiness and the textual, interactional, and informational importance of the lead are behind the application of what linguistically can be called *Maximal Relevance*, which guides decision-making, leads to variation across publications, and provides a craft benchmark.

News stories follow a set of reporting, writing, and editing rules that mainstream journalists by and large proceed from as standard operating procedure, rules of communicative practice that are taught explicitly in the classroom and the newsroom and reinforced implicitly through daily doing (Cotter 1999b; see also Bell 1991). While there is variation, a fact that leads us to consider elements of practice that relate more closely to social context, audience responsiveness, and the interpretive dimensions inherent in following rules of practice, the underlying norms of production have been routinized and conventionalized, accounting for a great deal of similarity across media outlets, a point noted in different ways by linguists (e.g., Cotter 1999b), communications scholars (e.g. Schudson 1987), journalism educators (e.g., Mencher 2006), and newspaper editors (Ben Bradlee and John Diaz, personal communication).

The news story is both *ordered* and ***sequenced*** (as embodied in the requisite *text goals* of appropriate lead, sentence structure, and story organization), and *content-driven* and ***atomic*** (evident in the required inclusion of quotes, attribution, background, and context). These reporting priorities, writing objectives, and story structure elements that journalists are expected to handle competently are necessary to a well-formed story; they are craft values that are integral to news practice. (On the theoretical-linguistic level, the sequential and atomic features that comprise news stories can be analyzed syntagmatically and paradigmatically.) "Good" stories are also influenced by a variable equation involving space and time, quality of the news, and audience (what the *community of coverage* needs to know as well as wants to know). The complexity behind the news story is backgrounded as rules of craft guide the reporter toward textual simplicity – as he or she strives to tell the story with an urgent eye on deadline.

Behind all these calculations, interpretations, and adherence to professional communicative norms is the lead. The importance or dictates of the lead cannot be overestimated in terms of its impact on story design overall. The lead distills the primary news element and establishes the hierarchical informational dimensions, often irrespective of chronology, that resonate throughout the story. The lead is intended to be "read" with ease of comprehension and, if things go well, with appreciation, particularly within the news community, who, like professional musicians, understand the practice "muscle" that is behind it.

In this chapter, we looked at the structure and function of the news story and the craft values behind it, and saw illustrated the ways in which language in its many instrumental permutations advances a range of news-centric discursive goals. In chapter 8, we will continue our exploration of the structure of news stories and consider the implications and sociopolitical influence that story design might also have.

8   "Boilerplate": Simplifying stories, anchoring text, altering meaning

KEY POINTS

- Boilerplate is recurring material inserted into stories extending longer than a single day to remind readers of prior context. It is a special type of "background" information.
- Boilerplate follows constraints on content and placement within a news text. Its discourse purpose is orientational, orienting the public to the status of a story to date.
- Key injunctions of newswriting are manifested in this seemingly throwaway material (often recycled wholesale from previous stories): to simplify, to maintain an authorial distance, and to summarize previously reported details of a story when reporting it afresh.
- Boilerplate is repetitious, unattributed, identifies and describes, summarizes, and is potentially expendable as text. Nonetheless, despite its "shorthand" language and a text design resulting from the pragmatic requirements of well-formed news discourse, its role in framing a news story may also end up influencing public debate.

A good news story is more than just scandal, victory, upset, or a tale of woe or triumph. A good news story is also marked by how artfully it is compiled, by the extent to which the reporter manages the injunctions and conventions of newswriting. Well-formed news discourse – the kind found in stories that would be considered well-reported and well-written by news practitioners themselves – is structured by a fairly strict set of rules that the reporter follows and acts on (as was articulated in Chapter 7). One primary task of the reporter writing a news story is to clarify and **simplify** the complex, a task that interacts with other discourse demands, such as maintaining **neutrality** and **summarizing** previously reported details of a story when covering it again.

On the textual level, the newswriting rules that involve simplification, neutrality, and provision of sufficient explanatory information are operating factors behind the production of all stories. They also lead to the production of "boilerplate," recurring material that is inserted into stories that continue longer than a single day to remind readers of prior context. Boilerplate summarizes, simplifies, and is presented as non-evaluatively as possible according to reporter codes of balance. Because of its very ordinariness and relative unimportance in relation to the "main point," or the most recent or newest dimension of a story (found in the lead), boilerplate is easy to overlook. Nonetheless, as an identifiable component of news discourse, it follows certain constraints on content and placement within the story. Its discourse purpose, while backgrounded to other communicative goals within the news story, is *orientational*, orienting the public to the status of a story to date.

Linguistically, then, boilerplate can be viewed as a manifestation of a complex discourse demand whose implications can become significant when the story is linked to more divisive issues. To illustrate how well-formed and well-reported news stories might unwittingly work against the informational clarity and balance that journalists are striving for, I will look at print media coverage of a contested California ballot initiative in the mid-1990s concerning the rights of illegal immigrants, characterizing what was included and what was left out of boilerplate summaries of a complicated social and political issue. My point is to show how the "shorthand" language and text design that result from the application of newswriting objectives may end up shaping public debate and even actions on important issues. The pragmatic implications of news discourse rules, not only those behind boilerplate, become especially significant when the underlying propositions of the language of a news story become linked to hot-button issues within the culture in which the discourse is situated.

In this chapter, I begin by briefly reviewing the newswriting elements considered necessary for well-formed news discourse (discussed at length in Chapter 7) which motivate the use of boilerplate and help to construct its genre conventions. Then I outline and illustrate the defining characteristics of boilerplate in terms of story content and structure. Finally, I consider the implications of boilerplate as a textual device that reports and thus represents the world to its readers. The case example is intended to underscore the value of looking at media discourse as a multifunctional, interactionally grounded system, and to show how one textual component is revealing of the complex relationship of journalists, their texts, and their audiences – and their role in the emergence of public understanding of social and political issues.

8.1   News discourse rules and boilerplate

Once we understand, from the "ethnographic insider" perspective, what is behind the construction of a news story, we can consider how journalistic practice relates, intentionally or not, to the public. A reporter who writes well is a well-socialized journalist, and explicitly or implicitly knows the requirements behind producing a good news story – the news *text*. He or she is operating, in the main, according to ethical, statutory, professionally circumscribed principles of fairness, balance, objectivity, and neutrality that characterize the profession – operating according to a journalistic *ideology*. What may not be as apparent, to journalists because they are in the middle of things and linguists because they are looking in a different direction, is the actual *impact* of the discourse, and how "small" discourse units that might be overlooked might have fairly big impacts on public understanding. (At the very least, we will better understand the composite textual and reportorial components that create a news story, in the tradition of sociolinguistic research that has focused on the previously underexamined: small talk, lists, discourse markers, back-channels, contextualization cues, language attitudes to some extent, etc.) Thus when I review in this section what I hope are by now the somewhat familiar newswriting injunctions behind well-formed news discourse – simplification, neutrality, and background (see Chapters 2, 3, and 7 for lengthier discussion) – I situate them in the context of the "small" discourse unit of boilerplate.

To illustrate what boilerplate is and how it and other types of background or explanatory material work functionally in continuing stories, I use examples from a corpus of stories that dealt with a major political issue in California in the 1990s – Proposition 187, a ballot measure that, as it has been described, "banned state benefits and public education for illegal immigrants," and whose implications are in the news to this very day. I also make reference to another ballot measure passed two years later, which banned preferences in hiring and other situations based on race and gender. This measure, Proposition 209, known variously and somewhat problematically as the anti-affirmative action, or anti-quotas measure, or California Civil Rights Initiative, is often linked with Proposition 187 in terms of its social impacts and underlying racist presuppositions. (All of the articles I cite from appeared in the three major California papers, the *Los Angeles Times* (*LAT*) the *San Francisco Chronicle*, and *The Sacramento Bee*, from June through November of 1994 and 1996, with selective sampling in 1995, and were collected using the Lexis-Nexis Database. Some 2,000 articles are in the corpus, from which examples have been selected primarily to illustrate fundamental issues concerning boilerplate.)

8.1.1   *Simplification and distance*

The injunction to **simplify** derives from the general rule of brevity (noted in Chapter 7). Daily, a reporter is charged with grasping the significant particulars about a complex situation, synthesizing those particulars, and writing accessibly about them – with a minimum number of words, often in a minimum amount of time, and for readers with a minimum amount of time and attention. For example, the descriptions of Propositions 187 and 209 in all three of the newspapers I examined amounted to one or two short paragraphs at most, as subsequent examples will show, whereas the language of the propositions themselves made a much lengthier legal document and was reproduced in entirety in the paper usually only once or twice during the election season.

Another discursive (and interactional) goal of newswriting and reporting is to maintain an authorial **distance** between reporter and story. Through discursive means reporters are expected to convey a sense of distance – of relation and ideology – between themselves and the material being reported. This principle derives from what I call the ***Neutral Authority Model***: the reporter adhering to the profession's ethical code will attempt to be neutral or balanced, to speak from a more distanced institutional or professional position rather than a personal one (see Chapter 6). This effort simultaneously supports the authority of the report as a compiled, vetted, multi-sourced, and neutralized text, and suppresses the potential perspective of the reporter as an individual self.

Various textual strategies allow manifestation of this principle, which tie into linguistic assessments of ***evidentiality***, or the distribution of responsibility for knowledge or the claims of an utterance. The *neutral authority principle* in particular governs lexical choices and influences the use of quoted material, as noted in chapter 7. Thus value-laden words relating to the ballot initiatives are supposed to be eliminated or marked as such. For example, before propositions are assigned numbers, like 187 or 209, they are given identificatory names by their authors – typically, names which frame the initiative so as to appeal to particular voters. By using quotation marks (Example 8.1(a)) and phrases like "so-called" and "dubbed" when referring to these names (Examples 8.1(b) and (c)), the reporter marks that portion of the utterance, distancing the journalist from the partisan conceptual context with which the meaning of the word or phrase is associated, as in the following examples:

Example 8.1
(a) *8/4/95 Chronicle*: The ideological divide was most evident on the issue of illegal immigration, the subject of November's Proposition 187, the "Save Our State" initiative.
(b) *8/12/94 Bee*: Venegas said he opposes Proposition 187, the so-called "Save our State" measure set for the November ballot that seeks to deny public education and social and health services – except for emergency medical care – to undocumented immigrants.
(c) *8/15/94 LAT*: In addition, the council will consider endorsing Proposition 187 on the November ballot. The controversial initiative, dubbed Save Our State, would bar illegal immigrants from receiving public schooling, non-emergency health care and social services.

The examples in 8.1 illustrate the use of particularly identifiable and obvious distancing devices. The quotative nature of these devices, like quotes them-selves, represents the material as coming from the source, and not the reporter.

8.1.2 Providing background

Another discourse requirement is to provide necessary **background** to ensure the reader has sufficient information at hand to understand the news. In the case of long-running stories that appear before the public frequently, or in stories that have been out of the public eye for a long while, this background material – boilerplate – is used as an efficient way of getting readers up to date. Boilerplate, defined by its unreflective, unoriginal replications, works in conjunction with the fact that reporters are to assume that each day's readers are unfamiliar with the previous material, and yet they must also simultaneously background the previous information *and* highlight the new information. On a textual level, it is a cut-and-paste process (initially instituted quite literally by time and technology demands, and one that computer technology has facilitated).

As a story progresses over time, relatively little attention is given to boilerplate by reporters or editors if it is factually or propositionally accurate. Boilerplate allows different reporters to cover a story at different points because it is assumed to be a comprehensive, neutralized summary of the main issues of the story to date – it is assumed to be given or rhemic information – and is repetitively inserted into stories. Boilerplate is also a textual aid that allows reporters to focus on breaking news or to develop a new angle without having to do all the reporting or research work from scratch.

The placement of boilerplate, in modifying clauses on first-mention and in paragraphs at or near the end of a story (where, if necessary, they could be cut, cf. the "inverted pyramid" mentioned in Chapter 7), demonstrates its secondary importance to the main angle of the story and allows an easy apprehension of what is new and old news in the story (what in linguistic terms is given or rhemic – "old" – and new information), as Example 8.2 shows:

Example 8.2
8/14/94 LAT: Supporters and opponents of the Nov. 8 ballot measure – which would deny schooling, non-emergency health care and other public benefits to illegal immigrants – have spent the summer gearing up countywide campaigns aimed at winning over voters.

The underlined phrase is the background material, set apart from the main framing of the story not only by the clausal structure of the sentence, but also by punctuation through the use of dashes.

The discourse rules of *simplification*, *distance*, and sufficient explanation or *background* work together in the construction of boilerplate. Boilerplate represents an extreme distillation of the simplicity rule as it eases the textual workload and reader comprehension, active goals of the newswriting enterprise as noted in previous chapters. Its characteristic generic, non-evaluative, and non-attributed format, as well as its subsidiary and thus expendable relation to the *current* installment of the story, follows the *principle of neutral authority*. Its rhemic nature means it becomes optional in relation to more salient issues, such as newness. Additionally, the summary structure of boilerplate as a piece or pieces of text repeated almost verbatim from story to story allows unmarked repetition over time, also easing the work of comprehension. But what boilerplate allows a reporter to achieve in relation to the larger requirements for the story (primarily those relating to newness) and for reader comprehension may have other consequences which invite examination, particularly when the story is controversial.

8.2   Features of boilerplate

Sacrificing chronology of events to the highlighting of the most newsworthy aspect of a story is a primary rhetorical characteristic of news genres, one that a reporter must learn how to do successfully, and one that also serves as a constraint on background or boilerplate material. Reporters are taught explicitly about presenting background and context within a story, and, indeed, students in beginning newswriting classes often have difficulty interpreting what counts as contextual and *necessary* and what is *expendable*, as some sorts of background material often are (cf. Chapter 7). Unsurprisingly, this difficulty occurs despite the definitions provided to novices that describe background in part as "material placed in the story that explains the event, traces its development and adds facts that sources have not provided" (Mencher 1997: 295).

Boilerplate, because of its often "canned" nature, can be viewed as a particular, more conventionalized form of background, as noted above. Mencher's definition of "background" refers to the explanatory, additive, and chronological nature of background – necessary to the extent that its addition makes news-of-the-moment intelligible. To call something "boilerplate" suggests additional features that make it a discourse subunit of its own: it is repetitious, unattributed, identificatory, descriptive, often expendable, and summarizes what have been interpreted previously by journalists as key "complicating actions" of a story (cf. Labov 1972b).

Example 8.3 stands as a reference example of boilerplate from which I will make other comparisons:

Example 8.3
Proposition 187 bars illegal immigrants from receiving social services and government-paid nonemergency health care. Federal law already forbids them getting those benefits.
The measure also bars illegal immigrants from public schools, even though the U.S. Supreme Court has ruled that unconstitutional.

(San Francisco Chronicle, April 27, 1999)

Example 8.3 bears structural and, more importantly, informational resemblance to Examples 8.1(a), 8.1(c), and 8.2, illustrating one feature of boilerplate: it is *repetitious.* Almost every example in my pre- and post-election corpus, as well as in randomly selected 1999 stories, contains mention of the following informational components down to the very words chosen:

- Illegal (or undocumented) immigrants.
- Deny (or bar, ban, restrict).
- Health, schooling, social services (or public benefits).

The examples also show how the boilerplate summary is repetitious from story to story, across newspapers and within newspapers, and across time. Additionally, this information is *not attributed* to a source, another characterizing feature. Despite the fact that attribution of information is a primary discourse requirement of a news story except in cases of common knowledge (cf. Chapter 7), boilerplate is thus viewed by the reporter – and hence viewable by the reader – as received information or common knowledge. Further, these examples show the *identificatory* positioning of boilerplate. Boilerplate identifies or describes what has occurred. Because it refers to the most observable, concrete aspects of a story, it is more *descriptive* than evaluative; interpreting and explaining is avoided, which allows brevity and repetition. It *summarizes* the story's key events (as in ongoing disaster, accident, or crime coverage) or the main necessary propositional information to date (as in coverage of government, political, or legal news). Boilerplate also responds to what has changed as the story has unfolded. Example 8.3, from 1999, contains information similar to Examples 8.1(b), (c), and 8.2 from before the measure passed in 1994. Challenges were subsequently filed in court after 1994 and then the measure's legal relationships were highlighted in news stories. Thus the 1999 story from which Example 8.3 is extracted contains relevant additional explanatory phrases ("<u>Federal</u> law already forbids them getting those benefits," "the <u>U.S. Supreme Court</u> has ruled that unconstitutional") which themselves are unattributed, identificatory, descriptive, and summarizing.

The physical-conceptual placement of boilerplate within the structure of a news story also positions it as background and allows for its potential *expendability*. It is material that can easily be cut to fit the fluctuating exigencies of the "news hole," the space allotted for that day's stories. Most boilerplate is placed near the bottom of the story where it can be cut (or ignored by readers) if necessary without sacrificing the completeness of the story. For instance, Example 8.3 represents paragraphs 14 and 15 in a seventeen-paragraph story.

There are further distinctions, such as the nature of the summarizing material appearing on first reference. This could be termed "first-reference boilerplate," examples of which follow in 8.4 from stories that are separated by nearly five years:

Example 8.4
(a) *8/13/94 Chronicle*: San Francisco's Social Services Commission voted unanimously Thursday to support a resolution by Supervisors Susan Leal and Tom Hsieh that would oppose Proposition 187, <u>which would deny public benefits to illegal immigrants</u>.

(b) *4/27/99 Chronicle*: While the whisperers and fingerpointers worked the Capitol corridors and phone lines, the federal appeals court accepted Davis' request for the mediator, a low-key method of handling the court challenge to the 1994 measure, which banned state benefits and public education for illegal immigrants.

When repetitious, unattributed, identifying material appears on first reference in the story itself, it is often in a modifying clause at the end of a paragraph, as in both Examples 8.4(a) and 8.4(b). Modifying clauses are easy to cut, often gaining an extra line when space is tight. But given its informational value in first-reference position, this would be the last resort and only if the copy editor (who generally will do the cutting) assumed a general knowledge within the readership. Interestingly, only stories in the corpus that appeared *after* the elections and passage of the propositions regularly eliminated first-reference boilerplate, suggesting that journalists were assuming a fair degree of shared knowledge on the part of readers by then (and pointing up the journalists' own mutable view of careful writing, enacted especially when something is officially or ritually disputed or under contention, as all electoral contests are).

There is even a hierarchical relationship within boilerplate itself, which relates to expendability. The newer legal-challenge information in Example 8.3, by its very location in the text – at the end of a paragraph, in a modifying clause at the end of a paragraph – is positioned as possibly expendable and thus subsidiary to the primary summary that has been integral to the Proposition 187 story from its beginnings. This hierarchy–expendability relationship is made clearer in Example 8.5, which more extensively shows the text from which Example 8.3 is extracted. Example 8.5 also illustrates the extent to which boilerplate is restricted as to *placement*, and points to the distinctions between boilerplate and background elements secondary to the story. Note that the underlined material in the example marks the primary "first-reference" summary of the issue, which predates the election, and the *italicized* material marks the additional facts of the issue, which occurred *after* the election. The most recent development in the story – the reason for publication – is marked by **boldface** type in the lead or first paragraph.

Example 8.5

PARAGRAPH (#)

(1) SACRAMENTO – A **feud** sparked by differences over Proposition 187 between
→ Governor Gray Davis and Lieutenant Governor Cruz Bustamante took a **new turn**
→ **yesterday over parking.**
(2–5) […]
(6) While the whisperers and fingerpointers worked the Capitol corridors and phone lines, the federal appeals court accepted Davis' request for the mediator, a low-key method of handling the court challenge to the 1994 measure, which banned state benefits and public education for illegal immigrants.

(7) *Nearly all of Proposition 187, passed by 59 percent of voters, has been blocked by U.S. District Court Judge Mariana Pfaelzer in Los Angeles.*

(8–13) [...]

(14) Proposition 187 bars illegal immigrants from receiving social services and government-paid nonemergency health care. Federal law already forbids them getting those benefits.

(15) The measure also bars illegal immigrants from public schools, even though the U.S. Supreme Court has ruled that unconstitutional.

(16) *Pfaelzer blocked the ban from taking effect, saying that regulating immigration is solely the job of the federal government.*

(17) *Davis said mediation would allow the state and the measure's opponents a chance to negotiate a settlement.*

(*San Francisco Chronicle*, April 17, 1999; emphases added)

The first five paragraphs of the story develop the lead, or new aspect of the ongoing story. Paragraph 6 relates the immediate situation of the parking feud ("While the whisperers and fingerpointers worked the Capitol corridors") to the current status of the proposition (it is in mediation) and reminds readers what the proposition (passed in 1994, five years earlier) was designed to do (ban state benefits). It is in a pre-emptive position: the reader must not be left too long to wonder about the relation of Proposition 187 to the immediate story. Nonetheless, the clause in the last sentence of paragraph 6 ("which banned ...") highlights the given or rhemic nature of the information, implying a status as background shared by the majority. As first-reference boilerplate, the clause contains identificatory elements that have gone along with the story since its inception ("ban," "benefits," "illegal immigrants"), mentioned in the examples in 8.1. Paragraph 7 builds on the background function as well as the propositional information in the preceding paragraph, which summarizes the court challenge, the most salient dimension of the story since the election.

Paragraph 7's position in relation to the identificatory material in paragraph 6 reaffirms the temporal order of the story, which serves reader comprehension and narrative coherence, and, by its second-order placement, also marks the identificatory facet of the proposition in paragraph 6 as essential. (Paragraphs 8 through 13 develop the feud story line – the new information – and are not included here.) This pattern is repeated in the concluding paragraphs (14–17) and follows the general order of the "inverted pyramid," the basic structure of news texts in which information is placed in diminishing order of importance or salience, the least important in last place. The story could easily be cut after paragraph 13 and still be well-formed; indeed, it could be cut after paragraphs 6 or 7 and still count as a fully fledged news story. Of course, what is cut out – either on the page at any optional moment or in the formulation of boilerplate as a standardized summary – influences what information the public has access to.

8.3   Implications of boilerplate

Boilerplate has implications for public understanding as it both responds to and frames the nature of a news story and its social entailments. Beyond its role in information structure affecting the reader and the public record, boilerplate also has a bearing on the reporter's own position in relation to the information being reported. It supports the ideology or professional stance of "being a reporter," because it marks a form of neutrality and distance. It is contingent – on the story process, its placement, and expendability – creating various editing options depending on what else needs to be addressed that day. It is only a partially representative summary that is never overtly evaluative. Nonetheless, given its characteristics, boilerplate as read or interpreted by both reporter and reader serves to background what can be viewed as a more covert evaluative dimension that may be embedded within the text and within the production of news.

8.3.1   Given and new status

Boilerplate's reflection of the general rules of well-formed news discourse as well as its unique characteristic features jointly support the backgrounding of what is presented. This backgrounding essentially renders uncontested (or incontestable) the information it sets apart, making the issue of "given" or pre-existing seemingly innocuous information key when one considers how the structure of texts and the meaning of their constituent parts have an impact on public understanding. The story as it is presented may be the only version of the event a reader has.

Boilerplate is essentially information about some facet of the story that predates the new angle being freshly reported; it is given (or rhemic) information that is assumed to be generally known but cannot be left out because it explicitly gives background or a history of the issue to date. As the given information that accompanies stories that are long-running, boilerplate is a standard textual element because reporters are always to assume a new and uninformed audience at the same time they must background the previously presented material and foreground the new information. Not knowing what prior discourse the audience has had access to, the reporter has boilerplate as a tool to serve a multifunctional discourse purpose. Its features (repetition, non-attribution, identification, structural placement) lead to an interpretation of genericness that allows a reader to either skim or ignore the information as given at the same time it can be read for its informational value by a first-time or forgetful reader. Either way, the framing of the issue, as we have seen in the example case of Proposition 187 in two different years, becomes part of the public record. If a story is an ongoing one, as most stories that have an impact on the sociopolitical sphere are, the preliminary depiction of the issue gets replicated and repeated through boilerplate.

8.3.2   The neutral authority model

Reporters spend a fair amount of professional and thus discursive energy distancing themselves and the news texts they produce from the claims, propositions, narratives, and beliefs they are reporting on. At the same time, an utterance has more credibility when it is directly or indirectly viewed as coming from a source other than the reporter, hence the tremendous emphasis in US journalism that is placed on attribution of information. The reporter thus positions himself or herself as a neutral authority, using professional identity and the resources of the text to do so. As mentioned earlier, the principle of neutral authority would account for words such as "so-called" or "dubbed," as in "Proposition 187, dubbed the Save Our State initiative." These quotative textual markers isolate the phrase that follows as not of the journalist's creation: "Save Our State" and its accompanying "SOS" acronym are interpreted as value judgments by the initiative's originators, that the state needs help. These distancing textual devices (including scare-quotes) allow the perpetuation of a neutral authority, and distance the reporter from the evaluative stance of the source.

Of course, despite the professional-ideological constraints governing personal affiliations to the matters being reported, the boundary between social self and professional self is semi-permeable, as are the issues of authorship in the discursive process of reporting the news in which one story is the outcome of many contributing participants. Boilerplate, despite the features that lead to a generic or neutral reading, nonetheless owes its origin to the primary framing of an issue. In the case of a ballot measure, the authors of a ballot proposition provide a baseline definition of an issue, creating and setting the terms for debate against this baseline. Given the source of what ends up as boilerplate, the use of "neutral" or unattributed information can better be seen as representing the journalist's *intention* to hold to a neutral authority model rather than cut-and-dried evidence of a neutral authority alone.

8.3.3   Contingencies in the story process

Boilerplate is contingent on the story process as it unfolds over time and changes to meet changing informational needs. In the data, there were substantive changes in the presentation of boilerplate after the elections, when modifying clauses after first mention – as in the examples in 8.1 – fall off and acronyms such as CCRI (the California Civil Rights Initiative) or SOS (Save Our State) to refer to Propositions 209 and 187 all but disappear. One could hypothesize that after the proposition becomes ratified by voters its presence becomes unmarked and viewable as shared knowledge; or that editors and reporters are less careful. Particular care is generally taken with stories before an election – by reporters *and* editors – because of the potential loss of credibility and status as a neutral authority, which news organizations (and individual reporters) want to maintain.

Boilerplate usage changes not only in response to actual events, but also in connection with developing social attitudes. In fact, the meaning of Proposition 187 and its implications changed over time from a legislative proposition with specific consequences for a specific group of people to a symbolic marker that invoked a larger and more abstract set of social meanings. Immigration-related stories that ran in 1995, the year after the proposition's passage, began to cite Proposition 187 in passing as tangential to the main point of whatever the current story was – as a way to illustrate what was viewed as a general decline in tolerance, particularly toward immigrants and minority communities generally. In this way, Proposition 187, which was viewed by opponents as punitive and racist, became linked to a new proposition in the next election cycle, Proposition 209, itself viewed by detractors as racist and exclusionary. The boilerplate phrasing remained the same, but the contingencies of its use and contexts in which it was embedded changed. Despite its relatively low textual value and its inert, below-the-radar information status, boilerplate can thus be viewed as both a highly contingent and situated discourse element.

8.3.4   Partial representation of an event

Related to its contingent status, boilerplate is only a partial representation of the fuller meaning of what it is characterizing. Although it does not carry an overt evaluative stance, it can be seen as offering a position by its presence. I have already noted that boilerplate in Proposition 187 coverage functions to identify the proposition by articulating only what it will do (limit benefits for a particular segment of the population). This information is drawn from the actual language of the ballot initiative, which itself can be viewed as separate from the social agenda or rationale of its authors. The *implications* of Proposition 187 are not included within the boundaries of boilerplate because implications are evaluative and therefore not compatible with "neutral," unattributed information.

There are a number of features of Proposition 187 that seldom appeared in the majority of the hundreds of summaries (both background and boilerplate) presented in the three California papers. These include the following:

• that it is a measure to get federal attention with the hopes of changing national immigration policy;
• that federal laws would supersede the state initiative (this fact comes out in boilerplate well after the election, as Example 8.6 shows);
• who the detractors and supporters of the measure are;
• the fiscal impacts;
• the partial unanimity across the opposing camps that the issue of illegal immigration needs to be addressed;

- the most dire implications raised by either side (at their worst: zero-sum diminution of life-as-we-know-it vs. unhealthy, uneducated, underserved underclass); and
- its relation to other events and anti-immigrant attitudes from California's recent past, such as Japanese-American internment during World War Two.

These details, which are less about identification and contain more socially complex implications, are often relegated to invisibility because they are not currently "new." And because they cannot easily be summarized without all the apparatus of proper reporting (e.g., balance, attribution, fairness to all positions, fresh quotes), they go unrepeated. Example 8.6 from the *Los Angeles Times* is a rare example that includes the points that are seldom raised or represented in boilerplate about Proposition 187 (issues under debate, jobs and the border, and the viewpoints of authorities outside of the political sphere, such as "scholars and other authorities"):

Example 8.6
8/10/94 LAT: But even as polls show the measure gathering widespread support among voters, its very premise – that public services and schools draw illegal immigrants – remains a matter of fierce debate. The initiative doesn't directly address jobs, widely considered by scholars and other authorities to be the principal lure for immigrants. Nor does Proposition 187 do anything about the porous U.S.– Mexico border.

One could also look at the presence of boilerplate in relation to a host of intertwined agendas, themselves inherently partial. Proponents and detractors have their own complicated political agendas, which become the content of what is reported, while journalists themselves, under the mantle of neutral authority, have a stated position of balance within journalistic practice that is intended to supersede personal political agendas. But the issue of balance itself is a negotiated and conventionalized notion, entailing a certain *kind* of journalistic balance: getting an equal number of (at least two) sides; quoting the originator of a claim, which is preferable to a third-party spokesperson quote; verifying and testing claims against the "other" side; and giving the person singled out a chance to respond, to voice another view.

From this perspective, journalistic partiality is rarely overt and instead becomes reflective of a mainstream orientation to or understanding of a topic, and of professional practice in handling text. But as the requirements of news discourse stand, the neutrality or balance rules sometimes work *against* balance when the issue is complicated and the meanings are negotiable or contested. This is where journalists can pause: not only are assumptions embedded within boilerplate, but more importantly, the summary of story is only partial. It is good to keep this in mind: the elements of a "complete," well-formed news story represent an interpretation of what is considered important on the journalistic level as well as on the level of shared, public knowledge.

8.3.5   Evaluation in "neutral" text

Although every effort may be made to eliminate value judgments in journalistic practice, there are discourse-level issues that can be seen as privileging an evaluative stance because they inherently contextualize information and how it may be interpreted. Quotes and repetition are two components of narrative structure that orient an audience to the material being presented. I have already mentioned the relation between the repetition of boilerplate and given vs. new information. From the journalistic perspective, repetition might be better viewed not so much a reinforcement of the propositions, but as a way of marking elements of the story so that a reader has what he or she needs to process the news of the moment – the emphasis being on what is new and comprehensible and not on what is comprehensive (see Cotter 1993).

The use of quotes by reporters serves not only to disavow responsibility for an utterance but to sometimes also point to a frame of reference or perspective that cannot be expressed personally or within the parameters of the reporter's textual participation. (Otherwise the "intrusion," or violation of expected journalistic norms, will be noted by editors and disallowed before it reaches print.) In the Proposition 187 coverage, restricted material such as the rare overtly racist or "politically incorrect" comment by sources was carried within quotations, as in the Example 8.7.

Example 8.7
8/10/94 LAT: "Illegal aliens are killing us in California," said Ronald Prince, a Tustin accountant who heads the Proposition 187 campaign. "Those who support illegal immigration are, in effect, anti-American."
8/13/94 LAT: "Thanks for sticking up for white people!" says a call-in listener from Del Mar Vista to Buck's radio show, pleased with the host's support of Proposition 187, which would take away most public benefits to illegal immigrants.

Even so, reporters may be so grounded within the professional ethic in which quotes are predominantly viewed and used as distancing devices that they do not also see another perspective: that reporters are co-responsible – along with the speaker being quoted – for the content they produce, including their choice of what they include within quoted material. But the responsibility does not only reside with the reporter and newsmaker. If the quote is an implicit way reporters can present information about the participants in a story without violating the discourse-level norms governing newswriting or the reporter's own perceived role in the discourse, the reader is also implicated. The reader becomes part of the inferential process, distributing responsibility for the construction of meaning beyond the newsroom and into the living room (or coffee shop or laptop or commuter train or wherever news is consumed).

8.4 Conclusion: responsibility and "neutral" text production

The discourse requirement to provide accessible synopses and background information in news stories leads to textual elements like "boilerplate" and other shorthand devices of reference. General journalistic writing rules – simplification of complex issues or events, authorial distance and the value of neutrality or balance, and the recurrence of sufficient given information to render all new versions of a story intelligible by the majority of intended readers – guide the production of boilerplate, which has intrinsic characteristics. It is repetitious, unattributed, identifies and describes, summarizes, and is potentially expendable as text.

Nonetheless, there are implications for the transmission of meaning that are inherent in even the most innocuous or expendable forms of text. For example, Santa Ana (1999, 2002) argues that the issues of immigration were formulated rhetorically by journalists to ultimately minimize humanitarian responses in discussions of Propositions 187 and 209, whether it was consciously intended or not. These meanings, which likely extended beyond journalists' intentions, were also potently interacting with social values held by the larger public collective (the propositions, after all, were voted in by the electorate). Nonetheless, they are potentially replicated in each iteration of the story because background material – which carries the story's history over time – is seldom challenged on behalf of its content. Boilerplate, for its part in a news story, contributes just as significantly to the orientation of the public debate as do the lead and other more highlighted textual components of a story.

Because boilerplate assists in responding to and framing the nature of public discourse, it is worth noticing by journalists, linguists, and the public. Like all linguistic and discursive elements situated contextually, it plays a multi-level role in shaping social action. Considered generic and uncontested information, boilerplate is also a textual device that allows the reporter to distance authorially from the material and helps to establish the professional persona of a neutral authority. As a summarizing mechanism, it only partially represents what it is characterizing, a feature that may have greater significance when the issue is complicated, socially contested, and relates to issues of authority, power, and responsibility in society. On their own, mainstream journalists generally resist changing or tinkering with the rules that they perceive as supporting free speech. But perhaps linguists can argue the point for them, by pointing out the rituals and routines of news production and texts, exploring the connection of text-level behaviors to social meaning, and thereby bring the discussion to another footing – one that could offer alternative readings and meanings in the presentation of contested issues to the public.

In keeping with my objective to develop the "ethnographic insider" perspective and have linguists and journalists better understand the other's professional points of view about language, meaning, social roles, and action, we will move on to chapter 9. There we will examine the attitudes journalists have toward language use, as news professionals and as members of the larger social world, and discuss how these influence, too, the shape of news texts.

9 Style and standardization in news language

KEY POINTS

- Journalists have a very self-conscious relationship to language, meta-talk about which is part of everyday practice. Their self-identity as "protectors" of the language is part of the professional discourse from textbook to trade publication; in other words, from student days to retirement.
- Journalists' language attitudes are conservative, prescriptive, and mainstream; their role in societal language standardization complex but robust. They reiterate culturally situated language norms through the processes of news production. But communicative needs can supersede prescriptive ones.
- Standardization in the journalistic realm is also discursive: Well-formed news discourse is structured by a fairly strict set of rules that govern how information is selected and presented, leading to an identifiable "news style."

While many people consider the media's handling of language an affront to good usage, the news media in fact have a fairly prescriptive and conservative, rather than innovative and laissez-faire, attitude toward language use. Print and broadcast media are concerned with maintaining their own style rules as well as upholding the mainstream language-use standards of society; copy editors (or sub-editors) actively aim to "preserve" the language. In this chapter, I orient the social and structural factors of language standardization to the practice and attitudes of the news media, noting journalism's role in influencing language style and accommodating to standard language ideologies. Additionally the news context offers something else which I detail: many instances in which communicative demands – instigated by interaction with the public or imposed by the rules of newswriting – supersede prescriptive habits. News language, thus, reflects the larger social status quo; at the same time it operates independently of it.

The general investigations in this chapter involve looking at news language – both the written word of print media and the planned oral/aural discourse in the case of broadcast news – as a reflex of social practice; observing how a pattern of usage reflects community norms; exploring the extent of the news media's participation in language standardization processes; and revealing unexamined assumptions about media processes, production, and language. The particular questions are: What is the news media's insider attitude toward language and usage? What role do journalists play in language standardization within the larger culture? What might a media practitioner actually do to promote (or subvert) standardization? Data come from a range of sources, including newswriting textbooks, journalism style guides, professional publications, field interviews and classroom teaching, published news-outlet "ombudsman" responses to questions by the public, and select case studies.

As my overarching objective is to shed light on the correlations between praxis and discourse – between reporting and writing in a range of media modalities – I will look at language style and standardization in both print and radio news contexts focusing on the language values that undergird journalistic identity, and the public complaints and professional injunctions concerning language production in the media. I also demonstrate that linguistic innovations and changes occur over time in the service of the communicative needs of news discourse, as when news practitioners expand standard genre forms or circumvent what I call the *prescriptive imperative*.

9.1   Background: language standardization

Language standardization is a process generally wrought by conscious intervention on the part of social groups, either in a collectively unreflective and somewhat ad hoc manner or very deliberately, either from within a speech community or from without (by, for example, government committee). The goal of language standardization, as Milroy and Milroy (1999: 6) succinctly put it, is the "suppression of optional variability in language," to minimize variety and choice. A standard language means that one form or variety of usage is preferred, privileged, and expected to be used in particular social contexts and discourse situations, and is considered the norm to aspire to. The parameters under which standardization and variation (optional or otherwise) occur are linguistic, sociolinguistic, social, and operational (see Table 9.1).

From a linguistic perspective, standardization favors one phonological, lexical, syntactic, or stylistic form over others. Is it "ee-ther" or "eye-ther," "HAR-ass" or "har-ASS"; is it "soda" or "soft drink," "kids" or "children"; is it "isn't" or "ain't," "have gone" or "have went"; is it "beverage" or "drink," an elaborated description or brief comment, "posh/fancy/la-de-da" (as some speakers gauge usage that marks status) or "normal/regular" (as others view usage that indexes

Table 9.1 *Standardization parameters*

Parameters	Mechanisms
• Linguistic	Favors one form over others:
	– *Phonological*
	– *Lexical*
	– *Syntactic*
	– *Stylistic*
• Sociolinguistic	Prestige carrier
	Norm function
	Written modality
• Social	Institutions
	Power, exercise and reinforcement of
	Implementation process (can be ad hoc or deliberate)
	Speech community inputs (or not)
• Operational	Prescriptive grammars
	Dictionaries
	Language mavens (cf. Pinker, R. Lakoff, Bolinger)

solidarity)? Sociolinguistically, the standard variety tends to be the prestige form, or the norm against which evaluations of use are calibrated, whether the ultimate goal is to support solidarity or social connection or to support status and relative hierarchy and position among speakers in a community.

Standardization generally refers to the written rather than the spoken variety. Indeed, as many scholars have pointed out (Bex 1996; Chafe 1984; Milroy and Milroy 1999, etc.), standard language practices have been facilitated by the rise of the written word – and of the "complaint tradition" that sprang up alongside it – enabled by the invention of the printing press and subsequent technologies. It is most often the case that the written variety trumps the spoken in all arguments about "correct" usage. The examples from the news media, which I note below, will also indicate this.

In the larger social context, institutions such as schools and funding bodies – power-holding entities in the economic and social senses – are the formal instigators of standardization, connecting economic status and social position, as well as community-valued goals such as literacy, social mobility, and community cohesion, to the outcomes of language choice. The implementation process of standardization, most visible through government-level language policy and planning, can be ad hoc or deliberate, politicized or pragmatic, and engaged with or without input from the speech community.

Operationally, the standardization process is supported by prescriptive grammars, dictionaries, and the constant intervention of "language mavens" (Pinker 1994), "language bosses" (Lakoff 1990), and "language shamans" (Bolinger

1980). Language mavens are published opinion leaders and columnists like the late William Safire in the US (see Aitchison 1997 for British examples), who for hundreds of years have helped to establish a "complaint tradition," correlating any variation and change in usage against the prescribed norm with the decline of civilization (cf. examples in Milroy and Milroy 1999). The process has generated prescriptive notions about language use (many of which linguists have learned to discount, but see also Cameron 1995), and a complex of responses about "correct language" that falls under the rubric of "standard language ideology," or the underlying assumption that only one form is right.

While the standard attempts to suppress optional variation in usage, difference does exist. Comparative examples from other geographical places with their different social and political histories – from the next county over to the next country over – illustrate the variation in approach, in meaning, and in the role of broader social concerns in dealing with language standardization and language use (see Bell 1991 and Leitner 1980, 1984, for comparative research on radio data). Indeed, linguists investigating usage within the sociology of language tradition (e.g., Lippi-Green 1997; Milroy and Milroy 1999) have argued that what comes to be recognized as the standard language in a society is more of an abstraction or target ideal that users strive in the direction of, and a function or result of an ideology of standardization, rather than a description of what is actually achieved. Given that perspective influences judgment, one will never be "correct enough" unless one expands one's contexts of interpretation.

9.2   Language standardization in the news context

Language standardization in the news context derives from the larger social context of which it is part as well as the demands of news production. In the news context, language standardization is an ongoing, socially motivated, responsive process internal to news organizations, evoking the factors that facilitate change and stability (cf. Cotter 2003). The metalinguistic attention that most language users possess and bring to bear in daily interactions and social evaluations is part of active, explicit, and everyday awareness throughout the profession, from reporter to editor, aspiring journalism student to journalism educator. Unsurprisingly, as they are not trained as linguists, in the absence of descriptive linguistic knowledge, the conclusions and assessments of news practitioners are prescriptive, and embody familiar "lay" notions of language, as examples in Chapter 7 evidenced.

News practitioners respond to socially motivated standardization pressures. At the same time, they work actively to honor the discursive metalinguistic norms and rules of their craft (as discussed in previous chapters, particularly

Table 9.2 *News language standardization tools and rules*

Operational tools

- Explicit and implicit standardization policies
- Style guides and in-house manuals
- Pronunciation committees
- Individuals charged with maintaining uniformity of presentation (e.g., editors)

Discursive-journalistic mechanisms

- Rules of writing for appropriate modality
- Newsgathering conventions
- Core journalistic ideals

2, 3, and 7). It is important to note that the issue of standard usage in and of itself ties in with and is somewhat inseparable from the journalistically motivated standardization that circumscribes news genre forms. Mainstream and journalistic ideologies intertwine; lay notions of usage are blended with journalistic ones. This intricate relationship is indicated by Jill Geisler, news director at a Midwestern television station, who made the following suggestion to broadcast reporters:

Study grammar. So much of what we do is *live*. A journalist's credibility is destroyed by usage errors. In live reporting, no editor can save you. Newsrooms should develop a culture in which appropriate English usage is paramount and immediate feedback is given. (Quoted in Utterback 1995: 237)

In the Geisler case, several assumptions about the relation of journalists to language are present:

- The importance of correct usage and its basis in maintaining a journalistic identity.
- The explicit connection of credibility – an essential journalistic goal and professional value – and language use.
- The exigencies of the medium: live reporting requires a special attention to language production, to performance.
- That editors, especially, function as usage monitors ("no editor can save you").

The reference to a "culture" of correctness within the newsroom implicates the physical and psychological boundaries of the professional setting, and with them the larger journalistic production/performance contexts that this book attempts to illuminate and the many insider-aware entailments that follow from them.

There are tools on hand to assist with the routinization or conventionalization of language as it appears in the news, as summarized in Table 9.2. These tools are both *operational* – bounded, physical, and atomistic in the form of documents or people one queries or consults for reference or for decisions on language use, writing, and editing – and *discursive* – shared *underlying* rules and conventions that are applied to the production of stories.

The operational tools are common, explicit, and take physical shape: any insider or outsider could read a style guide, check it online, or consult a copy editor. The discursive mechanisms are embedded within the news culture, drive actual daily process, practice and production of stories, and must be learned: knowledge of them is necessary, assumed, and reinforced by insiders (cf. Chapters 3 and 7).

Reporters, no matter their nationality, have easy access to style guides and in-house style manuals and are expected to consult them daily. For decades the *AP Stylebook* has been known as "the journalist's 'bible'" and is still the default throughout the profession in the US. At the same time, individual newsrooms have manuals listing local style conventions and local information. Some examples: the Redding (Calif.) *Record Searchlight* notes for incoming editorial staff and for forgetful veterans that nearby and visible Mt. Shasta, the peak, is 14,162 ft. high; the California State University, Chico *Orion* newspaper style manual specifies that it should be "California State University, Chico" on first reference in stories, not "Chico State" which is the common, everyday reference; and Fasold *et al.* 1990 quote guidelines for non-sexist language in the *Washington Post* style guide.

Copy editors (or sub-editors in the UK) are charged with maintaining consistency of style (following both in-house and prescriptive rules) and uniformity of presentation (headline sizes, font, etc.). The broadcast media, the oral transmitters, also have explicit and implicit standardization policies, supported by style guides, pronunciation committees, and individuals charged with maintaining a uniformity of presentation. A well-known example is the BBC's Pronunciation Unit, which arbitrates on language usage matters, cf. Bell 1991; Sangster 2005. Other circumstances will be discussed below.

9.2.1   *Journalistic and discursive standardization*

To understand standardization in the media context, it is useful to look at it as journalistic and discursive, as well as linguistically and prescriptively related to the larger culture's notions of correct usage. News discourse is rule-governed, routinized, and follows on from profession-specific norms and routines. Journalistically, standardization involves the rules of writing for the appropriate *modality* (e.g., writing for a listener and emphasizing "conversational style" in the case of broadcast, cf. Brooks *et al.* 2005), the news-gathering *conventions* of the profession (see previous chapters), and the proliferation of core journalistic *ideals* such as balance of sources, attribution of sources, and responsiveness to audience. Discourse-level activity is bound by awareness of the norms of speaking and writing. The ratified news community member will display this communicative competence in both domains.

Discursive standardization ties into sociolinguistic or ethnomethodological notions of communicative competence (Garfinkel 1972; Hymes 1972a, 1974), or using language appropriately within a community's sociocultural context. Print reporters and broadcasters show themselves to be ratified members of the journalistic community by writing, reporting, thinking, and responding "like a reporter," and through appropriate presentation (visually, aurally) of story elements, actions which are learned through socialization in the profession. In broadcast, that ratification display is through appropriate tone of voice (key), management of prosodic conventions and intonation contours, and knowing when to engage in the spontaneous chat that Goffman 1981 described as "fresh talk" on the air, or change footing. In print, reporters show similar communicative competence through appropriate use of Associated Press and local news style, management of newswriting conventions, and knowing how to orient discursively to different types of stories with different style and structure requirements (features vs. news, breaking news, second-day news, briefs, meeting stories, etc., as noted in Chapter 7) as well as through profession-specific display of "text-category indicators" (Nunberg 1990) like punctuation, headline style, paragraphing, graphics, physical positioning, and page layout.

The structure of news also plays a part in journalistic standardization, particularly as structure-related features are rule-governed, constantly managed (by reporters and editors), and their effective execution consequently a hallmark of communicative competence. Certain structural components are required (such as the *lead* or opening paragraph, as discussed at length in Chapter 7), topics are constrained (on newsworthiness grounds, as mentioned in Chapter 4), and sequences within stories and on news pages themselves (or within a broadcast or Web program) follow a proscribed format (noted in Chapters 7 and 8). These patterns are especially visible in the *hierarchy of information elements* (a reporter learns how to reorder the narrative sequences); in *placement of attribution* (and subsequent nuances of *evidentiality*); in *stylistic variation by genre* (news stories and feature stories and opinion columns in complementary distribution); and in aspects of *deixis* and *indexicality* – such as datelines which signify the place where the news has occurred, introduction of sources and their implied or explicit relevance, reference to time (see Chapters 4, 5, and 6), and in embedded notions of audience, readership, and journalistic role in the community outside the newsroom (see Chapters 5 and 6).

(Economic factors also influence the shape of the news program for both print and broadcast: story length and the ratio of news to advertising content are often directly tied to marketing mandates. The "news hole" is what is open to editorial content – news stories – after the advertising has been positioned.)

9.3   Journalists and language: complaints, values, and injunctions

9.3.1   The "complaint tradition"

Reporters and editors, highly self-conscious of the use of language, differentiate between "writing" and "reporting," on one hand privileging reporting and its skill set (as outlined in Chapters 2, 3, 6, and 7), and on the other expecting competence in the use of language in writing and editing stories. One cannot get hired without acceptable "reporting" or information-elicitation skills; reporting is what one does (someone who self-identifies as a "writer" vs. a "reporter" may not get hired, as I have witnessed in my own newsroom experience). At the same time, language meta-talk is part of everyday practice in the newsroom. "Wordsmiths" are valued (cf. Aitchison 2007 and industry publications).

In the newsroom, the copy editors are considered the word experts. (Copy editors deal with the particulars of language – usage editing – as opposed to content editing, which is what section editors primarily do.) Within the journalism realm, copy editors are viewed as the "protectors" of the language; indeed, one widely used copy-editing textbook (Baskette et al. 1986) titled a chapter on usage, "Protecting the Language." Journalism educators, many of them former or current reporters or editors, help support and perpetuate the language-maven approach to usage, making explicitly clear to students – and colleagues – the necessity of maintaining prescriptive rules. Their actions and attitudes follow logically and smoothly along the lines of the "complaint tradition," and the promotion of the larger culture's standard language ideology. At the same time these actions and attitudes support the communicative norms intrinsic to being a member of the journalist community, as the examples below will show.

Milroy and Milroy (1999) differentiate two types of complaint about language: "legalistic" and "moralistic." **Type 1** or legalistic complaints concern actual errors (grammar, punctuation, pronunciation); **Type 2** or moralistic complaints concern twists of meaning (semantic sleights-of-hand leading to the absence of clarity and honesty). The public airing of complaints about the breaking of prescriptive rules (Type 1) and "spin" or bias (Type 2) is part of the reinforcement of a society's standard language ideology as well as news language ideology. Complaints about infringements of "correct" language use in news stories come from both the public and from within the news profession itself.

To keep complaints and subsequent self-recriminations at bay, as well as maintain journalistic style consistency, there is day-to-day reliance on the operational tools like stylebooks and trade publications and textbooks. "Legalistic" issues upon which the news media expect consensus – such as spelling, abbreviations, numerals, addresses, etc. – are the province of stylebooks. "Moralistic" issues concerning clarity of expression and the relationship

Primary usage injunctions	Complaint tradition correlates
Journalistic language ideology "Accuracy equals credibility"	Type 1 (legalistic - correctness)
Journalistic craft ideology "Good writing equals clarity"	Type 2 (moralistic - truth)
Journalistic language values Precision and prescription **Goal**: To safeguard accuracy and clarity	Types 1 and 2

Figure 9.1 Profession-centric language ideologies

of accuracy and credibility (mentioned in Chapter 2) are discussed in trade publications, textbooks, and op-ed columns and repeated as needed in day-to-day newsroom interaction (see the examples below).

9.3.2   News language and craft ideologies

News practitioners have their own language ideology which leads to injunctions about usage profession-internally that are Type 1 or "legalistic" in scope. This language ideology can be summarized as: *Accuracy equals credibility.* Being accurate – with words as well as facts – is the foundation of journalistic credibility, without which journalistic actions are empty. At the same time, their "craft" ideology leads to injunctions about appropriate journalistic performance that are Type 2 or "moralistic" in tenor which can be summarized as: *Good writing equals clarity.* Clarity is an objective that is constantly striven for (and relates to larger issues of "truth," which I will not elaborate on here). The language values underlying these profession-specific ideologies are **precision** (for both *accuracy* and *good writing*) and, to maintain precision, **prescription**. Knowing, following, and maintaining the prescriptive rules about language use will ensure precision; precision helps to safeguard both accuracy (Type 1) and clarity (Type 2) and is thus a fundamental professional value.

   Figure 9.1 summarizes the language usage values and ideologies of journalists and their explicit discursive, linguistic, and practice-driven objectives, and correlates them with the Milroys' Complaint Tradition Type 1 and 2 elements. Figure 9.1 also shows schematically how journalistic language ideology and values, i.e., the explicit expectation of precision in language use, intermingles with the larger society's standard language ideology, or prescription of use. The journalistic view toward usage embodies both elements of the complaint tradition: the legalistic (is it correct?) and the moralistic (does it mean what it should?).

Examples of this language ideology embodiment in professional texts are easily "read" in primary sources of standardization information for journalists, e.g., *The AP Stylebook* and newswriting textbooks (which distill daily practice in idealized form). *The AP Stylebook*, as well as the comparable *Times*, *Guardian*, and *Economist* style guides in the UK, indicates what aspects of language use are standardized and are expected to be adhered to – specifics such as spelling, abbreviations, courtesy titles, numerals, addresses, datelines (cities than can "stand alone" without state, province, or country), etc. – and more general social issues involving representation of age, gender, ethnicity, and disability that stylebooks include guidelines on.

In a similar profession-specific vein, newswriting textbooks explicitly indicate the importance and rhetorical value of *precision* and *clarity* of written expression in news stories, without necessarily problematizing or situating these rhetorical expectations outside of their immediate journalistic purview (as linguists both ethnographic and critical, for instance, would do) as exemplified in Example 9.1:

Example 9.1

(a) Good writing is precise, clear and concrete. It also shows rather than tells and uses figures of speech. (Brooks *et al.* 1999: 153, emphasis added)

(b) Writers owe their audiences three major considerations; to compose with care, style and clarity. (Newsom and Wollert 1988: 52, emphasis added)

(c) [Writing] should be good, clear, concise English that avoids cliché. It is the bedrock of journalism. (Fletcher 2005: 100, emphasis added)

Example 9.1 summarizes what counts as good writing, and relates good journalistic practice with *precision* and *clarity*. The Newsom and Wollert extract (9.1(b)) additionally underscores the inherent responsibility to audience (readers, listeners) that reporters must uphold, linking journalistic craft ideology particular to the community of coverage with appropriate rhetorical action in their news stories.

9.3.3   Journalistic language values: prescribing precision

Beneath the language and craft ideologies are actual usage injunctions that maintain language values actively, both in meta-talk about practice (see chapter 2) and in the day-to-day achievement of it. The explicit expectation of *precision* in language is manifested in different ways leading to usage injunctions and assumptions that are the bedrock of newswriting and reporting. One professional injunction is that *precision equals accuracy*, as exemplified in Example 9.2:

Example 9.2

Words should be used precisely. They should mean exactly what you intend them to mean. You should never use "uninterested" when you mean "disinterested." Nor should you use "allude" for "refer," "presume" for "assume," "endeavor" for "try," "fewer" for "less," "farther" for "further." [...] You can make the mayor "say," "declare," "claim" or "growl" – but only one is accurate.   (Brooks *et al.* 1999: 153, emphasis added)

In this textbook extract, "accuracy" means choosing the correct lexical item. The examples are not unfamiliar to standard-variety speakers and are similar to a list a high school English teacher might provide to students. It also makes clear that using the reporting verb "said" when quoting sources is the "only" correct option. Using "said" as a reporting verb is a fundamental writing rule, and adherence to it is held to on the grounds of accuracy (cf. Chapter 7). In other words, there is only one attribution verb – *said* (or *says*) – so "only one is accurate." Anything else by extension is "wrong" as "accurate" means "correct" according to journalistic prescription. Taking the *precision equals accuracy* assumption one step further, Example 9.3 collates the legalistic and the moralistic objectives of prescriptivism:

Example 9.3
Precision means choosing the correct sentence structure [...] Far too often, grammar and punctuation errors obscure meaning. (Brooks *et al.* 1999: 155–157, emphasis added)

In other words, **accurate** practice, particularly with respect to grammar, punctuation, and sentence structure (Type 1 concerns), leads to **clarity** of meaning (Type 2 issues). "Errors" – lack of precision – "obscure" it.

In a more Type 2 or moralistic vein, there is the assumption that *precision equals truth*, in that precise language minimizes unwanted, unnecessary, or unintended moral judgment. Example 9.4, which mandates against the use of sexist and racist language, shows this:

Example 9.4
Even when used innocently, sexist and racist language, in addition to being offensive and discriminatory, is imprecise [...] Our language is bursting with derogatory racial terminology [...] they rain inaccurate stereotypes on a class of people [...] Some dismiss this concern for language as being politically correct. That implies we are afraid to tell the truth. What is the truth in any ethnic slang? The truth is that many words historically applied to groups of people were created in ignorance or hate or fear [...] As writers concerned with precision of the language, we should deal with people, not stereotypes.
                (Brooks *et al.* 1999: 153–154, emphasis added)

The textbook writers in Example 9.4 make clear that "precision of the language" should be a concern when reporting on ("a class of") people. They argue on legalistic grounds that sexist and racist language is "imprecise," and argue on moralistic grounds that "ethnic slang," much of it "created in ignorance or hate or fear," does not in fact convey any relevant "truth" about the person or people being reported on. They correlate the craft ideal of good writing with correct meaning, precision, and appropriate surface-level lexical choice.

As Example 9.3 also showed, behind the journalistic language value of *precision* are the prescriptive components that proscribe it: rules of grammar, rules of style, and appropriate (i.e., minimally claused) sentence structure (cf. Chapter 7). Prescriptive issues that are raised from the beginning in the journalism classroom tend to be Type 1 or legalistic, as in Example 9.5, which mentions a number of prescriptive rule violations that should be avoided:

Example 9.5
No one who aspires to be a writer will succeed without knowing the rules of grammar. Dangling participles, split infinitives, noun-verb disagreements and misplaced modifiers are like enemy troops: they attack your sentences and destroy their meaning. The best defense is to construct tight, strong sentences.

(Brooks *et al.* 1999: 157–158, emphasis added)

Here, the *precision equals accurate meaning* injunction is tied up with heeding the rules of grammar, the violation of which will "destroy" meaning. (The sentence structure of this example and underlying conceptual metaphor of doing battle – with the entailments of taking action, defending, and winning – concurrently provides an *in situ* model for learners becoming familiar with news style as well as explicit articulation of what good writing involves.) That learning and applying correct (or standard English) grammar is a foundational first step, and one that is not necessarily easy to achieve, and operates in tandem with other profession-specific prescriptive injunctions (that of following the unique set of discursive rules of the particular spoken or written medium) is indicated in Example 9.6:

Example 9.6
Newswriters **must** know and observe the style rules of standard English. And they have the additional burden of **obeying** the rules of the medium they're working for.

(Newsom and Wollert 1988: 53, emphasis added)

The authors in Example 9.6 are aware of and make clear the differences between the larger community and the journalistic one. For our purposes, it is significant to see that they are connecting the maintenance of a standard language variety to being a news professional, as a demonstration of being competent and establishing credibility, upon which rests the individual's and the news profession's reputation, value, and success of output or of achieving journalistic goals.

9.3.4   Complaints about usage from the public

Despite all the efforts from within the profession, news outlets routinely receive complaints about language from the public. For example, National Public Radio in the US, which through a series of independent local member stations covers the whole of the country with 26 million listeners (and is available worldwide via the Web),[1] receives frequent complaints from listeners that are addressed by the network's ombudsman, as Examples 9.7, 9.8, and 9.9 show.

Example 9.7
[Listener complaint]
   Please tell [news reader] Bob Edwards to look in any good dictionary (if NPR has one) and find the word "controversial." The correct pronunciation is "CON-TRO-VER-SHUL," not "con-tro-ver-see-al."

[News practitioner (ombudsman) response]
   Actually, there are frequent but <u>subtle</u> regional variations in NPR's pronunciations. Bob Edwards' Kentucky roots may be showing from time to time. <u>In my opinion</u>, regional pronunciations should be encouraged as long as those <u>locutions</u> don't <u>distract from the story</u>.					(Dvorkin 2002d, emphasis added)

In Example 9.7, the listener maintains that only one form of spoken "controversial" is correct, hearkens to the authority of a dictionary, and castigates the news organization's inattention to linguistic detail. In effect, he is acting like any self-respecting language maven by trying to suppress optional variation, maintaining the hallmark of language standardization. The ombudsman, in his response, defends the newsreader on the grounds of regional variation, thus allowing variation within the standard – but up to a point. His argument validates regional variation (such pronunciations "should be encouraged") at the same time it in effect supports and promotes the standard: none of the variations is out-of-line, instead, they are "subtle," their frequency indicating their normality. He allows for opposing positions to this stance through the phrase "in my opinion," and displays writerly credentials through an unfamiliar (and somewhat nonstandard) use of the word "locutions." Additionally, his argument supports **journalistic craft ideology** in that regional variation is acceptable as long as the "locutions don't distract from the story" – as long as clarity prevails.

   As well as in Example 9.7, Dvorkin, the independent ombudsman for the network at the time, responds as one might expect to the three listeners' complaints listed in Example 9.8, and as an unequivocal, responsible defender of the standard in Example 9.9 (below).

Example 9.8
(a) The <u>proper</u> way to speak a year is:
      2001 is spoken two thousand one.
   The improper way:
      2001 is not to be spoken two thousand and one.
      Leave the and out.
      William Tighe

---

[1] November 2008 figures (*source*: www.npr.org/about/).

(b) Please let the (reporter) who produced the story on the Library in Alexandria know the word "library" is not pronounced "libury." The story was wonderful, but I had trouble listening to it with her consistent mispronunciation of one of the more important words in her story.
      Jill Smith

(c) PLEASE tell your reporters that not only is "centered round" grammatically incorrect [...] as any first-year physics student will attest, it is a physical impossibility. One "centers on;" one "revolves around." Keep up the good work.
      R. Jones (Dvorkin 2002b, emphasis added)

The ombudsman in Example 9.9 responds to the charges of "improper" and "grammatically incorrect" usage and "mispronunciation," saying that he forwards all email complaints about usage to NPR's broadcast librarian, who regularly informs the staff about their usage and "lapses":

Example 9.9
      [She] reminds journalists about correct usage, any grammatical lapses as well as mispronunciations of foreign names and places in the news and that she and I have detected and that the listeners have brought to our attention.
      [...] Some of the issues raised by the listeners may be considered "picky," but if NPR gets the details right, it means that the rest of the reporting is also accurate.
                                                            (Dvorkin 2002b, emphasis added)

His response – both the tacit agreement that lapses can occur and the expectation that they can and should be remedied – falls along the linguistic lines of the complaint tradition. But his motivation is also journalistic and related to a common – and key – journalistic insider "slippery slope" notion that equates ground-level reporting and editing precision with overall accuracy: "Some of the issues raised by the listeners may be considered 'picky,' but if NPR gets the details right, it means that the rest of the reporting is also accurate." The larger cultural (and journalistic) language ideology of correctness and the journalistic craft ideology that highlights accuracy of expression are concurrently upheld.

The NPR case is interesting: it was a pioneer in radio format and use of sound since its inception in 1970, innovating in broadcast style and form (which will be discussed in Section 9.4). At the same time, like most institutions with a public function, there is a concurrent resistance to deviations in standard language usage in their outputs, made clear in the responses of the ombudsman, whose business it is to "assist, as required, with the writing and editing of NPR's guide to standards and practices" (The Mandate and Office of Ombudsman, www.npr.org). NPR counts more than 860 noncommercial public radio stations as members and serves an audience of over 26 million in the US and abroad through radio services and the Internet. It generates daily newscasts and more than 130 hours of programming a week.[2] It is the US's radio equivalent of the *New York Times, Washington Post,* CNN, and the major television networks – the media outlets of record and influence. Its position is different from commercial radio as it receives its funding from voluntary public donations through membership drives and private support. In terms of status and range of news and cultural programming, NPR is the US's closest equivalent to the BBC. Its audience is generally the educated mainstream interested in being informed culturally and politically. NPR's deployment of the standard variety – Bob Edwards's "subtle" regional variation notwithstanding – is a given, a backgrounded reflex of the reporters', announcers', and producers' education and practice.

9.4   Changes and innovation in news style

Investigating aspects of news organizations' language use and usage ideologies over time and across situation – diachronically and synchronically – provides a productive glimpse into the dynamics of *innovation* and *stability* that underpin language and genre change, as well as the role of discursive action and profession-specific decision-making constraints in shaping textual outcomes in a particular community of practice. The radio and print cases noted in this section have several objectives: (1) to illustrate the complex role of the standard variety (beyond the binary assessments of right or wrong, prescriptive or descriptive) in different sociocultural and communicative situations contributing to the notion of *standard variety privilege*; (2) to illustrate the influence of a particular news community's "mission" or communicative objective as a factor in the ways it deals with language choice, socio-interactional expectation, and textual outcomes; (3) to make clear that journalistic, economic, or cultural motivations – the *macro-contextual* – also work, to differing extents, on behalf of linguistic, sociolinguistic, and discursive variation across and within news outlets; and (4) to remind us that language changes occur either incrementally over time or consciously at a specific point in time, the changes particularly evident on the *journalistic* level being delivery style and genre form.

New technologies, particularly the Web and digital recording options, are also playing a role in altering discourse forms. Radio on the Web, for instance, has readily innovated by appropriating the visual, supplementing spoken text stories with actual images (both video and still). Print media online, as well as service-provider news pages like Yahoo!, have also implemented new-modality changes, linking audio, video, still photos, and relevant URLs to stories.[3]

---

[2] November 2008 figures (*source*: www.npr.org/about/).

[3] An example is the *Minneapolis Star Tribune*'s 2007 Mississippi River bridge collapse coverage: the homepage had audio, video, photo, and URL links.

9.4.1   Genre innovations: the NPR case

National Public Radio is recognized for expanding the genre forms of radio, capitalizing on the "radiophonic" possibilities of the medium. More than merely announcing or reading stories, NPR produces complex narratives involving sound, interview, and commentary. It has pioneered the use of "nat sound," or natural background noise or ambient sound "so you'll feel you're standing there, with the sounds of the people. The sound should be as good as getting you to smell it," according to NPR pioneer Susan Stamberg, one of the first hosts of the evening news program *All Things Considered* (quoted in Wenner 2002). It has consistently utilized more actualities or sound bites – quotations from multiple sources – as part of its production ethos. It has produced longer story forms, such as radio documentaries, and on the content level it is known for its depth of coverage. Its average news story length is about five minutes (cf. Dvorkin 2002c), compared with the "one-breath" duration of most commercial newscasts. In fact, according to the ombudsman for the network: "NPR has an aural reputation to uphold, going back to its early days. The 'sound' of NPR was and is unique" (Dvorkin 2001).

Radio has traditionally coupled the immediacy of speech with the form and convention of a printed text. As a medium, radio has relied on verbal "pictures" or descriptions to evoke images in the minds of listeners. NPR has not been immune to the broader changes in radio format and delivery instigated by changes in other broadcast media as well as the Web. For instance, in 2003 a new radio newsmagazine called *Day to Day* made its debut in several cities. "The show's format and style answers the needs of busy listeners, with NPR news, commentaries and features in shorter segments, and more stories in the hour" (press release, July 25, 2003). There are other considerations in the change process such as competition or influence from other media, such as CNN, which in the case of NPR has caused it to orient to a greater emphasis on *breaking news*, news that is reported in real-time on the air, and not prerecorded or produced (press release 1999). This creates differences in delivery style, leading to a perception of change: "NPR sounds different, too," in the aftermath of the station's new breaking news policy, observed Stamberg, who noted that "CNN has really driven the agenda" (quoted in Wenner 2002).

NPR also innovates in terms of its own institutional history and identity, strengthening its own radiophonic persona by exploring other genre forms in its cultural programming. It adapts the traditional in the radio diary format (in productions like *Laura's Diary*, about a young woman with cystic fibrosis). It develops new story forms made possible by new technologies. An example of this is the "SonicMemorial" – a collection of answering machine tapes, interviews, and three decades of other sound memorabilia related to the World Trade Center attacks of 9/11. There is also the "Yiddish Radio Project," a series of stories incorporating forgotten, one-off recordings of immigrant radio shows of the 1920s and 1930s, with real-time translation on the website. And there is *Lost and Found Sound*, a program featuring the earliest sound recordings that give some sense of how life sounded in the early days of the twentieth century.

As it innovates, NPR, which started small and given the longevity of its personnel still adheres to its founding ideals, often evokes its "rich history of highly produced cultural commentaries, interviews, and segments" (Dvorkin 2002a) in internal discussions. The dynamics of change exist in balance with inclinations toward stability, with attempts to keep things familiar as well as interesting (a human-factor dimension to language standardization processes that Cameron 1995 addresses but is not fully explored in other linguistic literature).

The format and genre changes NPR made earlier in the decade were significant enough that it caused remark: "Since radio is an intensely personal medium (existing inside the listeners' heads, hearts and imaginations), many people are nervous that the new NPR will be unrecognizable" (Dvorkin 2002a). At the same time as NPR has secured a journalistic reputation nationally and a unique communicative niche radiophonically, it has been criticized for getting staid (a frequent line of critique at public radio conferences I have attended). The "staidness" critique is another aspect of the innovation–stability balance dynamic and the tendencies toward *journalistic* standardization, particularly the characteristics that safeguard in-group identity, that seem to develop over time within news organizations. The Raidió na Life example (below) shows similar, although differently realized, innovation and standardization-stability traits, which are held in balance over time.

9.4.2   The standard across radio contexts

Commercial radio – centralization requirements   The persistence of the NPR broadcast "standard," marked in part by a delivery style which Wenner (2002) in an *American Journalism Review* article called "somnolent" in comparison with commercial radio, is in contrast with what is occurring in other broadcast venues: locally produced news on commercial stations is rapidly disappearing. Major markets aired thirty-seven minutes of locally produced news on weekdays in 2002, compared with eighty-six minutes in 1998, whereas small markets went from forty-eight to forty-one minutes (Wenner 2002). The amount of time devoted to news on the radio is shrinking to the extent that this factor, too, is altering the genre, creating concurrent changes in delivery and presentation. (In print the time equivalent is space – a smaller "news hole" means less room for stories.) The minimal time devoted to news, especially on niche stations or music stations, means that newscasts, typically three minutes and often less, are comprised of "one-breath stories," often with near-overlap when announcers resume after a correspondent's report. The manner of delivery has evolved from a prestigeful style to one that responds to market exigencies and expectations of a casual connection with the listener. The extent to which this is actually true has not been empirically established in linguistics, although journalism scholars have conducted survey research to characterize change, and anecdotal perceptions are many, as Examples 9.10 and 9.11 show.

Example 9.10
Radio news sure doesn't sound like it used to. Twenty-five years ago [...] Listeners knew when the news came on, because the regular programming stopped, and the sound of the voice changed. News delivery was formal, serious. Just like the stories.
(Wenner 2002: 32, emphasis added)

Example 9.11
There are strange stresses that some newsreaders are starting to put on their words. It's like they have their own way of delivering lines, a kind of lilt that isn't talking to people any more, it's a performance [...].
(Michael Aspel, *London Evening Standard*, August 7, 2007: 21, emphasis added)

As Example 9.11 indicates, worrying changes have also been recognized by veteran BBC broadcasters in the UK, who note irregularities in delivery style, interactional "fads" (like two announcers talking to each other and using first-name address forms), and pronunciation "mistakes."

What has come to be viewed as prestigeful standard language use on the radio (despite changes over time and circumstance), in tandem with what has become normative and standardized on the journalistic-discourse level for both practitioners and listeners, is not just the province of what can be considered the mainstream nationwide classic cases such as NPR in the US or the BBC in the UK. More than ever, the new commercial formats actually rely on and privilege Standard English, as "local radio" is no longer locally produced. Big companies now own multiple stations in different cities to the extent that even the music products sound the same. One former NPR radio reporter observed that a local station in the San Francisco Bay Area, for example, is served by Clear Channel, which produces music programming for several different cities on the West Coast but which is hosted by a DJ – "a generic guy" – in another state: "It's one guy [airing in all the cities]; people think it's local. They have canned [local] ads – you just press a button" (Bill Drummond, personal communication).

Of course to sustain the illusion of the local, the DJ's on-air delivery is devoid of regional variation that otherwise is typically found on local radio. "He could never sound like he's from Wisconsin – people in San Francisco would rebel. [He sounds] innocuous, like elevator music," said Drummond, acknowledging my own home state dialect's persistent regionally distinctive monophthongal characteristics. Drummond finds the trend "disturbing" not for journalistic reasons but for sociolinguistic ones: "the whole local identity of people [circumscribed by language] is being lost along with the things that give character to the country that radio used to enhance," he said, referring to local usage unique to and associated with particular speech communities throughout the US. This means the gradual erosion of non-standard local radio usages like, "Drive careful," which caught my prescriptive attention when I first moved to Northern California from the Upper Midwest as a new college graduate (and which I later, sociolinguistically, realized was a marker indexing the solidarity role of the media in a small community that prided its distance, independence, and historical difference from the big cities – Sacramento, San Jose, San Francisco, Los Angeles – that tended to define California to the larger world).

Raidió na Life – target ideal   A very different but important case involving innovation on the macro-sociolinguistic level alongside standard-language awareness is Raidió na Life (RnaL) in Dublin, Ireland. RnaL is a volunteer-run station which targets an urban, music-loving listenership of Irish speakers. Its signal extends only to the greater Dublin area with several thousand listeners, but programs are available on the Web. The RnaL case is important because its creation in 1993 was a consciously innovative maneuver on the part of language activists to counteract broad cultural standardization constrictions aimed to "preserve" a dying language that had a great deal of symbolic value despite declining domains of use. It was started to offer a media resource for people living in Dublin who had or wanted to improve their mostly non-native Irish by either working for the station or by listening to it, and to function as an antidote to narrow prescriptive attitudes and generations of poor language-learning pedagogy.

From the start, RnaL's mission has been to "normalize" the use of Modern Irish (long in decline) by having it occupy an unremarkable public space, presenting news, interviews, and music programming just as its English-language counterparts do without comment (cf. Cotter 1996a, 1999a, 1999c). It was intended to provide a counterweight to societal attitudes that privileged native speakers from the traditional coastal speech communities or Gaeltachts and created linguistic insecurity in many learners. Nonetheless, on RnaL, every utterance has been subject to scrutiny – both inside the station and by listeners – especially in its early days. This is because transmission is in an obsolescing language, one that uniquely comprises three dialect varieties that share prestige, as well as one "constructed" standard variety that is tolerated for utilitarian purposes in government and education and is generally the province of second-language (L2) speakers.

Evidence of the robustness of standardization (in its prestige entailments) and its transfer to media contexts comes from the Raidió na Life case. The founders' philosophy in part was to offer a corrective to many decades of linguistic insecurity by allowing any variety, any proficiency of Irish on the air, and to encourage non-native speakers. Their aim was also to provide a sound journalistic product within the medium of Irish, which made actual use of the language less self-conscious, and to "urbanize" and update the domains of use. Nonetheless, two years after the volunteer-run station's inception, the organizers produced a training tape to standardize on-air talk by broadcasters, whose proficiency at first varied markedly. The training tape was the station's first educational aid to address matters of phonology, grammar, and discourse for non-native Irish-language broadcasters. The tape, *Cúrsa Gaeilge* "Irish-language course," is also interesting for what is considered important linguistically and what is typically overlooked by the non-native speaker (including many of the broadcasters on the air). Despite the station's language ideology – the open-minded tolerance of many proficiencies of Irish – the station personnel were still responsive to outsider judgments about language production, which were many, and were sensitive to the role of standard language in their accruing prestige as a media authority. They were also aware of their own limitations as semi-speakers or L2 speakers.

Grammatical issues that are not included on the tape are significant also, as their absence or inclusion suggests what features of the language are or are not valued for their distinctiveness or "Irishness." In this way the tape fosters attention to a subset of linguistic features particular to the language that are then emphasized in the broadcasts. The station is generating attitudes toward the standard from within, and replicating select aspects of it on the air. Figure 9.2 summarizes the tape's primary topics. On the level of grammar and phonology, the tape discusses palatalized consonants that are distinctive to Irish phonology but not to English; initial mutation processes, a defining characteristic in Celtic languages that is nonetheless disappearing (their use varies considerably across the dialects); constructions using prepositions, of which Irish has many; the grammatical environments that condition phonological processes known as *lenition* and *eclipsis*, also distinctive of Irish (see Figure 9.2 and Glossary); the genitive case; and the gender of nouns and their influence on phonology. The translation of English clichés and names of Irish institutions and agencies, and the use of the vocative case (for interviews), question forms, idiomatic expressions relating to time, and impersonal verb forms, are all relevant to the discourse structures of the news setting. The training guide thus provides a useful reference or "operational tool" for standardization.

Other sections of the tape concern discourse features particular to the well-formedness of news talk, such as beginning and ending interviews, beginning and ending programs, and manner of delivery ("be friendly except when you're reading a news story"). In this way, the training tape is cultivating standard

---

Phonological:
- palatalized ("slender") and non-palatalized ("broad") consonants
- initial consonant mutation: lenition and eclipsis

      lenited form eclipsed form
p   —> f   —> b
b   —> v,w   —> m
t   —> h   —> d
m   —> w, v   —> NA
etc.

Grammatical:
- the genitive (e.g., *fear* "man" —> *fir* "man's", *bád* "boat" —> *báid* "boat's", *cainteoir* "speaker" —> *cainteora* "speaker's", *beithíoch* "animal" —> *beithígh* "animal's")
- gender of nouns
- translating English clichés and phrases
- Irish forms for institution and agency names

Discourse-level:
- use of the vocative case (in addressing an interviewee)
- question forms
- idiomatic expressions relating to time
- impersonal verb forms
- openings and closings
- delivery style

Missing:
- long and short vowel distinctions
- explanation of grammatical and morphological focus (or emphasis)
- use of discourse-level forms, such as connectives

Source: Cotter 1996a

Figure 9.2 *Cúrsa Gaeilge* contents summary

journalistic forms. The tape's presenters, who speak throughout in Irish, leave no doubt that the purpose of the tape is journalistic, and that they will be talking about language issues relevant for broadcasters. Throughout the tape, the volunteer broadcasters are advised to listen to announcers on Raidió na Gaeltachta (which is the national Irish-language station) or RTÉ (Ireland's equivalent of the BBC) to model their broadcast style. (Likewise, American broadcast trainees are also advised to listen to target announcers, as are heard on National Public Radio, to develop a professional delivery style.)

Adoption of standard features is by no means uniform. My collection of station news scripts over a one-month period in 1997, two years after the training tape was prepared, establishes this. The news scripts, prepared by the most fluent of the announcers, often translating from an English-language newswire, are read throughout the day by different news readers and show penned-in changes based on the dialect affiliation of the particular news reader. Also, there is more latitude in genres outside of news, which is the prestige genre, as the presenters suggest.

How the standard prevails   In all cases – the classic case (NPR), the unusual case (RnaL), and the economically motivated case (Clear Channel) – the standard variety prevails. NPR, *the classic case*, has been and continues to be innovative in form, but conservative in language use and usage judgments. For NPR, the standard variety, Mainstream US English (cf. Lippi-Green 1997), is the **unmarked default**, derived from and part of the larger cultural domain.

Raidió na Life, *the unusual case*, is innovative in how it has repositioned Irish usage norms within the public domain and how it supports this culturally radical effort with a "journalist first" ideology. At the same time, the language on the air is becoming increasingly standardized from within, as the station's training tape (and field interviews in subsequent years) indicates. For RnaL, the standard Gaeltacht variety of Irish is the **target ideal**. In the endangered-language context, it is the **marked choice**, evokes broad historical associations, and ratifies one's social position through the level of usage competence achieved. The linguistic forms consciously selected for standardization on RnaL happen to be among the most distinctive in relation to English, allowing for a type of shorthand indexing of Irish identity.

Commercial radio, *the economically motivated case*, requires a language variety that allows for centralization of broadcasts and, from a reception perspective, allows for the production of "one-breath" stories that can be heard without meta-linguistic distraction; local variations are necessarily suppressed. Variation would limit the extent of usefulness; thus Mainstream US English is the **economic choice**, much like global English. For commercial radio, variation is limited explicitly: the standard variety carries an **extralinguistic utility**, brings with it the requisite cultural capital, and helps to support the bottom line. In all three cases, the standard variety, for different reasons, obtains.

9.4.3   *Communicative need vs. prescriptive requirement (connectives)*

Situations in which the standard is the default, where prescriptivism is part of active discussion, allow insight into what might motivate or "unsuppress" the variations that do occur. As we saw with the previous radio cases, *communicative need* is a factor in creating change and variation, despite the authority of the standard variety. Communicative need is also relevant with respect to the prescriptive requirement itself and is one line of explanation to explore to understand the instances in which prescriptive rules get broken, particularly in a profession that prides itself on upholding the standard variety, the variety that relies most heavily on usage prescriptions (cf. Cotter 1999b).

The use of connectives in print news discourse is one case. The prescriptive rule that says that a sentence cannot begin with a conjunction like *and* or *but* has been in modern usage manuals for most of the twentieth century. That *and* and *but* began to appear in sentence-initial positions in news stories in mid-century (see Cotter 2003 for a diachronic account of this change), despite rules to the contrary, speaks to the force of a communicative need superseding a prescriptive rule, as I have argued elsewhere (Cotter 2003).

Linguists more consciously than journalists make the distinction between types of connectives, separating formal *meaning* from actual *use* – the *ideational* or *semantic* from the *pragmatic* or *functional*. The purpose is to isolate particular behaviors characteristic of each, as Traugott (1986, 1988) and others have done in exploring the semantic-to-pragmatic changes that connectives as grammatical function words have undergone. The sentence-initial connectives that appear most often in news stories are used *pragmatically*, suggesting that the well-documented multifunctionality of the connective (cf. Redeker 1990; Schiffrin 1987; van Dijk 1979), which captures features of spoken discourse and operationalize a multitude of discourse-level tasks in conversational exchanges, is also relevant in news texts.

The connective as a multifunctional discourse entity is also interesting with respect to standardization dynamics and journalistic practice, as the rule to avoid sentence-initial usage still remains robust, despite authoritative opinions to the contrary. Several contemporary usage guides explain why the connective rule, once a mark of good expository prose, is no longer necessary. William Zinsser, whose book *On Writing Well* (1985) has long been used as a reference by many journalists, refers to the once-robust prescription for "but" but then dismisses it as obsolete. Another standard journalism grammar guide directly addresses the functional applications of the connective in their various positions in the sentence. The authors note that connectives aid understanding by the reader by contributing to coherence of the text, and "provid[ing] needed transitions" (Kessler and McDonald 1988: 29).

Despite the blessing by prescriptive grammarians, the old rule still holds sway in many writers' minds, even among college-age journalism students, the new generation. One student copy editor said she tries to delete sentence-initial connectives from reporters' stories "but [she] can't get all of them" (field notes, 1996). Professional newspaper copy editors, who are very serious about their mission to preserve standard language, indicate that deleting incidence of sentence-initial connectives is still a common practice, despite what is said in the usage manuals (field notes, n.d.).

Given this prescriptive awareness and application, the connectives that do make it in print, then, are hardy survivors of the editing process, which suggests that their meaning is interpreted by these usage gate-keepers, by copy editors, on the level of the discourse, on a pragmatic plane. When connective use complies with the norms and practice of "good journalism," the *ands* and *buts* surface in print. One can argue (as I have done in Cotter 2003) that there is a high incidence of pragmatic connectives in news texts because newspapers exploit their pragmatic functions for communicative reasons. For example, in the prototypical news text we find *and* and *but* operating in these ways:

- *and* connecting short paragraphs rather than propositions, affording a sense of narrative (and logical) continuity while at the same time setting apart the utterance for prominence.
- *but* serving to signal a contrast within the discourse by introducing a new speaker, idea, or topic.

Examples 9.12(a), 9.12(b), and 9.13 illustrate these functions:

Example 9.12

(a) The rapid changes in law mean the welfare department can't provide training fast enough to keep the staff informed, she said.

And constant regulation changes mean frequent adjustments in the handling of individual cases – to the displeasure of recipients and welfare workers.

(Cotter 2003: 64)

(b) [...] Where it resembles an English caff is that it sells a lot of English goods.

And the centrepiece of the menu is the Full English Breakfast. [...]

(*The Independent*, July 26, 2007, emphasis added)

Example 9.13

The GAO report, which is sure to generate anti-government headlines around the country, conceded that the changing nature of professionalism in government accounts for [...]

But GAO said its on-the-spot probe of grading practices in half a dozen federal agencies led it to conclude that tighter controls are needed [...].   (Cotter 2003: 65)

In Example 9.12(a), *and* works pragmatically to help the reader know that the argument is being continued and developed; in Example 9.12(b) *and* helps to both coordinate the informational elements in two related paragraphs and to create a narrative focal point within the reporter's longish list-like description of lunch in Beijing. In Example 9.13, *but* is used to contrast information in the dependent clause, and not in the main clause. Superficially, it serves to unify a complex story containing contrasting perspectives.

Examples 9.14 and 9.15 also illustrate the realms in which sentence-initial connectives (which often mean paragraph-initial position in short-paragraph news texts) have become the norm: functioning on behalf of coherence, articulating the presence of new speakers or new ideas, regulating the logical flow of propositional information, allowing stylistic flexibility, and opening up greater options for narrative tone.

Example 9.14

[...] The line of Barney toys due from Hasbro this summer is expected to generate $100 million in sales.

And to think, it all began on an expressway in central Dallas.

Example 9.15

[...] He [judge] declared all timber sales illegal.

But the Washington Contract Loggers Association asked for a hearing [...]

The Forest Service also argues that the sales should proceed.
And labor organizations contend that further restrictions on logging would be onerous.

(Cotter 1996b: 276, emphasis added)

Evident in Example 9.14 is the way *and* can be used to establish a particular narrative tone, and set apart the upcoming utterance for prominence – in this case stylistic (rather than informational) prominence. Example 9.15 indicates the extent to which the arguments that underlie an issue are clarified by very small words: *but* underscores the opposition of the loggers in relation to the judge's decision. *And* makes it clear that labor organizations are on the side of the opponents to the decision, which include the Forest Service and the loggers association, implicating that the three disparate groups form a coalition. *But*, in its multiple meanings, also implies a disagreement that is not stated which a reader can infer; and *and* in this example has a different sort of stylistic role than in 9.14: it in effect links the third element in a series (a series of individual subjects, a collective of opponents, and a list of arguments).

Similar to the changes in radio news delivery which in early forms were essentially spoken renditions of written text (cf. Quirk 1982, 1986), the use of pragmatic connectives in print ultimately captures a progression from a text-oriented to an audience-oriented ethos within the production of news discourse. They help to solve rhetorical issues that the modality or genre form engenders, be they "one-breath" stories demanding easy reception or (short) single-sentence paragraphs requiring coherence and narrative continuity; and thus provide additional evidence of the ways in which language evolves in response to communicative need.

9.5   Conclusion: language awareness and journalistic identity

This chapter has sought to shed light on the news media's insider attitudes toward language and usage, which tend to be prescriptive and mainstream; the complex but robust role of journalists in language standardization processes within the larger culture; and the actions that are undertaken on behalf of the *prescriptive imperative* as well as the "pragmatic alternative" that is deployed when professional needs clash with prescriptive needs. The news media uphold standard language ideals through practice in a variety of ways – through how they report, write, edit, and self-critique, as well as what they report on. Journalists' attitude toward usage is conservative and resistant to deviations, and it reflects broader community norms; language, thus, is assessed in a particular way that is securely grounded in broader social assumptions. At the same time, communicative or pragmatic requirements can override prescriptive ones. Language awareness is part of journalistic identity and tied to "an ideology of technique and neutrality" (Schudson 1978: 184).

Standardization processes play a role in influencing language use and attitudes about use – and, inevitably, language in the media. Standardization ideologies emerged in the wake of the printed word and may be considered an extension of an intrinsic human propensity to equate moral stature with truthfulness and competence in language use, as Cameron (1995) has argued. We saw examples of this in emails from NPR listeners to the station (in Section 9.3). Whereas the traditional view holds that standardization ideologies are embodied in usage guides, style manuals, prescriptive grammars, and the centuries-long-running discourse of mavens whose task is to keep the public alert and on track, in the media context they are also embodied in the responses of listeners and readers, of members of the ordinary public who also work to keep certain standards alive, as the NPR listener letters indicate. Language ideologies are also embodied in journalists themselves who reiterate culturally situated language norms through processes of news production; they actively follow the *prescriptive imperative* that helps to create their professional identity.

In the print and radio cases noted here, the standard language ideologies of the larger culture play out in the media, reside in journalistic practice, and are evidenced in the language used and discourse produced by the media. The media are as inclined to standardization pressures as any other speech community member, responding prescriptively to language use (by themselves and their sources), making social judgments and evaluations when they hear deviations from the standard, and incorporating a subset of standard language practices from within their own profession. In-house style guides and articles on usage in professional journals are an explicit example of this; a more complex case is Raidió na Life, which developed explicit newsroom policies about language use and specific aids to creating a more uniform presentation of Irish on the air, linguistically and journalistically.

The radio and print examples illustrate the extent to which language ideologies coexist in a context that has special discourse and practice-based motivations that influence the shape of the news text in addition to heeding the grammatical and phonological changes that follow society at large. Genres proliferate or contract, as one can hear in the production of first-person radio diaries on NPR or the increasingly short "one-breath" newscasts on commercial stations; narrative elements are refashioned, as the Yiddish Radio Project recasts old recordings in a Bakhtinian sense of repurposing; and pragmatic relationships to the audience are altered – the SonicMemorial, for instance, is produced by NPR but created by audience contributions. And grammatical function words as ordinary as *and* or *but* play a significant role in ensuring narrative coherence, propositional continuity, and stylistic flexibility in news texts. The connectives case shows how news texts are an interesting repository for the *prescriptive imperative* in relation to the *pragmatic alternative*.

Language style and standardization in the news media, then, can be viewed as a dynamic process, a set of factors that are linguistic, discursive, journalistic, and situational (i.e., economic, technological, political) that facilitate the responsive processes of change and of stability.

Part IV

Decoding the discourse

10 The impact of the news process on media language

Throughout this book, I have looked at how news stories can be "read" in terms of the process and the participants involved, from the *conceptualization of news* to the *construction of the news story* – all of which are related to the impact of internal processes and practice on media discourse. Delivering the news is the next step in the news production process. In this chapter, I will briefly mention what is of linguistic and discursive relevance at this presentation and delivery stage (Section 10.1), detailing extra-linguistic process-based elements like physical space, time, and seasonal cycles that nonetheless have a concurrent impact on the structure and content of media discourse. In this regard, I also address the larger issue of textual coherence (Section 10.2) as a consequence of following newswriting rules, particularly those related to length.

The way news discourse is manifested as a result of reporting and writing rules also has consequences – for people who are or are not reported on. In Section 10.3 I will apply concepts discussed throughout the book to examine the impacts of the news process on a group I know very well, linguists who are quoted in the news. In this case study, I examine more generally the often contested (or omitted) role of "expertise" in news stories, highlighting an impact that affects the academic's public profile as well as the larger culture's knowledge base.

A conclusion follows with a short summary of key points developed in the book to remind us of what we can examine in our outsider "decoding" of news discourse, alongside suggestions for further study.

10.1 Delivering the news

Once the newspaper or broadcast is delivered, aired, or uploaded, the newsroom has already gone ahead to the next news cycle. Thus, the first acquaintance a reader has with the day's news product is generally the journalist's last (barring updates between editions or on the website). The first glance by a reader is the first indication of the priorities of the news practitioner, the first ordering of social meaning and the relationship between journalist, audience, and text. (This stage can also be thought of as another installment in a long and ongoing dialogue.) The physical manifestation of the news on the page or on the air, the recurrent patterns of news genres, and the real-world constraints behind publication inter-operate with the news process, journalistic values, and actual outcomes.

10.1.1   Arranging the news

The visual arrangement of news encapsulates news values and interacts with story-internal hierarchies, and thus journalists who produce this work see a very different newspaper or product than the reader, one that is based on practice, action, and profession-specific comportment. At its simplest, it is iconic, relative to size or style of typeface; to what is higher, earlier, first, fastest, longer, or more immediate in display; and to conventions of placement in physical position in the paper or on the news broadcast or on the website. On another level, it is embedded in the recursive actions and decisions, and trajectories of practice and process, and entails a series of deictic relations – of time, space, and social position – which are presented through elements of the text, visually and verbally, and help to articulate the newspaper's position in relation to journalist, audience, and story. Deadline, relevance, relationship, newsworthiness, story design, and craft (elements discussed at length in preceding chapters) are priorities of the profession and mean that the news product is read or seen by the news practitioner in terms of them.

10.1.2   News genres and iterativity

News is subdivided and categorized by the journalist in many ways, many of which the general reader is unaware. The rule-governed patterns of news discourse create genres of reporting, stories that can be classified according to type, such as the news story or feature story, hard news or soft news, column and editorial, calendar item and news brief, or business, sports, and food story. The iterations of news genres occur on other levels, as well. *Seasonal cycles* produce the pre-Thanksgiving travel story, the pre-Fourth of July fireworks safety story, fashion-week reporting, the heartwarming Mother's Day story, the inspiring war veteran's story, the back-to-school story, the stories pegged to religious holidays, the successive iterations of the anniversary story. Some iterativity is *story-internal*, relating to reporters' actions and repetition in the text, such as the recirculation of sources or updates between editions or use of boilerplate (see Chapter 8). Much of news practice is a response to the imperatives of these recurrent patterns, and helps to motivate the worldview of the practitioner.

Real-world constraints

A journalist fully vested in professional values and skills that result in news stories familiar to us all has something else to contend with: the constraints of the physical world. Time to deadline, amount of space allotted a story, requirements of the channel of transmission (print, broadcast, Web, live coverage, etc.), and the protocols imposed by these channels create conventions and contingency plans for writing and decision-making that have a significant impact on the shape of news texts, as has been described in earlier chapters (see Chapters 5, 7, and 9). Not to mention the less predictable consequences of dealing with other human beings: sources, editors, colleagues, the public. While self-evident to reporters, it is not always obvious to the reading and viewing public the extent to which technical and temporal constraints help to create what we read, see, and hear (see Bell 1995).

10.2   Coherence of the text

There are numerous aspects of the practice of newswriting and the priorities of the news process, such as the short turnaround time for a story or the need to gain and hold attention, that indicate a need to ensure coherence of the text. Coherence issues revolve around the journalist-driven goals of clarity, simplicity, etc. (cf. Chapters 7, 8 and 9) and reader speed and apprehension (as mentioned in Chapter 7). Thus coherence issues and devices will be generic to any writer (the use of transition words like *meanwhile*) or specific to the news realm (particular use of connectives like *and* in paragraph-initial position), and both visible to the reader and implied through familiarity with prior news discourse.

   Length is singularly relevant to news discourse, for both the coherence issues it raises and the coherence devices it engenders. Length is a primary discourse parameter that relates in the first order to the rhetorical newswriting goal of *brevity*. Length – of sentence, paragraph, or story – is proscribed within the profession. Sentences are short and often constitute a single paragraph (as evident in examples in Chapter 7 and Example 10.1 below). Story length varies according to the import of the story and the space available, but generally stories are meant to be "short," with a standard size varying according to publication to allow for more than one story on a page and to avoid continuations or "jumps" to subsequent pages.

   Length corresponds to the story's representation on the page, thus paragraphs are consciously short – to avoid a grey block of type. (The phrase, "White space increases readership," was a common refrain from the mid-twentieth century, a reminder of the need to allow for visual ease when both writing and laying out stories, which influenced paragraph length.) Non-journalistic paragraphing standards (such as one finds in academia) in which a new paragraph signals a new idea or elaboration of a proposition do not apply. Thus, in newswriting one can find single or related ideas spread out over four or five paragraphs, or seemingly arbitrarily divided across paragraph boundaries, as in Example 10.1, which shows the top six paragraphs of a lengthy 48-paragraph story about a hurricane-driven storm in the areas of Maryland, Virginia, and Washington, DC.

Example 10.1

Powerful winds and lashing rains from much-anticipated Hurricane Isabel smashed through a shuttered Washington region last night.

Fallen trees blocked major commuter routes and neighborhood streets as work crews hurried to clear them. Winds gusted above 50 mph, rain fell in sheets, and tree branches and power lines were strewn across roadways. As storm waters rose, residents in low-lying areas were urged to abandon their homes; everyone else was warned to stay inside.

[3]→ By midnight, the storm had created widespread problems.

More than 700,000 electric customers in the Washington area had lost power, and scores of traffic lights had gone dark. The outages affected businesses as well as residences. The Washington Post suffered an outage at its Springfield printing plant.

The Fairfax County Water Authority's three water treatment plants lost power, leaving the system with no more than 6 to 8 hours of clean water, some of which will be needed for firefighting. If power stays off for longer, customers on higher ground will start losing water pressure, followed by those in lower elevations.

"If we don't get power returned by daylight, the system will begin to deteriorate," James Warfield Jr., executive officer of the Fairfax County Water Authority, at 2 a.m. Friday. "More and more customers will start losing water."

(Sue Anne Pressley, *Washington Post*, September 19, 2003)

While physical length (and typeface) maneuvers on the page, to some extent, provide "visible coherence" through their conventional form and reader familiarity with them, there are consequent issues that arise from the news story's *brevity* and *length* norms. The need to maintain coherence of the narrative overall, as well as the proposition being fronted, the argument being reported, and the numerous sources being quoted are managed through a number of tools familiar to any writer, such as *transition words* like *meanwhile*, as just noted, and judicious use of *connectives* like *and* and *but* (cf. Chapter 9). Equally, reporters are taught that the "logic" of story design brings with it an internally consistent coherence – as seen by news professionals, at any rate – such that unnecessary words are not needed. Thus, news stories just as frequently are elliptical with respect to the absence of the "obvious" transition words. There were none in the entire story in Example 10.1, although several very short single-sentence paragraphs, such as "By midnight, the storm had created widespread problems" in paragraph 3, served a transition function. In the news realm, besides specific language, coherence can also be built by a story following the conventionalized physical form, a reporter utilizing narrative conventions, and the profession relying on reader familiarity with its outputs.

10.3   Linguists as "experts" in news stories

Linguists and anthropologists from time to time are interviewed by the news media, with mixed results and frustration, either because they have been misunderstood or their half-hour interview boiled down to one ostensibly irrelevant quote, or because they were not contacted at all. Instead, many news stories about language-related matters, from Ebonics to email, often quote and cite as an expert an English literature professor or a communications professor for whom language is certainly important, but for whom the systematic study of language in society has not been part of their training. The experts with the well-grounded insights about language and social life and language in use – the sociolinguists, linguistic anthropologists, and ethnolinguists – are often overlooked. I argue that we need to look at what propels and constrains journalists and academics culturally and discursively for insights into what limits the satisfactory exchange and reception of ideas.

Over the course of both of my careers in daily newspaper journalism and field-based linguistics, I have interviewed quite literally thousands of people. As a sociolinguist, I have now been interviewed several dozen times by the media – about topics as diverse as the lay use of the words "schizo" and "Holocaust," the sound of Monica Lewinsky's voice, airline pilots' circumlocutions, Queen Elizabeth's changing accent, George W. Bush's "Yo, Blair" exchange with Britain's former Prime Minister, use of the "heavy metal umlaut" (e.g., Maxïmo Park), and most recently, the popularity of acronyms. My interest in this matter, in why the views of linguists are generally not part of mainstream discourse exceptions notwithstanding, derives from the curiosity and challenge I have felt in describing and accounting for the ideologies and conventions of each profession. A secondary objective is to offer an insight into the significant differences between American news media and the press in Europe and Great Britain. Ultimately, I do not just describe how the media treats academics and other experts, using incidents from personal experience as well as newspaper examples culled from the Lexis-Nexis Database, but also try to formulate a rationale, looking as a linguistic anthropologist into the ways news discourse is structured and how these patterns relate to the norms and values of the journalistic community.

10.3.1   Journalistic skepticism and discursive distance

The key reasons that experts with sociolinguistic or anthropological training may be overlooked or overtly devalued in news stories about ways of speaking, language, and the linguistic behavior of certain communities is not merely an oversight or willfulness on the part of the reporter. Rather, it is because of a journalistic understanding of what an expert is supposed to be or do, and it is the manner in which expert knowledge is sanctioned within the news profession. It is useful to make a conscious distinction between the "expert" and the "linguist" in the journalistic context, because it is a distinction that underlies some journalistic choices. The narrative conventions specific to journalism, which create and constrain these choices, ultimately govern the positioning of the expert and/or the academic. This dynamic is created through the value and practice of *journalistic skepticism*, particularly as this quality is defined within American newspaper trends.

Journalists are trained to be skeptical, to question the veracity of information they receive and the credibility of their sources. This practice has manifestations in how news narratives are constructed as well in the institutionalized routines of reporting – and ultimately in how linguists, anthropologists, and other academics are viewed by the media. One complex identity a journalist inhabits is that of the "friendly authority," as noted in Chapters 2, 7, and 8. This role illustrates the paradox of journalistic "distance," composed of co-occurring solidarity and power, a paradox of connection and apartness that is often managed through language and discursive strategies (Cotter 1999b). *Neutrality* (a type of "distance") is a reporting skill that is emphasized in newswriting textbooks and goes by terms such as "objectivity," "balance," "fairness," and "skepticism."

One discursive distancing strategy is to borrow words from others, as noted in Chapter 7. To support the authorial "distance" that the skeptical approach inherently requires, journalists cite experts (Cotter 1999b). In an effort to maintain a non-evaluative stance, which is part of this authorial "distance," reporters actively attempt to not explicitly frame stories in terms of judgments or moral lessons to be learned but in an apparently more neutral way that allows readers to make judgments for themselves. Attribution of information to multiple or expert sources is intended to reinforce the news media's self-defined position as a cautious, reliable, and unbiased authority and reporter of what is happening in the world. The expert, then, plays an important role in supporting a primary journalistic identity, one marked by proximal distance. This is also where the "expert" and the linguist begin to separate.

There are three aspects to the journalistic consideration of experts that authorizes their selection. For one, experts are viewed as offering an objective commentary, one secured by a particular kind of advanced training or skill set; this makes experts compatible with the reporter's own self-view as a non-partisan conduit. Secondly, experts used by the media frequently "make sense" on two levels: they shed light on the issue at hand, and they present an indirect reinforcement of the prevailing worldview when that worldview is considered "common sense" or is unquestioned. So it is the individual who can "make sense" in a dual way – of the local complexity of an issue, and the global question of how to fit it in comfortably with what we already know – who is authorized by the media. When the sociocultural linguistic view of a situation is at odds with a dominant cultural reading – which happens often when language issues are standing in for social, cultural, or moral ones – the linguistically informed side of things is either ignored or, ironically, framed as evaluative and is thus viewed as more suspect. At that point, the "expert" is demoted to an "academic" (a reframing I have experienced more than once).

A third key point is that journalistic skepticism is a complex reflex of history and practice in any country for whom the mass media is a central form of cultural transmission. In the US the press has evolved through constitutional ideals of free speech, nineteenth-century government decentralization that created the need for community-based papers, the muckraking tradition of early twentieth-century social advocates and authors, and a pre-professionalized view of class and power. Reporters in the US did not always have the visibility they do today, nor a celebrity contingent (with salaries commensurate with sports stars and financial traders) whose own opinions are solicited by other media. (Media "elites" were in the minority until the latter third of the twentieth century.)

In earlier eras, reporters were romanticized and emerged in pop culture incarnations, much like cowboys or truck drivers. The work of news reporters has become professionalized only in the past two generations, taking the occupation past its largely blue-collar roots. Before that, reporting – when the press reflected on itself – was in large part motivated by a mission to hold those in power accountable. Despite the more recent development of media conglomerates, celebrity, white-collar professionalism, and media self-critique, there are journalism ideologies from the past that are still linked to an earlier advocacy of the "little guy" in relation to society's power-holders and embedded in everyday practice. Mainstream social values that support the "common person" myth still fuel the process of getting the story, and the Web and blogging inform this. In the US, as compared to France or Great Britain, for instance, this leaves the news profession focusing on practice over theory, production over introspection, as it covers daily events.

Given the role experts are tacitly expected to play in the news narrative, it is not surprising that sociolinguists and anthropologists can easily fall outside of the definitional boundaries. Our own disciplinary orientation to knowledge sets us apart in various ways. For one, we up-end "sense" through our own institutionalized practices of query and knowledge production: our job is not to find solutions or tidy responses, instead it is to problematize and dismantle, to understand a process or phenomenon more deeply. For another, our qualitative methodologies fail to meet the criterion of expert objectivity; not only are the "findings" we develop generally not quantified, but the ethnographic or interactional methodologies we engage in are overtly based on interpretive practice and judgment. And academics of our ilk can be viewed, according to mainstream attitudes particularly endemic to the US, as suspect members of a power elite – as intellectuals – especially when academic ideologies are profoundly at odds with mainstream or "lay" ones. The idea that one can split an infinitive or violate a prescriptive rule and still be considered a good speaker, or the idea that sexism or racism or power can be embedded in less obvious levels of discourse production, or the idea that text and email "language" might reflect a new relationship with literacy, technology, and community and does not signal a decline in intelligence or communicative skill – these are all perspectives at odds with most non-specialists.

10.3.2   Levels of skepticism and reference

Despite our training and specialized set of skills, linguists are often met with disbelief, if not hostility, to our claims about language and its position in society. But why should journalists hold any other view about language than the one we run into when we step outside our discipline? Indeed, even when the linguist has been particularly adept at explaining some phenomenon, as David Crystal was in a *New York Times* story (December 13, 2001) about the language of the Internet, the background against which expert assumptions rest is just as clearly part of the story. In this case, it is made evident as early as the headline: Pooh-Poohing the Purists, a Scholar Revels in Netspeak. Later in the story, the reporter writes, echoing a common concern about language change: "It is this hybrid of speech and writing [Netspeak] that Dr. Crystal analyzes, unworried that English will be ruined by its often casual treatment." And, "Dr. Crystal is opposed to this approach [prescriptivism]. He feels free to begin some of his e-mail with 'Dear,' depending on the recipient, as well as commit many other so-called errors." Interestingly, Crystal was not referred to at all as a linguist; on first mention he was described as "Dr. David Crystal, an eminent Welsh authority on language and the producer of many scholarly volumes [...]"

The contexts in which linguists and anthropologists are mentioned in news stories can be sorted into three categories: undisputed, disputed, and generic. The undisputed contexts *describe* linguists – as translators, as technical or computational experts, as polyglots. Sociolinguists and linguistic anthropologists are also cited in stories of dispute, when topics like language attitudes, race, parenting, or social asymmetry are reported on or backgrounded. Linguists and anthropologists are also cited generically, mentioned without name, as in "The Darwinian linguistic anthropologist might conclude that it should be left to succumb to the impact of stronger forces" (*The* (Glasgow) *Herald*, September 9, 2000), or "Jerry Mission was not surprised to see me. Linguists and anthropologists are regular visitors. Why not journalists?" (*Financial Times*, April 15, 2000).

Linguists whose expertise is not in dispute are quoted with a fair degree of respect, even when the story is humorous, as in a *Los Angeles Times* story (November 2000) about the apocryphal origins of the word "chad." An unprecedented *three* linguists were interviewed and quoted, their expertise and humor embodied in their quotes ("The irony gives people something to latch onto at a confusing and tense time ...," "there are all these distinctions among chads, hanging ones and pregnant ones. They're sexually loaded. They're humanizing. They're kind of anthropomorphizing") mirroring the curiosity and amazement of the general public at the time. That the query was for technical information – about a word that itself was a technical term for a piece of paper punched out of a ballot, and that only a few were aware of before the 2000 presidential election – and not about the social aspects of its use, undoubtedly paved the way.

It is notable how expertise is sanctioned by the media when it concerns technical matters. Anthropologist Frank Poirier, describing of his own experiences with the media, talked about what made anthropologists less-than-desirable spokespeople: "Rather than stick with anthropologists, media may go with scientists who speak with conviction … The media may value firmness of conviction over professional hesitation and reticence."[1] Similarly, linguists get full expert billing when the story concerns search engines or computers or product naming or even endangered languages – quite often anytime the content lies beyond judgments of language *use*.

This does not mean that the technical side is accurately reported. Technical terms are often misappropriated, despite best efforts. Many years ago linguist Charles Adams did extensive linguistic and ethnographic fieldwork in the hills of Northern California to become expert on a community "lingo" spoken primarily before World War Two in the hills of Northern California. The lingo, which operates according to regularly occurring linguistic rules which Adams describes and indexes a rich and deeply rooted complex of social relations in the community over time, is known by its speakers as Boontling and is generally agreed to be, technically, a "jargon." Adams's frustration with the media is evident in a footnote in his book (Adams 1971: 41):

Example 10.2
After a thirty-minute telephone interview in which the full technical [and social] implications of the jargon classification had been discussed, the resulting Los Angeles Times article asserted, "Adams has classified Boontling as a jargon, which is defined by the dictionary as a 'confused, unintelligible language'."

Technical elements have the advantage of purporting a sense of objectivity. Their disadvantage is falling victim to the journalistic injunction to simplify the complex (as noted in chapter 8). In Adams's case, the dictionary became the expert, overriding his expertise, because it aided a more urgent journalistic objective to simplify.

In the matter of representation, as observed in the Crystal example, the professional designation is not always specified. In my sample, it was often just "professor, lecturer, author, language specialist." Often linguists aren't linguists at all. They are "amateur linguists" – which means a non-professional with a keen personal interest in language. Or, they are polyglots: "A fabled

---

[1] Speaking at an invited session, Anthropology's Public Face: Encounters with the Media, at the annual meeting of the American Anthropological Association in San Francisco in 2000.

linguist, speaking five languages"; "An expert linguist who speaks seven languages"; "A gifted linguist, speaking French, Spanish." Related to the polyglot rendering, *linguist* often is synonymous with "translator," as in Example 10.3:

Example 10.3
Scandiffio said he has about two dozen translators and linguists ... if none speaks a particular language, a database will be used to search names of about 1,400 language experts.   (*The Washington Post*, February 15, 2001)

Then there is the generic appropriation of linguists, who may be included in a list of experts, but not quoted or referred to outside of that list, as in Example 10.4:

Example 10.4
[The group included] crossword puzzle experts, linguists, chess masters, mathematicians, and [refugee intellectuals].   (*New York Times*, October 9, 2000)

Or, linguists may be included in a list of experts to which some linguistically inappropriate claim is being made, as in this example:

Example 10.5
A proposed language purification law aimed at repelling English words is receiving support from academics, linguists and politicians, The London Observer reports.
(*Straits Times*, February 12, 2001)

Scholars, linguists and anthropologists among them, are also positioned to illustrate contention, reflecting the agonistic structure of hard news stories, by pitting experts against each other, both within and outside of the discipline, as Example 10.6 shows:

Example 10.6
Is baby signing really language? The answer depends on how you define language – an issue that has divided experts in a longstanding and bitter debate.
(*Washington Post*, March 13, 2001, emphasis added)

The observation is true, but it is not a main point of the story; nor are the motivations behind the "longstanding and bitter debate" also described. Similarly, what is of intellectual interest and examination is not necessarily a flashpoint for scholars, as suggested in a *Christian Science Monitor* story: "But scholars still debate what is a separate language and what is simply a variation (or dialect) of that language." In this case the "debate" is part of the scholarly activity of figuring out a complex intellectual puzzle without easy answers, accounting for linguistic phenomena, and contributing to human knowledge and understanding.

Sometimes, the linguistic authority is matched against a lay person who has the last word, or who is meant to argue "the other side." In Example 10.7 the claims of the linguist in the lead or opening paragraph are "balanced," quite reasonably, by the comment by one of the students affected by the claims.

Example 10.7

A language expert has claimed that Scottish students at a university accused of elitism are too ashamed of their accents to speak during lectures, leaving their southern British counterparts to do the talking.

[…]

→ But Louise Evans, 21 […] said she had few problems about speaking in tutorials and was proud of her Scottish accent. She said: "Being Scottish is a good thing and many people find my accent nice to listen to. I do not have any problem at all when it comes to asking questions in tutorials. My grades are definitely not suffering because I have a Scottish accent."   (*The Scotsman*, October 13, 2000)

The student's comments in support of the positive "side" come after the linguist has explained that negative attitudes toward regional dialects have to some extent been improving, mitigating the proposition of the lead, and after another student was quoted supporting the downbeat aspect of the linguist's claim.

Similarly, in a story from the US, to counterbalance the explanatory, linguistically descriptive statements about the impact of technology on vocabulary made by sociolinguists Deborah Tannen and Pamela Munro, the *Los Angeles Times* quoted the counter-opinion of a high school French teacher, who cited the declining literacy skills of her teenagers as evidence of the "changes the Internet has wreaked on English," as the reporter put it.

These last examples illustrate the point that the extent to which information that disrupts "common sense," that disrupts the ideological alignment journalists share with their audience, is not considered expert knowledge at all. In these cases, the information in the stories I looked at can be viewed as qualified in some way, or marginalized according to the news hierarchy conventions that operate in the media.

10.3.3   *Trying to co-function as a linguist and journalist*

In my own personal experience, I lost whatever cachet I had with reporters on two occasions when I let my identity as a linguist supersede other considerations, when my language ideology clashed with theirs. Notably, when the debate over whether Ebonics (African-American Vernacular English) should be formally recognized in the Oakland, California schools was in the news in winter 1996–7, I presented information to a group of reporters from all over the country who were in Washington, DC, as journalism fellows. In an effort to contextualize African-American Vernacular English, I talked about non-standard varieties of a language, which are always marked socially, whose pejoration often stands in as a mechanism for working out or expressing larger social tensions. While I had initially aligned myself as a former reporter – one of you – it became clear that I no longer qualified for membership in a community I had been a part of for nearly a decade. Based solely on the ideas I was propounding, and despite my best efforts at packaging the information for the journalistic "ear," I was reappropriated to the category of academic, a category that is highly suspect, and thus expendable. With my identity so went my ideas or hopes of illuminating their thinking on language. Their observable response was quite hostile.

On another occasion I was interviewed on a national cable TV program about the word "niggardly," which bears an unfortunate phonological resemblance to the "n-word," possibly the most offensive word one could use as a white person in an American mixed-race context. A Washington, DC, city official, a Caucasian male, had caused unintended offense when he used the word in the course of his workday and had resigned to curtail further upheaval. The news anchors assumed that I would agree that the situation was ridiculous, that anyone who misheard the word was merely illiterate. When it became clear I was aligning with the DC official, who was sitting next to me at the anchor desk and essentially saying that social evaluations of language are often based on how we feel about a particular person or group, their relation to me changed. This change of affiliation was marked discursively by a change in their terms of address, from my first name, "Colleen," to a rather ironic and distancing rendering of "professor," as in "Well, professor, you're the expert. What would you say to that caller?"

Another time, the characterization of my sociolinguistic expertise in print matched my expectations. I explained to a *USA Today* reporter why pilots in cabin announcements might use generic terminology like "turbulence" instead of more specific "lightning storm," basing my response on ethnographically situated work I had done on aviation discourse with my father, a pilot himself. Of course my reading of pilot talk was perfectly in line with the industry experts they quoted. I had not challenged, as an academic, the safety-first language and communication ideology of a large industry. In fact, a colleague who read the story responded, "the airline industry is going to love you." Trained as I have been as a journalist, to feel that you are doomed if your sources are happy with how you report a controversy, it made me nervous, and led me to re-examine the way in which my own alignments with "common sense" or other language ideologies might allow me to get past the journalist's "skepticism" radar.

10.3.4   (De)constructing expertise

Here are some points that both academics and journalists can ponder as they cultivate their interactions with each other:

(1) Scholars need to see expertise as constructed and contingent, an insight that a great deal of the discourse literature on expert testimony in legal contexts

establishes. Expert status does not exist a priori, and cannot be expected to, just because we know ourselves to be experts in some domain. At the same time, journalists can reconsider what motivates their own appropriation of expert knowledge, particularly when it is at odds with a prevailing worldview.

(2) Language using and the attendant judgments about use need to be seen by anthropologists and linguists as normative practice, a point Cameron (1995) makes about expert and popular discourse on language – thus enabling the possibility of a challenge to these norms (see chapter 9). Journalists can reconsider how language judgments stand in for other meanings in society. Linguists and anthropologists can respond to reporters as they would a speech community under investigation and look at how journalistic decisions reflect its own kind of normative practice.

(3) Narrative conventions, for journalists and academics, both curtail and create the shape of texts. Journalists can reflect on how aspects of their practice impact how they are perceived. Academics can reflect on how these journalistic conventions become internalized by the community and reflected in their texts. A reporter colleague once read anthropologist Clifford Geertz's work on Bali and said he was very suspicious of his claims. Why? Because Geertz did not use any direct quotes, as a journalist would (Joe Cutbirth, personal communication). Instead of claiming authority for themselves, reporters assign it to the sources – through attribution and quotes – which brings us back to the notion of expert. The reporter saw enough similarity between anthropological and journalistic methods to be skeptical of Geertz's claims, on textual grounds, and to consider rejecting them.

My objective as it relates to journalistic "skepticism" in relation to the production of a news text has been to offer clarification and insights into different communities of practice, to understand better the processes that motivate the particular ways language is used and embedded within social life, and to consider how the making of the news narrative and the specificities of the process can reveal, reflect, and reaffirm journalistic values with respect to different priorities within a shared cultural context.

Conclusion and key points

In this book, I have attempted to view news discourse in ways that characterize the dynamic behind its production and the interrelationships that are integral in the process. For the purposes of academic discussion, I have set up these interrelationships in trichotomies that would be familiar to news practitioners: (1) in terms of news *content*, news *structure*, and the role of *interaction* between the communities of practice and the communities of coverage, among both individuals and groups; or (2) as *author*, *audience*, and *text* (the reporter-editor-source as *author*, reader-viewer as *audience*, and news product as *text*). The language–audience–media triumvirate is the basis of my ethnographic and interactional linguistic approach, but can be oriented to analytically – in ways that would be familiar to researchers – in different combinations and foci.

The journalistic values of **craft**, **community**, and **credibility** are integral to communicative competence within the news community. *Craft* and *credibility* are important in self-identity and *community* is an important framing concept for what counts as news. These three primary values put into perspective the importance of writing processes and the form and function of their discursive outputs and language norms (*craft*); relationship and interaction in the course of everyday journalistic work (*community*); and the professional ideologies (*credibility*) that become interpreted locally and underpin journalistic action and identity as news practitioners report, edit, and comment.

There is a **craft ethos** behind news production, to which reporters are socialized and which signals the acquisition of journalistic-communicative competence. To achieve this there is an **apprentice model** behind a reporter's socialization into journalistic practice. Novice reporters learn the roles, rules, relationships, and hierarchies within and outside of the news organization. They learn issues of text production and story construction; distinctions and firewalls with respect to news content, structure, and interaction; news priorities and news values – values which look different from the inside than the outside.

Linguistically, this **socialization matrix** operates within different speech situations, involving relations within the *community of practice* and with the *community of coverage*. The interaction-based nature of journalism involves some necessary degree of *reciprocal transmission* between the news practitioner and the news recipient-consumer. It is a special-case "pseudo-dyad," one that constitutes what we can refer to as a *pseudo-relationship*, of which the interactions are distinctively partial.

The set of reporting and editing rules that mold news language influences the structure of the text and the shape of the stories we read and hear. Selection of information elements in effect is based on Gricean conversational principles; the basic news story is a good example of Grice in action. In the journalistic realm, decisions about newsworthiness involve the application of *maximal relevance*; decisions about language use integrate with a *neutral authority* principle. Additionally, the attitudes of reporters to language, and the linguistic features of media language (which comprises characteristics of more than one domain), are bound to a profession-specific *prescriptive imperative* that aligns with societal norms.

Behind the rules of newswriting and norms of journalistic practice is an *interpretive dynamic*, one that allows both pattern and variation in news discourse. We can evaluate what is patterned and distinctive about news story design, as well as examine the implications of news discourse both story-internally (e.g., deixis, inference) and socioculturally and interactionally (framing, alignment of participants, stance, positioning). Which brings us to a discussion of the ways we can study news language, by incorporating ethnographic insight with other linguistic methods of analysis.

The basis of this book has been to provide a rationale for situating news media research in socially grounded, context-based, dynamic paradigms such as interactional sociolinguistics and ethnography of communication. Thus, I have emphasized the importance of evaluating media discourse from the ethnographic or participant-centered perspective whether the data under scrutiny, ideally acquired under fieldwork conditions, are ultimately subject to micro or macro analyses. Breaking down how a story goes from conception to reception is essential to understanding media language. In short, news stories can be understood in terms of the process – and what the participants bring to that process.

From that perspective, I want to highlight two points that relate to the actual compilation of a news story (*elements of practice* and *reporters as writers*), and the multiple ways news language operates (*news language and linguistics*) and how we can study it (*future research*), concluding with some final thoughts.

Elements of practice   While the rules of constructing news stories are simple and shared, because the process of information gathering is multifaceted and interaction-based, and stories are compiled by many participants, their output becomes complex. This point has been raised in different ways in this book, which has also focused on the acquisition of profession-specific communicative competence by journalism practitioners, their socialization with the *community of practice*, the role of the *community of coverage*, news language as performative and culturally constrained, and the organizing principles behind the construction of news (ideologically in terms of press freedoms and discursively in terms of craft).

Reporters as writers   Simplifying complex ideas for reader or viewer comprehension is one of the *discourse purposes* that attend the construction of news stories that appear in daily newspapers and broadcasts. News practitioners also situate themselves in opposition to writers of more florid or convoluted styles and pride themselves on their ability to quickly grasp the many significant particulars of a complex situation, synthesize them, and write about them accessibly (as the examples throughout the chapters make clear). They also value what is collectively viewed as "good writing" in the process of telling a story (cf. Chapter 4), as well as following norms of standard language usage (cf. Chapter 9).

News language and linguistics   To talk about language and news media, and to examine the relation of media to our understanding of language itself, is to consider language both *in* and *of* media. Linguistically, this comprises attention to sound, form, and meaning, and the micro and macro aspects of language function and structure: from the small grammatical segment to the longer stretch of discourse, from phonetics to philosophy, variation to policy (cf. Chapters 4 and 9). We can study how language operates within the boundaries of the news profession, how language is made unique through the constraints, exigencies, practice-rules, and ideologies of the news process (cf. Chapters 7 and 8). We can look at language resulting from specific processes and "production ways" in the media: the operations of journalists, the participants comprising the media, and that which is associated with, connected to, or produced by the media.

It also bears repeating that the language of news operates at the **intersection** of important linguistic and social dichotomies and the resources of language and communication that are used to manage these tensions. These traditional dichotomies, which media language data serve to challenge, include formal and informal, public and private, written and spoken, prestige and accommodation, authority and solidarity.

Future research   There are many options for further study of news language, such as I have attempted to outline, consider, and point to in this book. We can: focus linguistically on the production of text (in all manners of output), make use of the fuller range of news media data, look at news practice systematically, consider "everyday" or smaller-market or alternative journalism, examine the impacts of news content on the recipient,[1] examine the impacts of economy and culture on the news product, continue critical work on language and ideology,[2] or sufficiently synthesize or incorporate a wider range of theoretical and methodological frameworks offered by discourse analysis, sociolinguistics, and linguistic anthropology.

In terms of the Web and other new media, there are numerous possibilities for future research: the different textual constraints imposed by the medium; how we might come to different understandings of "interaction" and genre, or how technology is changing expectations of what counts as news; the sometimes contentious relationship between online and traditional reporters and editors and how that plays out in the texts we read; and "reciprocal transmission" issues pertaining to audience or geographical coverage area.

Accessibility (and relationship) is made more transparent as the traditional media uses "new media" and additional channels of communication like email, RSS newsfeeds, podcasts, and peer-to-peer networking technologies. Also worth serious consideration are the implications of the financial impacts on the profession, including loss of expert knowledge through staff cuts, and changing expectations of its textual, reportorial, and civic-minded outputs;[3] and how blogging, in terms of technology and practice, both reinforces long-held reporter values of observation, description, good story-telling (showing not telling), and speed (Van Hout 2008), and is affecting the journalist's relationship to the text, sense of professional identity, and internal discussions of ethics (Tenore 2008).

Final words – for now   News media discourse is best understood when the reporters, their intended audience, and the stories they write are considered holistically, as related parts contributing to a whole. As I have argued, analytic approaches that allow a focus on practice, cultural and

---

[1] For example, Jannis Androutsopolous (personal communication) argues for an expanded view of what constitutes interaction by linguists who study language variation and discourse in the media; while communications scholar Joe Cutbirth (personal communication) examines the impact of popular culture renditions of news events on political understanding.

[2] Some of its multifaceted potential is outlined in Jaworski 2007.

[3] "Technology has not only changed the way people get information – timeliness, the ability to use Internet tools to retrieve, sift and collate the news that interests them – but it has added the expectation that all this should be free. The result is an implosion of the business model that has generated robust double-digit profit margins for most newspapers [...] for the last half century. Some of the staples of newspapers that have lured and retained subscribers – stock tables, baseball box scores, TV listings, weather forecasts – are not only no longer our exclusive domain, there is no way we [print models] can compete with online sources for timeliness" (John Diaz, personal communication, emphasis added).

communicative competence, and an understanding of the norms and constraints of social interaction will give a more complete view of the language that is produced by the media. Within the ethnographic-interactional scope, the tools of discourse analysis and sociolinguistics can be fully implemented to consider language structure, function, social organization, and worldview. Focusing on media processes from the perspective of the norms and routines of the practitioner – part of an ethnographic discourse analytic approach to news language – draws attention to the discourse purpose particularities underlying news practice.

To this end, I hope I have brought into focus the **textual requirements of news stories**, the **metatextual issues concerning journalists**, and the **complexities of the journalistic objective**. News stories follow parameters of form (short paragraphs, short sentences, multiple sources, attribution, inverted pyramid structure), style (minimalist, each word must count), and prescriptive language rules (which are strongly held and part of an accuracy ethos). Metatextual issues that concern journalists and are part of everyday practice relate to prescriptive language attitudes (standard language ideology), interactional needs (connecting with the reader or listener), and a specific relation to a moment in time (writing the "first-draft of history" and later understanding the socio-historical position). Complexities of the journalistic objective revolve, very simply, around authority-proximity tensions, and how to resolve them.

The main objective of the book has been to develop an ethnographic view of the language of everyday journalism and an interactional sensibility in analyzing it, in which we come to understand how and what language is produced by the news community, and its relation to an intended public.

Epilogue

It is a truism in the news bizz that you have succeeded in writing a "balanced" story if all your sources take issue with and are unhappy with it. I never bought that (nor do others follow the precept). I much preferred it when both (all?) sides of story I had written – about a complex, grey-area, politicized local issue – were satisfied. It meant that I had listened and heard what might have been contradictory, divergent, or didn't add up and conveyed that both sides had something relevant to say. It also meant that I had succeeded in writing a "balanced" story in the expectations of my peers. I was an "insider" operating within the journalistic world, functioning as my community expected.

The way I have set up this book – focusing on practice more than problematizing the outputs, sometimes essentializing the journalist or over-simplifying the process – will undoubtedly mean I have pleased none of the people all of the time* (but, I would hope, all of the people some of the time). Which is as it should be. My goal is dialogue between journalists and linguists, among linguists, among journalists: to open up discussion, rather than shut it down. Linguists have the tools; journalists have the material; all have the interest. Let the dialogue begin.

---

* Based on responses from "both sides" over the years, I can predict that some journalists will say I have been too academic and jargonful. Some linguists and anthropologists will say I have not been sufficiently critical. This is a predictable consequence. Indeed, one journalist friend who read a version of chapter 4 said his eyes "glazed over" reading about *emic* and *etic* constructs. A short while later, a linguist colleague who read the same chapter emailed to say he loved the *emic/etic* concept application and wanted more. That "minimal-pair response" reinforced my understanding of what is differently relevant to both communities.

Appendices

Appendix 1: Story samples

A. *TYPICAL NEWS STORY DESIGN*
384 words, 15 paragraphs

Headline>	**One gene may be key to coveted perfect pitch**
Byline>	**By Julie Steenhuysen**

1. **Lead>**
   Attribution>
   Time element>

   CHICAGO (Reuters) – Musicians and singers work for years to develop their sense of pitch but few can name a musical note without a reference tone. U.S. researchers on Monday said one gene may be the key to that coveted ability.

[at 33 words fits within 25–35-word guideline]

2. **Context>**

   Only 1 in 10,000 people have perfect or absolute pitch, the uncanny ability to name the note of just about any sound without the help of a reference tone.

[supports newsworthiness]

3. **Quote>**
   Context>

   "One guy said, 'I can name the pitch of anything – even farts,'" said Dr. Jane Gitschier of the University of California, San Francisco, whose study appears in the journal Proceedings of the National Academy of Sciences.

4.

   She and colleagues analyzed the results of a three-year, Web-based survey and musical test that required participants to identify notes without the help of a reference tone. More than 2,200 people completed the 20-minute test.

[Attribution not needed as published source already named in previous paragraph]

5. **Attribution>**

   "We noticed that pitch-naming ability was roughly an all-or-nothing phenomenon," she said.

6.

   That led researchers to conclude that one gene, or perhaps a few, may be behind this talent.

239

7. **Attribution>** | Gitschier said those with perfect pitch were able to correctly identify both piano tones and pure computer-generated tones that were devoid of the distinctive sounds of any musical instrument.

8. **Attribution>** | She said people with perfect pitch were able to
   Connective> | pick out the pure tone with ease. And they also tended to have had early musical training – before the age of 7.

[Sentence-initial and connective supports discourse coherence]

9. **Attribution>** | "We think it probably takes the two things," she said.

10. **Indirect attrib>** | They also found that perfect pitch tends to deteriorate with age.

11. | "As people get older, their perception goes sharp. If a note C is played, and they're 15, they will say it's a C. But if they're 50, they might say it's a C sharp."

[Typical paragraph conventions]

12. | "This can be very disconcerting for them,"
    Attribution> | Gitschier said.

13. **Background>** | The most commonly misidentified note, based on the study, is a G sharp. That may be because G sharp is overshadowed by A, its neighbor on the scale, they said. A is often used by orchestras in the West as a tuning reference.

[Background info can be deleted; usually placed near end of story.]

14. **Attrib>** | Gitschier said she and her colleagues were focusing on identifying the gene responsible for perfect pitch, which will involve gene mapping. Then
    Inference> | they will try to figure out what is different in people with absolute pitch.

[Absolute pitch inferred to be synonym for perfect pitch, given word-economy objective.]

15. **"Good quote"/** | **"We'll have to play it by ear, so to speak,"** she
    Attrib> | said.

["zinger"-type quote often used to end story; functions as rhetorical closure]

B. *BRITE*
333 words, 13 paragraphs

Headline>	**5th-grader finds mistake at Smithsonian** 11-year-old catches sign error that has rankled staffers for 27 years
Byline>	The Associated Press

1. **Dateline>** ALLEGAN*, Mich. – Is fifth-grader Kenton
   8-word lead> Stufflebeam* smarter than the Smithsonian?

[the question lead sets up the premise]

2. **Background*>** The 11-year-old boy, who lives in Allegan* but attends
   Alamo Elementary School near Kalamazoo, went with
   Time element> his family during winter break to the Smithsonian
   Context> Institution's National Museum of Natural History in
   Washington.

[time element is scene-setting, not news-related; all the WHERE questions are answered]

3. **Context>** Since it opened in 1981, millions of people have para-
   ded past the museum's Tower of Time, a display
   involving prehistoric time. Not one visitor had reported
   The "story"> anything amiss with the exhibit until Kenton noticed that
   a notation, in bold lettering, identified the Precambrian
   as an era.

4. **The "story"** Kenton knew that was wrong. His fifth-grade teacher,
   John Chapman, had nearly made the same mistake
   in a classroom earth-science lesson before catching
   himself.

5. **Quote>** "I knew Mr. Chapman wouldn't tell all these students"
   Attribution> bad information, the boy told the Kalamazoo Gazette
   Time element> for a story published Wednesday.

6.

Time element>

Partial quote>

So Kevin Stufflebeam took his son to the museum's information desk to report Kenton's concern on a comment form. <u>Last week</u>, the boy received a letter from the museum acknowledging that his observation was "<u>spot on</u>."

[follows first-name reference conventions for children; avoids repetition: "Kenton," "the boy"]

7. **Quote>**

Attribution>

"The Precambrian is a dimensionless unit of time, which embraces all the time between the origin of Earth and the beginning of the Cambrian Period of geologic time," <u>the letter says</u>.

8. **Indirect quote>**

Attribution>

The solution to the problem would not involve advanced science but rather simply painting over the word "era," <u>the note says</u>.

["note" avoids repetition with "letter" in prior paragraph]

9. **Quote>**

Attribution>
Job title>

"We did forward a copy of the comment and our paleobiology department's response to the head of the exhibits department," <u>said Lorraine Ramsdell, educational technician for the museum</u>.

10.

Attribution>

While no previous visitors to the museum had brought up the error, it has long rankled the paleobiology department's staff, who noticed it even before the Tower of Time was erected 27 years ago, <u>she said</u>.

11.**Quote>**
   Attribution>

"The question is, why was it put up with that on it in the first place?" <u>Ramsdell said</u>.

12.

Excited as he was to receive the correspondence from museum officials, he couldn't help but point out that it was addressed to Kenton <u>Slufflebeam*</u>.

13.

In <u>Allegany*</u>.

Comments:
This unbylined story is set up to reveal a punchline in paragraphs 12 and 13 at the same time it presents as a well-structured news story with the news element in lead position. Words with asterisks in paragraphs 1 and 2 set this up. Relevance rules are ostensibly broken – through name identification in lead and repetition of non-newsworthy town of residence (I wondered why the reporter was focusing on these details) – until the

rationale for this repetition is made clear at the end. From a story-design perspective, it is a masterful journalistic "performance," illustrating deictic control.

C. COLUMN
(See discussion in chapter 4.)

Some Are Less 'Newsworthy' Than Others
By Colbert I. King
The Washington Post

On Nov. 28, 2003, shoppers swarmed Washington area malls hunting for bargains as the holiday season kicked off; hard-line Protestant and Catholic political parties in Northern Ireland triumphed in local legislative elections; two major oil companies in Russia abruptly suspended their landmark merger; and here in Washington, Marion Fye of V Street NE vanished. All of the foregoing, except Fye's disappearance, was duly reported in the Nov. 29 edition of The Post.

Marion Fye's name first appeared in the news, and only in this newspaper, last June 10, when The Post reported that her live-in boyfriend, 33-year-old Harold D. Austin, aka "Devine," had been charged with her murder. On Feb. 1 a D.C. Superior Court jury found Austin guilty of killing Fye. Her body was never found.

A note from a reader who is also a federal prosecutor contrasted the handling of Fye's disappearance with the media frenzy that followed last year's disappearance of a "young, pretty, white," straight-A Alabama high school graduate named Natalee Holloway, who was vacationing in Aruba.

"Was it because Ms. Fye was 36 years old, a single mother of five children, unemployed and African American?" the reader asked. "Who knows, but kind of sad, don't you think?"

He asked whether media attention during the first days after Fye's disappearance would have helped. Answering his own question, he suggested a news story would have alerted the public and possibly drawn information that could have helped the police. Perhaps.

But did Fye's race make a difference? Certainly it didn't to the D.C. police. The department received well-earned praise for the way in which it responded to reports of Fye's disappearance. Police conducted an authorized search of Fye's home about a week after Austin reported her missing. On Dec. 24, 2003, the D.C. police issued a news release seeking the public's help in locating Fye, who was described in detail. The Post didn't use it.

After an exhaustive 18-month investigation by Detective Christopher Kauffman of the violent crimes branch, the police obtained a confession from Austin, who was put on trial in January and found guilty two weeks ago. Kauffman received the Detective of the Year medal for 2005 for successfully closing the second "no-body" case in police department history. So the police did their job.

Disparate racial treatment in the coverage? Compared with what? The Post has given extensive coverage to the murder of a 15-year-old youth in Southeast Washington and the arrest of another youth for an unconnected murder; both are grandsons of a prominent former member of the D.C. Council – all African Americans.

The real question, which the reader also posed, is how we decide whether one story is more worthy than another. How do we determine the merits of a case? The answer, in my judgment, lies at the heart of newspaper industry's downward spiral in circulation.

The decision to go with one story rather than another turns on what we in this business consider "newsworthy." It's an amorphous term, but editors claim to know it when they see it. Unfortunately, in my view, that decision seems to boil down to what those of us in newsrooms, and not readers, care about.

And there's the problem. What draws the interest of people in the news business (what they like to read and write about) often bears little relationship to what people who live in communities like Marion Fye's care about.

And that's how a single mom in Northeast Washington who disappears from her home, leaving behind all her children and possessions, doesn't make it into the newspaper.

It's because someone may have decided that a story like hers, of a woman nobody has ever heard of, won't have much significance to readers. It's because someone has concluded that there is nothing out of the ordinary about an adult black single mom walking out on her family. It's because such behavior is considered commonplace, too routine to warrant precious space.

Marion Fye is not alone.

Two weeks ago, the D.C. police asked for the public's help in finding an 88-year-old black woman, about 120 pounds, wearing a salt-and-pepper wig, suffering from dementia, and unable to care for herself, who was last seen at her daughter's doctor's office. The Post didn't print it.

Neither did we tell you that on Dec. 1 the police were trying to locate a 42-year-old black man wearing a Dallas Cowboys hat, eyeglasses, a blue coat and gray pants, who requires medication and was last seen on Nov. 20.

Sometimes there are legitimate reasons for not publishing a report. For example, the missing person is found before the story goes to press. But the fact is that inner-city events that some editors regard as routine – the loss of a young man to gunfire, a mom separated from her children, kids left to fend for themselves – are the kind of issues that people who live in those communities really care about.

Tough nuggies. Marion Fye's disappearance, in the judgment of those who get to decide such matters, just wasn't worthy of the news.

D. FEATURE STORY

Life's been blooming for him
By Colleen Cotter
The (Appleton, Wis.) *Post-Crescent*

If you ask Paul Lochschmidt, Kimberly, which kind of flower he likes best, he'll tell you the question "isn't fair."

Lochschmidt, 87, has in his garden nearly 20 flowers which start blooming in early spring and last late into the fall. As far as Lochschmidt is concerned, each flower has its own beauty in its own time. "There's always something new," he said.

Lochschmidt sat with his wife Kate in the screened patio next to his garage and listed with great familiarity the flowers in his garden. "I don't know what all their names are," he said. "I'm liable to call them Pat and Mike. Of course when you want to buy a certain flower you can't just ask for Pat and Mike."

Although reluctant to show favoritism, Lochschmidt admitted he was fond of cosmos, because they "bring the canaries." He said the "tall flower dries up and the seed pod opens like a little trough. The canaries twine their tiny feet around the stem and put that old beak of theirs into the seeds. The male, of course, is a brilliant yellow fella."

When Lochschmidt talks about his garden, he describes the colors. He even has black Holland tulips, he said, which have been cross-bred. He points to an old painted grill which holds geraniums of various and subtle red and pink shades. "They're just heaven," he said.

"Every time I see a different flower, I buy it," claims Lochschmidt, who reads magazines about flowers.

Kate, who tends the plants in the house, shares his enthusiasm and said it is a "good hobby." They don't have a car, she said, and her husband's colorful circle of flowers attracts people to their house.

"The neighbors enjoy it," Lochschmidt agreed, and said he takes care of the flowers of his 95-year-old next-door neighbor, Mrs. Martin Wydeven. "I plant flowers there every spring, and she likes looking out her window at my garden," he said.

Lochschmidt's night-blooming cactus, which blossoms at midnight when it is in season, has been the occasion of several neighborhood parties.
[...]

The Lochschmidts go to Arizona every year to visit a few of their 14 children. They often exchange plants. "Some don't grow here, and some from here don't grow in Arizona," said Kate, who mentioned that her husband saved the seeds and sent packets of them to friends and relatives across the country.

Lochschmidt started his backyard mountain ash tree from a seed. It flowers every spring. "There have never been blossoms as pretty as this year," Kate said.

Green berries replace the flowers on the mountain ash, Lochschmidt said. "When the berries are dead ripe, I don't know how many hundreds of robins come every day at five for supper," he said. "The red berries must be real strong in something. The birds eat so many that they get tipsy and stagger around on the ground as if they had a jag on."

Lochschmidt, who had been custodian for the Kimberly school district for 36 years before his retirement [...] raised the mountain ash at the high school.
[...]

The flowers at Kimberly Savings and Loan are Lochschmidt's doing. He had been a director there for 34 years, he said, and in charge of the building and grounds committee.
[...]

Lochschmidt has the quiet sense of perspective and humor one acquires from working close to the earth. He has cultivated, besides his flowers, an appreciation for the unusual in the ordinary.

"The Lord God knows I've been on my knees most of my life," he said.

© The (Appleton, Wis.) Post-Crescent.
Comments:
This story (written during a summer internship before my senior year in college, and reproduced as published except for deletions noted by ellipsis, despite an urge to do some editing) is a typical community-oriented feature story intended to highlight something

unique or noteworthy about an individual who has made a contribution to the community in which he or she lives. It is not necessarily a story that would "make the wires" and be transmitted elsewhere (although I have had that experience with seemingly "small stories" during my career). Nowadays the Web, of course, would allow greater distribution, should the community paper be online. The assignment from the city editor was likely: "Cotter: this old guy's garden is the talk of the neighborhood. One of his neighbors called to tell us about it. Check it out for Saturday. We're low on features." Note the intern's attempt to include numerous quotations, to "show, don't tell," and to situate the individual and his actions explicitly within the community.

Appendix 2: Outline guide for the analysis of news media language

Below are ten topics relevant to our understanding of news language from the linguistic and journalistic perspectives.[1] Primary linguistic concepts are listed, followed by deliberately open-ended questions to encourage further thought, research, and understanding from several analytical points-of-view: structural, functional, theoretical, social, linguistic, practice-oriented, and journalistic.

1. USAGE NORMS AND EXPECTATIONS

- speech
- writing
- influence of written norms on spoken language
- influence of spoken language on written norms
- influence of channel or modality (Web, broadcast, print) on usage
- influence of Web on news-story style

Questions: How can we "read" the news media knowing that different modalities of transmission comprise different sets of norms? How does what reporters are taught about newswriting influence the shape of the narrative? Where do journalistic usage norms differ from or correspond to expectations in the larger culture?

2. USAGE AND SOCIAL EVALUATION (SOCIAL FACTORS)

- speech community
- communicative competence
- language attitudes and prejudice
- social stratification: language choice and its implications

Questions: How can the media be accounted for in a community? How would speech community norms influence usage in the media? How does standard language ideology figure in? How does the news media reinforce or subvert standard language, innovation in language, society's attitudes toward non-standard language users?

---

[1] With thanks to Sherzer and Darnell 1972.

3. USAGE AT THE DISCOURSE LEVEL (STRUCTURAL FACTORS)

- planned and unplanned discourse ("color commentary," live reporting, blogging, newswriting, etc.)
- the linguistics of punctuation (Nunberg 1990)
- visual communication

Questions: How can structural factors – elements that are foundational – be considered in a comprehensive description of media language? How can we account for non-verbal or visual communication that is meaningful and journalistically salient? How can we make claims about news discourse that are defensible ethnographically?

4. THE EFFECTS OF GENRE

- narratives and stories – constraints on "text" and its shape, order, and detail
- "rules and roles"– constraints on participants and what they (can) say and write

Questions: How can one begin to identify recurring stories or themes or presentation styles in the media? Are there genres unique to the media? What features or patterns help us to identify these genre forms?

5. THE AUDIENCE

- audience design (Bell 1984)
- language planning effects (e.g., Fasold *et al.* 1990; Vandenbussche 2008)
- nationality and language (e.g., Leitner 1980)
- pseudo-relationship/reciprocal transmission (Cotter 1996b; also this volume)

Questions: Linguistics offers a variety of "tools" to understand the role of the audience in media language contexts as well as to understand the formulation of the language itself. How can various linguistic approaches be taken further in this regard? Why look at linguistic evidence anyway?

6. THE WAYS JOURNALISTS WORK

- copy editors (sub-editors) and their gate-keeper function
- stylebooks and their standardization function
- standard language ideology and the perpetuation of negative linguistic stereotypes
- social history and understanding media practice
- reporters and their role within communities
- the objectives of reporting, interviewing, and editing

Questions: How does practice influence language use? At what levels? How do declines in newsroom staffing or corporate oversight influence news language? What differences occur cross-culturally?

7. PRESCRIPTION AND STANDARDIZATION

- complaint tradition
- types of complaints
- linguist vs. lay view of language
- standard language ideology

Questions: How do these concepts relate to and influence media language, directly and indirectly? What is the role of the news media in maintaining usage standards? Where can variation occur? Where might there be flexibility? How does a reporter quote non-standard language?

8. VARIATION IN MEDIA LANGUAGE

- influence vs. causality
- presupposition and shared cultural knowledge
- visual and textual information
- out-group interpretations of media discourse

Questions: How can we explain variation and standardization as influential dynamics in the construction of media language? What are other causes of differentiation across news media contexts? How can one study variation of news outputs and practice across cultures over time?

9. THE "ETHNOGRAPHIC ADVANTAGE"

- process of news production
- speech events and situations
- communities of practice
- relationships within the profession and outside

Questions: How does the news community work? What are its values? Who makes up the community and what role do they play? What counts as communicative competence? How is it embedded in the larger social world? What are the components of the news process? What are the community-identified routines that comprise "doing" journalism? How can we characterize practice and its embodiments? What are constraints on practice? What counts as "ethnographic" in terms of data, analysis, methodology? How can we develop ethnographic approaches?

10. NEWS MEDIA DISCOURSE

- information structure
- context
- situated activity
- interaction within process and practice

Questions: What are the rules behind the reporting and writing of news stories? How does the process of information gathering shape news discourse? How does it shape relationships between and among news practitioners, their sources, the public? How is media language embedded or situated in the context of social relationships? Where does responsibility reside? Why does a journalist see outputs in the media differently than a non-journalist?

Appendix 3: Society of Professional Journalists Code of Ethics

SOCIETY OF PROFESSIONAL JOURNALISTS

Code of Ethics

Preamble

Members of the Society of Professional Journalists believe that public enlightenment is the forerunner of justice and the foundation of democracy. The duty of the journalist is to further those ends by seeking truth and providing a fair and comprehensive account of events and issues. Conscientious journalists from all media and specialties strive to serve the public with thoroughness and honesty. Professional integrity is the cornerstone of a journalist's credibility.

Members of the Society share a dedication to ethical behavior and adopt this code to declare the Society's principles and standards of practice.

Seek Truth and Report It

Journalists should be honest, fair and courageous in gathering, reporting and interpreting information.

Journalists should:

► Test the accuracy of information from all sources and exercise care to avoid inadvertent error. Deliberate distortion is never permissible.

► Diligently seek out subjects of news stories to give them the opportunity to respond to allegations of wrongdoing.

► Identify sources whenever feasible. The public is entitled to as much information as possible on sources' reliability.

► Always question sources' motives before promising anonymity. Clarify conditions attached to any promise made in exchange for information. Keep promises.

► Make certain that headlines, news teases and promotional material, photos, video, audio, graphics, sound bites and quotations do not misrepresent. They should not oversimplify or highlight incidents out of context.

► Never distort the content of news photos or video. Image enhancement for technical clarity is always permissible. Label montages and photo illustrations.

► Avoid misleading re-enactments or staged news events. If re-enactment is necessary to tell a story, label it.

► Avoid undercover or other surreptitious methods of gathering information except when traditional open methods will not yield information vital to the public. Use of such methods should be explained as part of the story.

► Never plagiarize.

► Tell the story of the diversity and magnitude of the human experience boldly, even when it is unpopular to do so.

► Examine their own cultural values and avoid imposing those values on others.

► Avoid stereotyping by race, gender, age, religion, ethnicity, geography, sexual orientation, disability, physical appearance or social status.

► Support the open exchange of views, even views they find repugnant.

► Give voice to the voiceless; official and unofficial sources of information can be equally valid.

► Distinguish between advocacy and news reporting. Analysis and commentary should be labeled and not misrepresent fact or context.

► Distinguish news from advertising and shun hybrids that blur the lines between the two.

► Recognize a special obligation to ensure that the public's business is conducted in the open and that government records are open to inspection.

Minimize Harm

Ethical journalists treat sources, subjects and colleagues as human beings deserving of respect.

Journalists should:

► Show compassion for those who may be affected adversely by news coverage. Use special sensitivity when dealing with children and inexperienced sources or subjects.

► Be sensitive when seeking or using interviews or photographs of those affected by tragedy or grief.

► Recognize that gathering and reporting information may cause harm or discomfort. Pursuit of the news is not a license for arrogance.

► Recognize that private people have a greater right to control information about themselves than do public officials and others who seek power, influence or attention. Only an overriding public need can justify intrusion into anyone's privacy.

► Show good taste. Avoid pandering to lurid curiosity.

► Be cautious about identifying juvenile suspects or victims of sex crimes.

► Be judicious about naming criminal suspects before the formal filing of charges.

► Balance a criminal suspect's fair trial rights with the public's right to be informed.

Act Independently

Journalists should be free of obligation to any interest other than the public's right to know.

Journalists should:

► Avoid conflicts of interest, real or perceived.

► Remain free of associations and activities that may compromise integrity or damage credibility.

► Refuse gifts, favors, fees, free travel and special treatment, and shun secondary employment, political involvement, public office and service in community organizations if they compromise journalistic integrity.

► Disclose unavoidable conflicts.

► Be vigilant and courageous about holding those with power accountable.

► Deny favored treatment to advertisers and special interests and resist their pressure to influence news coverage.

► Be wary of sources offering information for favors or money; avoid bidding for news.

Be Accountable

Journalists are accountable to their readers, listeners, viewers and each other.

Journalists should:

► Clarify and explain news coverage and invite dialogue with the public over journalistic conduct.

► Encourage the public to voice grievances against the news media.

► Admit mistakes and correct them promptly.

► Expose unethical practices of journalists and the news media.

► Abide by the same high standards to which they hold others.

Sigma Delta Chi's first Code of Ethics was borrowed from the American Society of Newspaper Editors in 1926. In 1973, Sigma Delta Chi wrote its own code, which was revised in 1984 and 1987. The present version of the Society of Professional Journalists' Code of Ethics was adopted in September 1996.

Glossary of news and linguistic terms
(a supplement to discussion within the chapters)

Actuality   The actual recording, used in radio broadcasting, of what the news-maker or interviewee has said, not the newsreader or news reporter's voice. It is comparable to a "quote" in print. Known outside of the industry as a "sound bite." (See **Chapter 9**.)

AP   The Associated Press. (See "Wire service" below.)

Boilerplate   Information that provides additional background to the story that gets repeated (often without any change to the text) in subsequent stories. It is informative, but not "news," and thus easily deletable. Boilerplate is also a term used in the legal profession to refer to language that is repeated again and again, and is known generically in that sense. (See **Chapter 8**.)

Breaking news   News that is occurring at the moment it is being reported. (See **Chapter 7**.)

Brite   See "Zinger." (See **Chapter 7** and **Appendix 1B**.)

Byline   The name of the reporter who wrote the story (used when the story warrants it), usually positioned at the top of the story.

Copy editor   A person responsible for editing news stories for appropriate style, usage, grammar, and punctuation, as well as placement on the page and writing headlines. They are instrumental in maintaining consistency, upholding usage norms, querying facts, and locating inadvertent errors of all sorts. The **News Editor** oversees the copy editors on the **copy desk** (or "desk"). In the UK, a copy editor is known as a *sub-editor*.

Dateline   The place where the news has occurred or where the reporter has reported from; usually in upper-case letters before a story begins, e.g., "LONDON – The Royal Parks Half-Marathon got off to a running start today with a record number of …"

Deck   A line of headline. A "three-deck hed" is a headline composed of three lines of type.

Graf   Paragraph.

The "Five W's" The basic reporting questions: who, what, when, where, why – and how. They also function as an internalized checklist while the story is being written, edited, or evaluated.

Hed Headline.

Journo A slang term for "journalist," used primarily in the UK, by both journalists and members of the public. *Hack* is also used by members of the UK news community as a positive term of insider reference. Outside of the news community it is often used pejoratively, often to discredit writing ability and prose style.

Jump (noun, verb) *Noun*: The part of the story that continues onto a subsequent page: "the jump." *Verb*: Also the process of continuing the story inside: "let's jump that; that will have to jump." US papers tend to jump stories, sometimes over more than two inside pages, although they try to minimize it as readers stop reading ("losing readers on the jump" is a common problem); UK papers try to avoid doing so except on Page One. A *jump page* is one reserved for stories that are continued from Page One, as well as to accommodate last-minute additions and changes to stories.

Lead The beginning or top of a news story. Also spelled *lede* in US newsroom contexts. (See **Chapter 7**.) In the UK, it is called the *intro*; and "lead" is used to refer to the story's news angle (or focus).

Leader In the UK, the term for what in the US is called the *editorial*, the genre of newswriting that highlights opinion and takes a position on an issue or situation.

ME Managing Editor: the person who oversees the "news side," as opposed to the editorial/opinion or business sides, of a news organization. He or she tends to lead the story meetings. (See **Chapter 5**.)

Nat sound Natural sound recorded to set a scene, to position a radio reporter in a specific place, and to evoke an interpretive response in the listener, e.g., traffic noise, sounds in nature or places like amusement parks, concerts, etc. (See **Chapter 9**.)

News tip An idea for a story generally delivered by members of the public via telephone, email, or face-to-face interaction; also solicited and sought after by the news organization. (See **Chapter 3**.)

Newspaper of record The newspaper designated within a community to function as a primary source (and archive) for the official publication of legal notices and information of public and civic importance. The principle extends into the news-editorial realm to include other community-relevant, although not necessarily "newsworthy," information such as routine decisions (and vote counts) of civic and government entities.

Nut graf   A paragraph that summarizes the essence (metaphorically the "nut") of a news story, allowing for more flexibility in how the reporter writes the lead; a synopsis. (See **Chapter 7.**)

Op-ed   1. The term of reference for the Opinion page itself and its practitioners. 2. A genre of newswriting characterized by editorials ("leaders" in the UK), columns, news analysis, and opinion. 3. The section of the paper that deals with editorials, opinion pieces and columns, and letters to the editor.

Pull-quote   A comment or quote from a story that is extracted and featured through boldface or larger or different type. It functions to break up the grey type of the story and to alert a reader to the story's content or to an aspect of the story that is not obvious in the headline or lead. It is used to enhance graphic-informational display. (See **Chapter 7.**)

Sidebar   A story that accompanies a longer story, generally drawing out and focusing on one aspect or impact of the news focus. (See **Chapter 7.**)

Skybar   When the top of a newspaper is used to draw attention to stories elsewhere in the paper that space is referred to, by some news organizations, as a skybar. (See **Chapter 5.**)

Story meetings   Also known as **budget meetings** or **news meetings**. Regular meetings of editors for the purpose of determining what stories the news organization will lead with (broadcast and print) and keeping up to date with what is happening in other departments. (See **Chapter 5.**) In the UK they are known as *editorial meetings*.

Wire service   Stories that are not reported, written, or produced by a news organization's staff generally come from "the wires," from one or more "wire services" or news services which provide stories or "news feeds" to subscribers. Most news organizations have a **Wire Editor** who keeps tabs on wire transmissions. Examples of news or wire services are: The Associated Press, Reuters, Press Association of Britain, Canadian Press, Agence France-Presse, Los Angeles Times-Washington Post, Market Wire, etc.

Zinger   A humorous or unusual story, referred to in different ways by different news organizations (e.g., "A-head" at the *Wall Street Journal*). The equivalent in the UK is the very common "*and finally*" segment at the end of a news broadcast. (See **Chapter 7** and Appendix 1B.)

LINGUISTIC TERMS FOR JOURNALISTS AND OTHERS

Community of coverage   The term I have coined to refer to the members of the public – reader, listener, viewer, audience, news consumer – which news practitioners take into account and have in mind when they report, edit, write, and produce. It is a companion term, of sorts, to "community of practice," intended to facilitate discussion of the interaction between news practitioners and the public they actively write for. (See **Chapter 2**.)

Community of practice   The term I use to refer to the community of news practitioners (reporters, journalists, editors, writers, columnists, producers, photographers, videographers, Web designers), following Lave and Wenger 1991, who introduced the concept to help linguists analyze communicative action and interaction as well as aspects of language particular to a group. (See **Chapter 2**.)

Conversational maxim   The late philosopher H. Paul Grice summarized the rules of conduct necessary for well-formed and successful communication: Say only what needs to be said for the situation, be truthful, be brief and clear, be relevant (Grice 1975). As I note in **Chapter 7**, Grice's conversational maxims succinctly summarize the basic rules of newswriting and can be used to analyze news stories' shape.

Deixis   Orientation to place, person, time, and social context in relation to ourselves and what we are speaking about. This is accomplished through words like "this," "there," "yesterday," as well as verb tense and pronoun use. In the news context, datelines, bylines, quotes, story position, time element, etc. contribute to the journalistic "deictic display." (See **Chapter 1**.)

Discourse analysis   A systematic approach to studying longer stretches of language (not just the sounds or forms of words and sentences) as it is used in interaction. Conversation, written language, genre forms like lectures and sermons (and news stories), question-and-answer pairs, formality and informality, etc., are some of what is investigated. Different approaches to the analysis of discourse derive from philosophy, sociology, linguistics, anthropology, and critical theory and may or may not involve the study of context alongside the study of the text or talk under scrutiny (see Schiffrin 1994). *Ethnography of communication* and *interactional sociolinguistics* are two frameworks used in discourse analysis, and are useful for situating communicative phenomena within culture and context.

Eclipsis   In Irish and other Celtic languages, the way the first – or initial – consonant sounds in words change in certain environments internal to the language. For example, eclipsis occurs to the noun for *house* (*teach*) after the preposition for *in* (*i*): *i dteach* "in a house." The [t] sound changes to [d] and the spelling (orthography) reflects that change. (Also see *lenition* and **Chapter 9**.)

Ethnography of communication   A fieldwork-based approach to analyzing language use (or ways of speaking and interacting) in society based on the principle that to understand communication, one has to understand the community. The ethnography of communication framework combines anthropology (tools to understand culture) and linguistics (tools to analyze language).

Evidentiality   The distribution of responsibility for knowledge or the claims of an utterance. When we as speakers and writers make claims or share information, we also indicate the extent to which we are affiliated with it, often by including the source of information or the "evidence" behind it. Journalistically, evidentiality is expressed in the way information is attributed or the voice of the reporter is authorized. (See **Chapters 5** and **8**.)

Indexicality   The connotations within and behind our interactions, used strategically or not, that allow us to affiliate with, orient to, and establish social meaning and group membership.

Interactional sociolinguistics   An approach to analyzing discourse that prioritizes context and determines both the sociocultural and linguistic elements that constitute interaction. As such, it acknowledges prior and emergent meanings within interactions; the role of culture and how it affects the interpretation of interactions by participants; and the community-specific patterns behind structures of talk (spoken discourse) and text (written discourse).

Interlocutor   A participant in a conversation or communicative exchange; as a technical term it is a more general and inclusive term than Speaker or Hearer.

Language maven   Language mavens (to use Steven Pinker's 1994 term, following William Safire) are published opinion leaders and columnists who adhere to socially prescriptive (as opposed to linguistically descriptive) notions about "correct" language and are viewed as self-appointed experts in that domain. Their pronouncements in print, often based on the often unquestioned assumption that only one form is right, have helped to establish the longstanding "complaint tradition" about any variation and change in usage that goes against the prescribed norm. (See **Chapter 9**.) Indeed, even the use of the word "maven" reflects the vitality of language in use: the term was adopted, from the Yiddish *meyvn*, into mainstream American colloquial English through advertising and television to define an expert or specialist in some area. The term has become more internationally widespread, particularly as it correlates to trends and market information, since Malcolm Gladwell's 2000 best-seller *The Tipping Point*. Scrabble aficionados (such as this author's mother) can play the word-assembly game on the computer against the artificially intelligent "Maven" – another context in which expertise and language (and rules governing form) are intertwined.

Lenition   Like *eclipsis* (see above), lenition is another process of systematic sound change at the beginnings of Irish words based on certain underlying language-internal or grammatical conditions. For example, lenition occurs to the noun for *house* (*teach*) after the possessive pronoun *my* (*mo*): *mo theach* "my house." The [t] sound changes to [h] and the spelling (orthography) reflects that change. (Also see *eclipsis* and **Chapter 9**.)

Participant framework   A term that refers to the way participants in an interaction (conversation, email, interview, news broadcast, etc.) are constituted, the roles they play, and the constraints on what they can or cannot say.

Pragmatics   Analyzing and understanding language and communication in *use*, often in terms of what is *not* said (inference and intention), as well as examining what conditions our interpretations of what speakers say or write.

SPEAKING grid   A mnemonic developed by Hymes (1972b), used to help researchers (in the initial stages of analyzing communication in social contexts) to isolate relevant components of communication as it is occurring and see their relationships: Setting of the speech situation and its role, Participants in the interactions, Ends or objectives of interaction, Act sequence or message form and content, Key or tone, Instrumentality or mode of communicative delivery, Norms of interaction and speaking, Genres that are relevant to the speech community.

Speech community (discourse community)   A community that shares a language (or language variety) and shares an understanding of how it is used and what it means in situations that comprise the community's social life and work. A **discourse community** (and *community of practice*, see above) shares an understanding of how to communicate – how to produce discourse – in the community's particular contexts. The workplace, or professions like academia or journalism or medicine, can be seen as discourse communities or communities of practice; they exist within the larger speech community.

Speech event   An activity involving speaking (or communicating) that has underlying rules, understood roles, and a particular purpose known and fostered by the participants associated with it. I refer (in **Chapter 5**) to the daily story meetings as a speech event: editors understand what takes place, how the meeting begins and ends, and who speaks and when; they know how the story meeting is structured and what its function is.

Standard language ideology   Based on prescriptive notions about language use, and a variety of non-linguistic but socially meaningful responses about "correct language," it is the underlying assumption that only one form of language is right. (See **Chapter 9**.)

Text   In sociolinguistic circles (as opposed to cultural studies, rhetoric, or mobile telephony), "text" is a term of reference for a piece of discourse data (spoken as well as written) that the researcher is examining.

Utterance   An interval of speech, of any length or form, in an interaction. As a technical term, it is more general and inclusive than "sentence."

References

Abate, Tom. 2005. "Circulation of US weekday newspapers takes 2.6% hit." *San Francisco Chronicle*. November 8, 2005, p. D1.

Adams, Charles C. 1971. *Boontling: An American Lingo*. Austin and London: University of Texas Press.

Agar, Michael H. 1980. *The Professional Stranger: An Informal Introduction to Ethnography*. New York: Academic Press.

1986. *Speaking of Ethnography*. Newbury Park, CA: Sage Publications.

Agha, Asif. 2006. "Registers of language." In Alessandro Duranti (ed.), *A Companion to Linguistic Anthropology*. Oxford: Blackwell, pp. 23–45.

Aitchison, Jean. 1997. *The Language Web: The Power and Problem of Words – The 1996 BBC Reith Lectures*. Cambridge: Cambridge University Press.

2007. *The Word Weavers: Newshounds and Wordsmiths*. Cambridge: Cambridge University Press.

AJR Staff. 2000. "Motto a go-go." *American Journalism Review* (April), 14; also at www.ajr.org/Article.asp?id=3074.

Allan, Stuart. 1999. *News Culture*. Maidenhead and Philadelphia: Open University Press.

ASNE (American Society of Newspaper Editors). 1999a. *Examining Our Credibility: Perspectives of the Public and the Press*. Reston, VA: American Society of Newspaper Editors (ASNE).

ASNE Readership Issues Committee. 1999b. *The Local News Handbook*. Reston, VA: American Society of Newspaper Editors (ASNE).

Atkinson, Max. 1984. *Our Masters' Voices: The Language and Body Language of Politics*. London: Routledge.

Bakhtin, Mikhail. 1986 [1953]. "The problem of speech genres." In Caryl Emerson and Michael Holquist (eds.), *Speech Genres and Other Late Essays*. Austin: University of Texas Press, pp. 60–102.

Barnhurst, Kevin G. and John Nerone. 2001. *The Form of News: A History*. London and New York: The Guilford Communication Press.

Baskette, Floyd, Jack Z. Sissors, and Brian S. Brooks. 1986. *The Art of Editing* (4th edition). New York: Macmillan Publishing Company.

Bauman, Richard. 1977. *Verbal Art as Performance*. Prospect Heights, IL: Waveland Press.

1986. *Story, Performance, and Event: Contextual Studies of Oral Narrative*. Cambridge: Cambridge University Press.

1993. "Disclaimers of performance." In Jane H. Hill and Judith T. Irvine (eds.), *Responsibility and Evidence in Oral Discourse*. Cambridge: Cambridge University Press, pp. 182–196.

Bauman, Richard and Joel Sherzer (eds.). 1989. *Explorations in the Ethnography of Speaking* (2nd edition). Cambridge: Cambridge University Press.

Beaman, Karen. 1984. "Coordination and subordination revisited: Syntactic complexity in spoken and written narrative discourse." In Deborah Tannen (ed.), *Coherence in Spoken and Written Discourse*. Norwood, NJ: Ablex Publishers, pp. 45–80.

Beeman, William O. 2007. "The performance hypothesis: Practicing emotions in protected frames." In Helena Wulff (ed.), *The Emotions: A Cultural Reader*. Oxford: Berg Publishers, pp. 273–298.

Beeman, William O. and Mark A. Peterson. 2001. "Situations and interpretations: Explorations in interpretive practice." *Anthropological Quarterly* 74(4), 159–162.

Bell, Allan. 1984. "Language style as audience design." *Language and Society* 13(2), 145–204.

1991. *The Language of News Media*. Oxford and Cambridge: Blackwell.

1994. "Telling stories." In David Graddol and Oliver Boyd-Barrett (eds.), *Media Texts: Authors and Readers*. Clevedon: Multilingual Matters Ltd., pp. 100–118.

1995. "News time." *Time and Society* 4, 305–328.

1996. "Text, time and technology in news English." In Sharon Goodman and David Graddol (eds.), *Redesigning English: New Texts, New Identities*. London: Routledge.

1998. "The discourse structure of news stories." In Allan Bell and Peter Garrett (eds.), *Approaches to Media Discourse*. Oxford and Malden, MA: Blackwell, pp. 64–104.

2001. "Back in style: Re-working audience design." In Penelope Eckert and John R. Rickford (eds.), *Style and Sociolinguistic Variation*. New York: Cambridge University Press, pp. 139–169.

Bell, Allan and Peter Garrett (eds.). 1998. *Approaches to Media Discourse*. Oxford and Malden, MA: Blackwell.

Besnier, Niko. 1993. "Reported speech and affect on Nukulaelae Atoll." In Jane H. Hill and Judith T. Irvine (eds.), *Responsibility and Evidence in Oral Discourse*. Cambridge: Cambridge University Press, pp. 161–181.

Bex, Tony. 1996. *Variety in Written English: Texts in Society: Societies in Text*. London and New York: Routledge.

Bird, Elizabeth. 1992. *For Enquiring Minds: A Cultural Study of Supermarket Tabloids*. Knoxville: University of Tennessee Press.

1999. "Gendered representation of American Indians in popular media." *Journal of Communication* 49(3), 61–83.

Bleyer, Willard Grosvenor. 1913. *Newspaper Writing and Editing*. Boston: Houghton Mifflin Company.

Blommaert, Jan and Jef Verschueren. 1998. *Debating Diversity: Analysing the Discourse of Tolerance*. London: Routledge.

Bolinger, Dwight. 1980. *Language, the Loaded Weapon*. London: Longman.

1982. "The network tone of voice." *Journal of Broadcasting* 26, 725–728.

1986. *Intonation and Its Parts*. Palo Alto: Stanford University Press.

1989. *Intonation and Its Uses: Melody in Grammar and Discourse*. Palo Alto: Stanford University Press.

Boorstin, Daniel J. 1987 [1961]. *The Image: A Guide to Pseudo-Events in America*. New York: Atheneum.

Bourdieu, Pierre. 1977 [1972]. *Outline of a Theory of Practice*. Cambridge: Cambridge University Press.

Briggs, Charles L. 1986. *Learning How to Ask: A Sociolinguistic Appraisal of the Role of the Interview in Social Science Research*. Cambridge: Cambridge University Press.

Brooks, Brian S., George Kennedy, Daryl R. Moen, and Don Ranly (The Missouri Group). 1999. *News Reporting and Writing* (6th edition). New York: St. Martin's Press.

Brooks, Brian S., James L. Pinson, and Jean Gaddy Wilson (The Missouri Group). 2005. *News Reporting and Writing* (8th edition). Boston: Bedford/St. Martin's Press.

Bucholtz, Mary. 2000. "The politics of transcription." *Journal of Pragmatics* 32, 1439–1465.

Bucholtz, Mary and Kira Hall. 2006. "Language and identity." In Alessandro Duranti (ed.), *A Companion to Linguistic Anthropology*. Malden, MA: Blackwell, pp. 369–394.

Bunton, Kristie, Thomas Connery, and Mark Riley Neuzil. 1999. *Writing Across the Media*. New York: Bedford/St. Martin's Press.

Caldas-Coulthard, Carmen Rosa. 1997. *News as Social Practice*. Florianópolis, Brazil: Federal University of Santa Catarina Press.

Cameron, Deborah. 1995. *Verbal Hygiene*. London: Routledge.

Cappella, Joseph, N. and Kathleen Hall Jamieson. 1997. *Spiral of Cynicism: The Press and the Public Good*. New York: Oxford University Press.

Chafe, Wallace. 1984. "Speaking, writing, and prescriptivism." In Deborah Schiffrin (ed.), *Meaning, Form, and Use on Context: Linguistic Applications (Proceedings of the Georgetown University Round Table on Language and Linguistics)*. Washington, DC: Georgetown University Press, pp. 95–103.

Clayman, Steven. 1992. "Footing in the achievement of neutrality: The case of news-interview discourse." In Paul Drew and John Heritage (eds.), *Talk and Work: Interaction in Institutional Settings*. Cambridge: Cambridge University Press, pp. 163–198.

Clayman, Steven and John Heritage. 2002. *The News Interview: Journalists and Public Figures on the Air*. Cambridge: Cambridge University Press.

Conboy, Martin. 2006. *Tabloid Britain: Constructing a Community Through Language*. London: Routledge.

Cotter, Colleen. 1993. "Prosodic aspects of broadcast news register." *Proceedings of the Nineteenth Annual Meeeting of the Berkeley Linguistics Society*. Berkeley: Berkeley Linguistics Society, pp. 90–100.

1996a. "Irish on the air: Media, discourse, and minority language development." University of California, Berkeley. Unpublished PhD dissertation.

1996b. "Engaging the reader: The changing use of connectives in newspaper discourse." In Jennifer Arnold, Renée Blake, Brad Davidson, Scott Schwenter, and Julie Solomon (eds.), *Sociolinguistic Variation: Data, Theory, and Analysis (selected Papers from NWAV 23 at Stanford)*. Stanford: CSLI Publications, pp. 263–278.

1999a. "From folklore to 'News at 6': Managing language and reframing identity through the media." In Mary Bucholtz, Anita C. Liang and Laurel Sutton (eds.), *Reinventing Identities: The Gendered Self in Discourse*. New York: Oxford University Press, pp. 369–387.

1999b. "Language and media: Five facts about the Fourth Estate." In Rebecca S. Wheeler (ed.), *The Workings of Language: From Prescriptions to Perspective*. Westport, CT: Praeger Publishing, pp. 165–179.

1999c. "Raidió na Life: Innovations in the use of media for language revitalization." *International Journal of the Sociology of Language* 140, 135–147.

2001. "Discourse and media." In Deborah Schiffrin, Deborah Tannen, and Heidi E. Hamilton (eds.), *Handbook of Discourse Analysis*. Oxford: Blackwell, pp. 416–436.

2003. "Prescriptions and practice: Motivations behind change in news discourse." *Journal of Historical Pragmatics* 4(1), 45–74.

Cotter, Colleen and James A. Cotter. 1998. "Miscommunication in the aviation context: Linguistic factors as human factors." *Aviation Communication: A Multi-Cultural Forum (Proceedings of the 1997 Aviation Symposium)*. Prescott, AZ: Embry-Riddle Aeronautical University, pp. 103–113.

Cotter, Colleen and Daniel Marschall. 2006. "The persistence of workplace ideology and identity across communicative contexts." *Journal of Applied Linguistics* 3(1), 1–24.

Coy, Michael (ed.). 1989. "Introduction." *Apprenticeship: From Theory to Method and Back Again*. Albany: State University of New York Press, pp. 1–12.

Cupaiuolo, Christine. 2000. "Deconstructing the journalistic experience." Paper presented at Georgetown University Round Table on Languages and Linguistics (GURT), Washington, DC.

Davies, Bronwyn and Rom Harré. 1990. "Positioning: The social construction of selves." *Journal for the Theory of Social Behaviour* 20: 43–63.

Davis, Howard and Paul Walton (eds.). 1983. *Language, Image, Media*. Oxford/ New York: Basil Blackwell/St. Martin's Press.

Dégh, Linda. 1994. *American Folklore and the Mass Media*. Bloomington: Indiana University Press.

Dorgan, Howard. 1993. *The Airwaves of Zion: Radio and Religion in Appalachia*. Knoxville: University of Tennessee Press.

Downie, Leonard, Jr. and Robert G. Kaiser. 2002. *The News about the News: American Journalism in Peril*. New York: Alfred A. Knopf.

Drew, Paul and John Heritage (eds.). 1992. *Talk at Work: Interaction in Institutional Settings*. Cambridge: Cambridge University Press.

DuBois, John W. 1993. "Meaning without intention: Lessons from divination." In Jane H. Hill and Judith T. Irvine (eds.), *Responsibility and Evidence in Oral Discourse*. Cambridge: Cambridge University Press, pp. 48–71.

Duranti, Alessandro. 1988. "Ethnography of speaking: Toward a linguistics of the praxis." In Frederick Newmeyer, ed., *Linguistics: The Cambridge Survey IV*. Cambridge: Cambridge University Press, pp. 210–228.

1997. *Linguistic Anthropology*. Cambridge: Cambridge University Press.

2001. *Linguistic Anthropology: A Reader*. Malden, MA: Blackwell.

Duranti, Alessandro and Charles Goodwin (eds.). 1992. *Rethinking Context: Language as an Interactive Phenomenon*. Cambridge: Cambridge University Press.

Dvorkin, Jeffrey A. 2001. "NPR: It's journalism! No, it's radio! Stop! You're both right!" www.npr.org/yourturn/ombudsman/2001/010305.html

2002a. "Changes at NPR: Making some listeners nervous" www.npr.org/yourturn/ ombudsman/2002/020429.html

2002b. "Details, details…" www.npr.org/yourturn/ombudsman/2002/021114.html

2002c. "It's about time: Have NPR reports become too short?" www.npr.org/yourturn/ ombudsman/2002/021107.html

2002d. "NPR listeners have excellent hearing" www.npr.org/yourturn/ombudsman/ 2002/020208.html

Fairclough, Norman. 1992. *Discourse and Social Change*. Cambridge, MA: Polity Press.

1995. *Media Discourse*. London: Edward Arnold.

Fasold, Ralph, Haru Yamada, Steven Barish, and David Robinson. 1990. "The language-planning effect of newspaper editorial policy: Gender differences in the *Washington Post*." *Language in Society* 19(4), 521–539.

Fletcher, Kim. 2005. *The Journalist's Handbook: An Insider's Guide to Being a Great Journalist*. London: Macmillan.

Fowler, Roger. 1991. *Language in the News: Discourse and Ideology in the Press*. London: Routledge.

Friedersdorf, Colin. 2006 (March 30). "Small can be big in newspaper blogging." Blue Plate Special.net, http://journalism.nyu.edu/pubzone/blueplate/issue1/ smallbig/.

Gans, Herbert J. 1979. *Deciding What's News: A Study of CBS Evening News, NBC Nightly News, Newsweek and Time*. New York: Pantheon Books.

Garfinkel, Harold. 1972. "Remarks on ethnomethodology." In John J. Gumperz and Dell Hymes (eds.), *Directions in Sociolinguistics: The Ethnography of Communication*. New York: Holt, Rinehart & Winston Inc., pp. 301–324.

Geertz, Clifford. 1973. *The Interpretation of Cultures*. New York: Basic Books.

Glasgow University Media Group. 1976. *Bad News*. London: Routledge & Kegan Paul.

1980. *More Bad News*. London: Routledge & Kegan Paul.

Goffman, Erving. 1959. *The Presentation of Self in Everyday Life*. New York: Doubleday (Anchor Books).

1974. *Frame Analysis: An Essay on the Organization of Experience*. New York: Harper & Row.

1981. *Forms of Talk*. Philadelphia: University of Pennsylvania Press.

Gonzalez, Andrew B. 1991. "Stylistic shifts in the English of the Philippine print media." In Jenny Cheshire (ed.), *English Around the World: Sociolinguistic Perspectives*. Cambridge and New York: Cambridge University Press, pp. 333–363.

Goodwin, Charles. 1992. "Rethinking context: An introduction." In Alessandro Duranti and Charles Goodwin (eds.), *Rethinking Context: Language as an Interactive Phenomenon*. Cambridge: Cambridge University Press, pp. 1–42.

Goodwin, Marjorie Harness. 1990. *He-Said-She-Said: Talk as Social Organization among Black Children*. Cambridge: Cambridge University Press.

Greatbatch, David. 1992. "On the management of disagreement between news inter-viewees." In Paul Drew and John Heritage (eds.), *Talk at Work: Interaction in Institutional Settings*. Cambridge: Cambridge University Press, pp. 268–301.

1998. "Conversation analysis: Neutralism in British news interviews." In Allan Bell and Peter Garrett (eds.), *Approaches to Media Discourse*. Oxford and Malden, MA: Blackwell, pp. 163–185.

Grice, H. Paul. 1975. "Logic and conversation." In Peter Cole and Jerry L. Morgan (eds.), *Syntax and Semantics*, Volume III: *Speech Acts*. New York: Academic Press, pp. 41–58.

Gumperz, John J. 1968. "Types of linguistic communities." In J. A. Fishman (ed.), *Readings in the Sociology of Language*. The Hague: Mouton, pp. 460–472.

1982a. *Discourse Strategies*. Cambridge: Cambridge University Press.

(ed.). 1982b. *Language and Social Identity*. Cambridge: Cambridge University Press.

1984. "Communicative competence revisited." In Deborah Schiffrin (ed.), *Meaning, Form and Use in Context: Linguistic Applications (Proceedings of the Georgetown University Round Table on Languages and Linguistics)*. Washington, DC: Georgetown University Press, pp. 278–289.

1992. "Contextualization and understanding." In Alessandro Duranti and Charles Goodwin (eds.), *Rethinking Context*. Cambridge: Cambridge University Press, pp. 229–252.

Gumperz, John J. and Dell Hymes. 1964. "The ethnography of communication." *American Anthropologist* 66(6), part II.

(eds.). 1972. *Directions in Sociolinguistics: The Ethnography of Communication*. New York: Holt, Rinehart & Winston Inc.

Hall, Stuart. 1994. "Encoding/Decoding." In David Graddol and Oliver Boyd-Barrett (eds.), *Media Texts: Authors and Readers*. Clevedon: Multilingual Matters Ltd., pp. 200–211.

Hanks, William F. 2000. *Intertexts: Writings on Language, Utterance, and Context*. Lanham, MD: Rowman & Littlefield Publishers Inc.

Heath, Shirley Brice. 1983. *Ways with Words*. Cambridge: Cambridge University Press.

Hill, Jane H. 2007. "Crises of meaning: Personalist language ideology in US media discourse." In Sally Johnson and Astrid Ensslin (eds.), *Language in the Media: Representations, Identities, Ideologies*. London: Continuum, pp. 70–88.

Hill, Jane H. and Judith T. Irvine (eds.). 1993. *Responsibility and Evidence in Oral Discourse*. Cambridge: Cambridge University Press.

Holmes, Jennifer and Meredith Marra. 2005. "Narrative and the construction of professional identity in the workplace." In J. Thornborrow and J. Coates (eds.), *The Sociolinguistics of Narrative*. Amsterdam: John Benjamins, pp. 193–213.

Horner, Kristine. 2004. "Negotiating the language-identity link: Media discourse and nation-building in Luxembourg." State University of New York at Buffalo. PhD dissertation. Ann Arbor, MI: University Microfilms International.

Hough, George A., 3rd. 1988. *News Writing* (4th edition). Boston: Houghton Mifflin Company.

Howley, Kevin. 2005. *Community Media: People, Places, and Communication Technologies*. Cambridge: Cambridge University Press.

Husband, Charles and Jagdish M. Chouhan. 1985. "Local radio in the communication environment of ethnic minorities in Britain." In Teun A. van Dijk (ed.), *Discourse and Communication: New Approaches to the Analysis of Mass Media Discourse and Communication*. Berlin: Walter de Gruyter, pp. 270–294.

Hymes, Dell. 1972a. "On communicative competence." In J. B. Pride and J. Holmes (eds.), *Sociolinguistics*. Harmondsworth: Penguin, pp. 269–293.

1972b. "Models of the interaction of language and social life." In Dell Hymes and John J. Gumperz (eds.), *Directions in Sociolinguistics: The Ethnography of Communication*. New York: Holt, Rinehart & Winston Inc., pp. 35–71.

1974. *Foundations in Sociolinguistics: An Ethnographic Approach*. Philadelphia: University of Pennsylvania Press.

1984. "Linguistic problems in defining the concept of 'tribe'." In John Baugh and Joel Sherzer (eds.), *Language in Use*. Englewood Cliffs, NJ: Prentice-Hall Inc., pp. 7–27.

Itule, Bruce D. and Douglas A. Anderson. 1991. *News Writing and Reporting for Today's Media* (2nd edition). Boston: McGraw-Hill.

Jacobs, Geert. 1999. *Preformulating the News: An Analysis of the Metapragmatics of Press Releases*. Amsterdam and Philadelphia: John Benjamins.

Jacobs, Geert, Henk Pander Maat, and Tom Van Hout. 2008. "Introduction: The discourse of news management." *Pragmatics* 18(1), 1–8.

Jaffe, Alexandra. 1999. *Language Politics on Corsica*. Berlin: de Gruyter.

2007. "Corsican on the airwaves: media discourse in a context of minority language shift." In Sally Johnson and Astrid Ensslin (eds.), *Language in the Media: Representations, Identities, Ideologies*. London: Continuum, pp. 149–172.

Jaworski, Adam. 2007. "Language in the media: Authenticity and othering." In Sally Johnson and Astrid Ensslin (eds.), *Language in the Media: Representations, Identities, Ideologies*. London: Continuum, pp. 271–280.

Johnson, Sally and Astrid Ensslin (eds.) 2007. *Language in the Media: Representations, Identities, Ideologies*. London: Continuum.

Kaniss, Phyllis. 1991. *Making Local News*. Chicago: University of Chicago Press.

Keating, Elizabeth and Maria Egbert. 2006. "Conversation as a cultural activity." In Alessandro Duranti (ed.), *A Companion to Linguistic Anthropology*. Malden, MA: Blackwell, pp. 169–196.

Kelly-Holmes, Helen J. (ed.) 2002. *Minority Language Broadcasting: Breton and Irish*. Clevedon: Multilingual Matters/Channel View Publications.

Kelly-Holmes, Helen J. and Atkinson, David. 2007. "'When Hector met Tom Cruise': Attitudes to Irish in a radio satire." In Sally Johnson and Astrid Ensslin (eds.), *Language in the Media: Representations, Identities, Ideologies*. London: Continuum, pp. 173–187.

Kessler, Lauren and Duncan McDonald. 1988. *When Words Collide: A Journalist's Guide to Grammar and Style* (2nd edition). Belmont, CA: Wadsworth Publishing Company.

King, Colbert I. 2006. "Some are less 'newsworthy' than others." *Washington Post*, Saturday, February 18, 2006, p. A33.

Knight, Alan and Yoshiko Nakano (eds.). 1999. *Reporting Hong Kong: Foreign Media and the Handover*. Surrey: Curzon.

Knudson, Jerry W. 2000. *In the News: American Journalists View Their Craft*. Wilmington: A Scholarly Resources Inc. Imprint.

Kress, Gunther and Robert Hodge. 1979. *Language as Ideology*. London: Routledge.

Kulick, Don and Bambi B. Schieffelin. 2006. "Language socialization." In Alessandro Duranti (ed.), *A Companion to Linguistic Anthropology*. Malden, MA: Blackwell, pp. 349–368.

Labov, William 1972a. *Sociolinguistic Patterns*. Philadelphia: University of Pennsylvania Press.

1972b. "The transformation of experience in narrative syntax." *Language in the Inner City*. Philadelphia: University of Pennsylvania Press, pp. 354–396.

Lakoff, George. 2006. *Thinking Points: Communicating Our American Vision*. New York: Farrar, Straus & Giroux.

Lakoff, Robin. 1982. "Some of my favorite writers are literate: The mingling of oral and literate strategies in written communications." In Deborah Tannen (ed.), *Coherence in Spoken and Written Discourse*. Norwood: Ablex Publishing Corp, pp. 239–260.

1990. *Talking Power: The Politics of Language in Our Lives*. New York: Basic Books.
Lakoff, Robin Tolmach. 2000a. *The Language War*. Berkeley: University of California Press.
2000b. "The neutrality of the status quo." *The Language War*. Berkeley: University of California Press, pp. 42–85.
Lamb, Sharon and Susan Keon. 1995. "Blaming the perpetrator: Language that distorts reality in newspaper articles on men battering women." *Psychology of Women Quarterly* 19(2), 209–220.
Lanson, Gerald and Mitchell Stephens. 1994. *Writing and Reporting the News* (2nd edition). Fort Worth: Harcourt Brace.
LaRocque, Paula. 1999. "Language and lost credibility: Poor writing skills can jeopardize reader trust." *The Quill* 87(8), 38.
Lauterer, Jock. 2006. *Community Journalism: Relentlessly Local* (3rd edition). Chapel Hill, NC: University of North Carolina Press.
Lave, Jean and Etienne Wenger. 1991. *Situated Learning: Legitimate Peripheral Participation*. Cambridge: Cambridge University Press.
Leitner, Gerhard. 1980. "BBC English and Deutsche Rundfunksprache: A comparative and historical analysis of the language on the radio." *International Journal of the Sociology of Language* 26, 75–100.
1984. "Australian English or English in Australia: Linguistic identity or dependence in broadcast language." *English World-Wide* 1, 55–85.
LeVine, Philip and Ron Scollon (eds.). 2004. *Discourse and Technology: Multimodal Discourse Analysis*. Washington, DC: Georgetown University Press.
Lippi-Green, Rosina. 1997. *English with an Accent: Language, Ideology, and Discrimination with the United States*. London and New York: Routledge.
Lorenz, Alfred Lawrence and John Vivian. 1996. *News: Reporting and Writing*. Boston: Allyn & Bacon.
Love, Alison and Andrew Morrison. 1989. "Readers' obligations: An examination of some features of Zimbabwean newspaper editorials." *ELR Journal* 3, 137–172.
Mahoney, Mark. 2007. "Getting back to basics." *The American Editor* (Fall 2007), p. 5.
Martin, Judith. 2007. "A doctorate in rudeness." *Washington Post*, December 26, 2007, p. C10.
McElhinny, Bonnie. 1998. "'I don't smile much anymore': Affect, gender, and the discourse of Pittsburgh police officers." In Jennifer Coates (ed.), *Language and Gender: A Reader*. Malden, MA: Blackwell, pp. 309–327.
Meinhof, Ulrike H. 1994. "Double talk in news broadcasts: A cross-cultural comparison of pictures and texts in television news." In David Graddol and Oliver Boyd-Barrett (eds.), *Media Texts: Authors and Readers*. Clevedon and Philadelphia: Multilingual Matters Ltd, pp. 121–223.
Mencher, Melvin. 1997. *News Reporting and Writing* (7th edition). Madison, WI: Brown and Benchmark.
2006. *News Reporting and Writing* (10th edition). New York: McGraw-Hill.
Milroy, James and Lesley Milroy. 1999. *Authority in Language: Investigating Language Prescription and Standardisation* (3rd edition). London and New York: Routledge.
Milroy, Lesley. 1987. *Language and Social Networks* (2nd edition). Oxford: Basil Blackwell.
Modan, Gabriella G. 2007. *Turf Wars: Discourse, Diversity, and the Politics of Place*. Malden, MA: Blackwell.

Morgan, Marcyliena. 2006. "Speech community." In Alessandro Duranti (ed.), *A Companion to Linguistic Anthropology*. Oxford: Blackwell, pp. 3–22.

Naro, Anthony J. and Maria Marta Pereira Scherre. 1996. "Contact with media and linguistic variation." In Jennifer Arnold, Renée Blake, Brad Davidson, Scott Schwenter, and Julie Solomon (eds.), *Sociolinguistic Variation: Data, Theory, and Analysis (Selected Papers from NWAV 23 at Stanford)*. Stanford: CSLI Publications, pp. 223–228.

Nash, June (ed.). 1993. *Crafts in the World Market: The Impact of Global Exchange on Middle American Artisans*. Albany: State University of New York Press.

Neuharth, Al. 2008 (May 23). "On 225th birthday, newspapers dying?" USAToday.com, http://blogs.usatoday.com/oped/2008/05/on-225th-birthd.html.

Newsom, Doug and James A. Wollert. 1988. *Media Writing: Preparing Information for the Mass Media* (2nd edition). Belmont: Wadsworth Publishing Company.

Newton, Eric. 2006. "A look back at Bob Maynard, who was always looking ahead." Poynteronline, June 16, 2006, www.poynter.org

Nunberg, Geoffrey. 1990. *The Linguistics of Punctuation*. Cambridge/Stanford: Cambridge University Press/CSLI.

Ochs, Elinor. 2001. "Socialization." In Alessandro Duranti (ed.), *Key Terms in Language and Culture*. Malden, MA and Oxford: Blackwell, pp. 227–230.

Ochs, Elinor and Bambi B. Schieffelin (eds.). 1983. *Acquiring Conversational Competence*. Boston: Routledge.

Pan, Yuling, Suzanne Wong Scollon, and Ron Scollon. 2002. *Professional Communication in International Settings*. Malden, MA and Oxford: Blackwell.

Perrin, Daniel. 2006. "Progression analysis: An ethnographic, computer-based multi-method approach to investigate natural writing processes." In L. Van Waes, M. Leijten, and C. Neuwirth (eds.), *Writing and Digital Media*. Amsterdam: Elsevier, pp. 175–181.

Perrin, Daniel and Maureen Ehrensberger-Dow. 2006. "Journalists' language awareness: Inferences from writing strategies." *Revista Alicantina de Estudios Ingleses* 19, 319–343.

2008. "Progression analysis: Tracing journalistic language awareness." In M. Burger (ed.), *L'analyse linguistique des discours des médias: théories, méthodes en enjeux. Entre sciences du langage et sciences de la communication et des médias*. Québec: Nota Bene.

Peterson, Mark A. 1996. "Writing the Indian story: Press, politics and symbolic power in India." Unpublished PhD dissertation. Brown University.

2001. "Getting to the story: Unwriteable discourse and interpretive practice in American journalism." *Anthropological Quarterly* 74(4), 201–211.

2003. *Anthropology and Mass Communication: Media and Myth in the New Millenium*. New York: Berghahn Books.

2007. "Making global news: 'Freedom of speech' and 'Muslim rage' in US journalism." *Cont Islam* 1, 247–264.

Philips, Susan U. 1989. "Warm Springs 'Indian Time': How the regulation of participation affects the progress of events." In Richard Bauman and Joel Sherzer (eds.), *Explorations in the Ethnography of Speaking* (2nd edition). Cambridge: Cambridge University Press, pp. 92–109.

1998. *Ideology in the Language of Judges: How Judges Practice Law, Politics, and Courtroom Control*. New York: Oxford University Press.

Pike, Kenneth Lee. 1967. *Language in Relation to a Unified Theory of Structure of Human Behavior* (2nd edition). The Hague: Mouton.

Pinker, Stephen. 1994. *The Language Instinct*. New York: HarperPerennial.

Quirk, Randolph. 1982. "Speaking into the air." In Richard Hoggart and Janet Morgan (eds.), *The Future of Boadcasting: Essays on Authority, Style and Choice*. London: Macmillan Press.

    1986. *Words at Work: Lectures on Textual Structure*. Harlow, Essex: Longman.

Rampton, Ben. 1995. "Language crossing and the problematisation of ethnicity and socialisation." *Pragmatics* 5(4), 485–515.

    2001. "Language crossing, cross-talk, and cross-disciplinarity in sociolinguistics." In Nikolas Coupland, Srikant Sarangi, and Christopher N. Candlin (eds.), *Sociolinguistics and Social Theory*. London: Longman, pp. 261–296.

Randall, David. 2000. *The Universal Journalist* (2nd edition). London: Pluto Press.

Redeker, Gisela. 1990. "Ideational and pragmatic markers of discourse structure." *Journal of Pragmatics* 14(3), 367–381.

Richardson, John E. 2007. *Analysing Newspapers: An Approach from Critical Discourse Analysis*. Basingstoke: Palgrave Macmillan.

Robinson, Eugene. 2007. "Spike the obit; newspapers still rock." *The American Editor* (December), p. 17.

Rogoff, Barbara. 1990. *Apprenticeship in Thinking*. New York: Oxford University Press.

Rosenberg, Scott. 1999. "Fear of links: While professional journalists turn up their noses, weblog pioneers invent a new, personal way to organize the Web's chaos." www.salon.com/tech/colrose/1999/05/28/weblogs

Sangster, Catherine. 2005. "What is BBC English?" Paper presented at the Language in the Media conference, University of Leeds, UK; see also "Received Pronunciation and BBC English" at www.bbc.co.uk/voices/yourvoice/rpandbbc.shtml.

Santa Ana, Otto. 1999. "Like an animal I was treated: Anti-immigration metaphor in US public discourse." *Discourse and Society* 10(2), 191–224.

    2002. *Brown Tide Rising: Metaphors of Latinos in Contemporary American Public Discourse*. Austin: University of Texas Press.

Satoh, Akira. 2001. "Constructing imperial identity: How to quote the imperial family and those who address them in the Japanese Press." *Discourse and Society* 12(2), 169–194.

Saville-Troike, Muriel. 2002 [1989]. *The Ethnography of Communication: An Introduction* (3rd edition). Cambridge, MA: Blackwell.

Schieffelin, Bambi B. and Elinor Ochs. 1996. "The microgenesis of competence: Methodology in language socialization." In Dan Isaac Slobin, Julie Gerhardt, Amy Kyratzis, and Jiansheng Guo (eds.), *Social Interaction, Social Context, and Language*. Mahwah, NJ: Laurence Erlbaum, pp. 251–264.

    (eds.). 1986. *Language Socialization Across Cultures*. Cambridge: Cambridge University Press.

Schieffelin, Bambi B., Kathryn A. Woolard, and Paul V. Kroskrity (eds.). 1998. *Language Ideologies*. New York: Oxford University Press.

Schiffrin, Deborah. 1987. *Discourse Markers*. Cambridge: Cambridge University Press.

    1994. *Approaches to Discourse*. London: Blackwell.

Schnurr, Stephanie, Meredith Marra, and Janet Holmes. 2007. "Being (im)polite in New Zealand workplaces: Māori and Pākehā leaders." *Journal of Pragmatics* 39(4), 712–729.

Schudson, Michael. 1978. *Discovering the News: A Social History of American Papers*. New York: Basic Books.

1987. "Deadlines, datelines, and history." In Robert Karl Manoff and Michael Schudson (eds.), *Reading the News: A Pantheon Guide to Popular Culture*. New York: Pantheon, pp. 79–108.

Schudson, Michael and Danielle Haas. 2007. "Who hates the press?" *Columbia Journalism Review* (November/December), 70.

Scollon, Ron. 1997. "Attribution and power in Hong Kong news discourse." *World Englishes* 16(3), 383–393.

Scollon, Ron and Suzanne Wong Scollon. 1997. "Point of view and citation: Fourteen Chinese and English versions of the 'same' news story." *Text* 17(1), 83–125.

2003. *Discourses in Place: Language in the Material World*. London and New York: Routledge.

Sherzer, Joel and Regna Darnell. 1972. "Appendix 2: Outline guide for the ethnographic study of speech use." In John J. Gumperz and Dell Hymes (eds.), *Directions in Sociolinguistics: The Ethnography of Communication*. New York: Holt, Rinehart & Winston Inc., pp. 548–554.

Simon, David. 2008. "Does the news matter to anyone anymore?" *Washington Post*, Sunday, January 20, 2008, p. B01.

Sperber, Dan and Deirdre Wilson. 1985. *Relevance: Communication and Cognition*. Oxford: Blackwell.

Spitulnik, Debra. 1992. "Radio time sharing and the negotiation of linguistic pluralism in Zambia." *Pragmatics* 2(3), 335–354.

2001. "The social circulation of media discourse and the mediation of communities." In Alessandro Duranti (ed.), *Linguistic Anthropology: A Reader*. Malden, MA: Blackwell, pp. 95–118.

Suleiman, Camelia. 1999. "Pronouns and self presentation in public discourse." In Yasir Suleiman (ed.), *Language and Society in the Middle East and North Africa*. London: Curzon Press, pp. 104–121.

2000. "Pronoun use in television interviews: Social interaction and the Middle East peace process." Unpublished PhD dissertation. Georgetown University.

Swales, John M. 1990 *Genre Analysis: English in Academic and Research Settings*. Cambridge: Cambridge University Press.

Tannen, Deborah. 1984. *Conversational style*. Norwood, MA: Ablex Publishers.

1989. *Talking Voices: Repetition, Dialogue and Imagery in Conversational Discourse*. Cambridge: Cambridge University Press.

1994. *Talking from 9 to 5: Men and Women at Work*. New York: William Morrow and Co. Inc.

1998. *The Argument Culture: Moving from Debate to Dialogue*. New York: Random House.

Tenore, Mallary Jean. 2008. "Live blogging: How it makes us better journalists." Poynteronline.org. April 10, 2008. Accessed April 11, 2008.

Terrio, Susan J. 2000. *Crafting the Culture and History of French Chocolate*. Berkeley: University of California Press.

Thurlow, Crispin and Adam Jaworski. 2003. "Communicating a global reach: Inflight magazines as a globalizing genre in tourism." *Journal of Sociolinguistics* 7(4), 579–606.

Toye, Margaret. 2006. "Interaction in the production and fanship of Train 48: An Interactional Sociolinguistic Study." Unpublished PhD dissertation. Georgetown University.

Traugott, Elizabeth Closs. 1986. "On the origins of 'and' and 'but' connectives in English." *Studies in Language* 10(1), 137–150.

1988. "Pragmatic strengthening and grammaticalization." *Proceedings of the Fourteenth Annual Meeting of the Berkeley Linguistics Society.* Berkeley: Berkeley Linguistics Society, pp. 406–416.

Tuchman, Gaye. 1978. *Making News: A Study in the Construction of Reality.* New York: Free Press.

Turner, Will. 2007. "Spinning spin." Paper presented at Language Ideologies and Media Discourse conference, University of Leeds, UK.

Tyler, Alina. 2006. "The role of humour in the newsroom." Unpublished ms.

Ungerer, Friedrich (ed.). 2000. *English Media Texts Past and Present: Language and Textual Structure.* Amsterdam: John Benjamins Publishing Company.

Utterback, Ann S. 1995. *Broadcast Voice Handbook: How to Polish Your On-Air Delivery* (2nd edition). Chicago: Bonus Books Inc.

Van de Velde, Hans. 1996. "A trend study of a trendy change." In Jennifer Arnold, Renée Blake, Brad Davidson, Scott Schwenter, and Julie Solomon (eds.), *Sociolinguistic Variation: Data, Theory, and Analysis (Selected Papers from NWAV 23 at Stanford).* Stanford: CSLI Publications, pp. 501–514.

van Dijk, Teun A. 1979. "Pragmatic connectives." *Journal of Pragmatics* 3(5), 447–456.

1985. *Discourse and Communication: New Approaches to the Analysis of Mass Media Discourse and Communication.* Berlin and New York: Walter de Gruyter.

1988. *News as Discourse.* Hillsdale: Lawrence Erlbaum Associates Inc.

1991. *Racism and the Press.* London: Routledge.

2001. "Multidisciplinary CDA: A plea for diversity." In Ruth Wodak and Michael Meyer (eds.), *Methods of Critical Discourse Analysis.* London: Sage, pp. 95–120.

Van Hout, Tom. 2008. "Need for speed: (Re)productive strategies in news production." Paper presented at the NewsTalk and Text Research Seminar, Ghent University.

Van Hout, Tom and Geert Jacobs. 2008. "News production theory and practice: Fieldwork notes on power, interaction and agency." *Pragmatics* 18(1), 59–84.

Van Hout, Tom and Felicitas Macgilchrist. In press. "Framing the news: An ethnographic view of financial newswriting." *Text and Talk.*

Van Maanen, John and Stephen R. Barley, 1984. "Occupational communities: Culture and control in organizations." *Research in Organizational Behavior* 6, 287–365.

Vandenbussche, Wim. 2008. "Standardisation through the media: The case of Dutch in Flanders." In Evelyn Ziegler, Peter Gilles, and Joachim Scharloth (eds.), *Variatio Delectat.* Frankfurt: Lang.

Verschueren, Jef. 1985. *International News Reporting: Metapragmatic Metaphors and the U-2.* Amsterdam and Philadelphia: John Benjamins Publishing Company.

Waugh, Linda. 1995. "Reported speech in journalistic discourse: The relation of function and text." *Text* 15(1), 129–173.

Weizman, Elda. 1984. "Some register characteristics of journalistic language: Are they universals?" *Applied Linguistics* 5(1), 39–50.

Wenger, Etienne. 1998. *Communities of Practice: Learning, Meaning and Identity.* Cambridge: Cambridge University Press.

Wenner, Kathryn S. 2002. "Bang, bang, bang." *American Journalism Review* (November), 32–33.

Woo, William. 1999. "Credibility is built by a *paper*, not just a newsroom." *The American Editor* (May–June), 7–8, 26.

(and Philip Meyer, editor). 2007. *Letters from the Editor: Lessons on Journalism and Life*. Columbus: University of Missouri Press.

Wortham, Stanton E. F. 2005. "Socialization beyond the speech event." *Journal of Linguistic Anthropology* 15(1), 95–112.

Zelizer, Barbie. 1995. "Text, talk and journalistic quoting practice." *Communication Review* 1(1), 33–51.

Zinsser, William. 1985. *On Writing Well* (3rd edition). New York: Harper & Row.

Index

Internet
  influences of, 28, 39, 45, 60, 62, 202
  interactivity and, 131
interpretive stability, 70
intertextuality, 101
interviewing, 39, 54, 149
interviewing skills, 50, 51, 62
intonation contours (radio), 28, 140, 152
inverted pyramid, 26, 27, 28, 140 *see also* story
  design
Irish Emigrant Newsletter, 71
iterativity, 158, 185
  news genres and, 218
Itule, Bruce D. and Douglas A. Anderson, 77,
  120, 123

Jacobs, Geert et al., 4
Jaffe, Alexandra, 4, 22, 53
Jaworski, Adam, 21, 233
Johnson, Sally and Astrid Ensslin, 22
Journal Sentinel (Milwaukee, Wis.), 162
"journalism of conscience", 70
journalism school, 7, 61, 136
journalistic skills and relation to
  ethnography, 29
journalistic standardization
  BBC, 204
  commercial radio, 204, 208
  language ideology behind, 212
  NPR, 203
  Raidió na Life, 205–206, 208
journalists and linguists, 10, 23, 220–221,
  235 *see also* linguistics and journalism
  linguists as sources, 217
J-School. *see* journalism school

Kaniss, Phyllis, 46
Karush, Sarah, 160
Kelly-Holmes, Helen, 22
  and David Atkinson, 54
Kermode, David, 127
King, Colbert I., 77, 78, 80, 243
Knight, Alan and Yoshiko Nakano, 22, 101
Knight-Ridder Washington Bureau, 70
Knudson, Jerry, 31
Kulick, Don and Bambi B. Schieffelin, 16, 33, 52

Labov, William, 86, 111, 163, 176
Lakoff, George, 47
Lakoff, Robin, 5, 21, 47, 63, 109, 130, 189
language. *see also* news language; standard
  language ideology
  attitudes about, 10, 26, 211 *see also*
    complaint tradition
  communicative function and, 16

credibility and, 42–43
discourse and, 16
news practice and, 24
prescription. *see* prescriptive imperative
prescription and pragmatics, 209
standardization in media contexts, 208, 212
style and variation, 22
Lanson, Gerald and Mitchell Stephens, 73, 76,
  84, 141, 153, 155
LaRocque, Paula, 42
Lave, Jean and Etienne Wenger, 19, 23, 25, 35,
  111, 255
leads, 9
  "bad ledes", 167
  cliché leads, 167
  label leads, 168
  question leads, 168
  feature leads, 153–155
  good leads, 163
  importance of, 170
  second-day leads, 157
  traditional leads, 153
  types of, 152–153, 155–157
    anecdote, 155
    brite, 155
    narrative, 155
    zinger, 155, 156
Leitner, Gerhard, 53, 86, 190
lenition, 257
LeVine, Philip and Ron Scollon, 3
linguistic anthropology, 2, 3, 19, 33, 47, 233
linguistics and journalism, 2, 16 *see also*
  journalists and linguists
local priority emphasis, 90, 98–100
  importance of, 119–122
local values in US journalism, 45–47 *see also*
  community factor; local priority
  emphasis; community of coverage
Lohn, Martiga, 157
Lorenz, Alfred Lawrence and John
  Vivian, 68
Los Angeles Times, 6, 81, 83, 98, 173, 225
Love, Alison and Andrew Morrison, 101

Mahoney, Mark, 46
managing editor, 91, 253
Marra, Meredith, 62
Marschall, Daniel, 35, 62
Martin, Judith, 60
Mason Valley News, 59
Maximal Relevance, 161, 162, 169, 231
Maynard, Bob, 90
McCullagh, Declan, 36, 40, 44, 115
McElhinny, Bonnie, 62
McLuhan, Marshall, 15